DICKIE BIRD
MY AUTOBIOGRAPHY

DICKIE BIRD
MY AUTOBIOGRAPHY

Dickie Bird
with
Keith Lodge

Hodder & Stoughton

Copyright © 1997 Dickie Bird

First published in Great Britain in 1997
by Hodder and Stoughton
A division of Hodder Headline PLC

The right of Dickie Bird to be identified as the Author of
the Work has been asserted by him in accordance with the
Copyright, Designs and Patents Act 1988.

10

A CIP catalogue record for this title is available
from the British Library.

ISBN 0 340 68457 7

Typeset by Palimpsest Book Production Limited,
Polmont, Stirlingshire
Printed and bound in Great Britain by
Mackays of Chatham PLC, Chatham, Kent

Hodder and Stoughton
A division of Hodder Headline PLC
338 Euston Road
London NW1 3BH

To my late Mum and Dad for giving me such a very happy start in life, to my sister Marjorie for her love and day-to-day support over all these years, and to my sister Sylvia who was so close to me, and who died tragically young.

CONTENTS

ACKNOWLEDGEMENTS

I particularly want to thank my lifelong friend Keith Lodge, the well-respected Sports Editor of the *Barnsley Chronicle*, for the care he has taken in helping me to put my story down in book form. It has been an honour working with him.

I would also like to thank my publisher Roddy Bloomfield for regularly making the journey from London to Barnsley for our meetings. He encouraged me at all times and gave me much helpful advice. We also had a lot of laughs and a lot of fun while working on the book.

Finally I would like to thank the TCCB (now the England and Wales Cricket Board) for all their support throughout my career. It has been much appreciated, as has all the support given to me by the press.

Photographic Acknowledgements

For permission to reproduce copyright photographs, the author and publisher would like to thank the *Herald Express*, Torquay; Walkers Studios Ltd, Scarborough; A. Wilkes & Sons; The Press Association Ltd; County Press Photos, Wigan; Times Newspapers Ltd; Patrick Eagar; *The Yorkshire Post*; Ken Kelly; *The Evening Post*, Wellington, NZ; *Barnsley Chronicle*; *Daily Mirror*; Sheffield Newspapers Ltd; John Ireland; Sports-Line Photographic; Colin Stanhope; Post Studios Ltd; Popperfoto.

FOREWORD

by Michael Parkinson

I THINK I love cricket, but not like Dickie Bird. I have never
met anyone with such a passion for the game. I love the game,
warts and all, but Dickie doesn't see the blemishes. I speak from
experience having known the man for near on fifty years. I
remember when I first saw him. He was circling the edge of
our ground like some wary animal exploring new territory. He
could be forgiven his caution. Barnsley Cricket Club, in those
days, was a big deal. It had a pavilion with a balcony and a bar,
a shed for indoor cricket and, most impressive of all, a proper
scoreboard which you only saw on county grounds. Best of all
was the wicket. For any young man with ambition to open for
Yorkshire (and in those days that would account for 99 per cent
of the male teenaged population) the strip, prepared by a great
groundsman called John Matthewman, offered the best chance
for displaying his talent. If the fast bowlers bent their backs it
bounced, but in the main it was the sort of wicket you wanted
to roll up and take with you. To Dickie and the rest of us who
played club cricket on pitches best described as whimsical, the
chance of playing at Barnsley was not to be passed by. Dickie's
main problem was he didn't look like an athlete. Even then he
had a slightly geriatric stoop and the pallor of a man who worked
underground. He was, I seem to recall, carrying his belongings in

a carrier bag. None of us were well off – apart from the captain whose father owned a brewery – but somehow Dickie seemed to have less than any of us. I don't mean he was raggy arsed or emotionally deprived. Indeed he was as meticulous about his appearance then as he is now and deeply attached to his family. But there was something forlorn about him. It wasn't easy for him. As he recalls, at first he was advised to go home but a chance meeting with a sympathetic member changed all that. We all practised in those days. We had to. If you didn't then you were not even considered for selection. But Dickie set new standards in diligence and application. The rest of us perspired slightly, but Dickie sweated it out and by doing so transformed himself from a good club player into a Yorkshire cricketer.

We shared the same ambition. Our fathers were both miners and came to know each other, so it seemed almost natural we should open the innings for Barnsley and become friends. We made runs together, shared the collection money on occasions (if we got to it before our fathers did) and discovered the reality of playing Yorkshire League cricket. I remember Dickie being felled by a young Fred Trueman, I went to administer first aid and sympathy. After Dickie had revived I made my way back to the bowler's end where the aforesaid F. S. Trueman was squatting on his haunches.

'How's thi' mate?' he asked.

'I think he'll live,' I said nervously.

'That's all right then, but think on tha'rt next,' he said.

We went to the Yorkshire nets together, the ultimate test. He passed, I didn't. I went away to do my National Service and when I returned I found a young man called Geoffrey Boycott had taken my place. The selectors sensibly got rid of him and gave me my place back. I scored a century. To his credit, Geoffrey tells the story in his autobiography and, in any case, Dickie and I always remind him of it. There was a time when the three of us sat in the same dressing-room at Barnsley dreaming of what might happen. One went on to play for Yorkshire and England and be acclaimed as our greatest opening batsman, the other played for Yorkshire and Leicestershire and then became a first-class umpire and one of the best loved and respected men the game has ever produced. One or two things happened to me as well but I always regarded myself as the failure.

Most importantly the friendships have endured. Whenever the three of us meet it is as if we have never been apart. Sometimes Dickie comes to stay and when he does there is always something worth reporting. Like the time he was sitting in my back garden having coffee and toast when the window cleaner appeared around the corner of the house. Dickie leapt to his feet and rushed across the garden, hand extended.

'Dickie Bird, first-class umpire,' he said. Another fan claimed, another anecdote to add to the legend.

It is interesting that in the book Dickie attempts to correct the popular notion that he is naive, accident prone, nervous or a mixture of the three. There is little doubt he has been caricatured from time to time but I hope it doesn't offend. He should realise that all the stories told about him are based on affection, and only someone who is beloved rather than beliked can claim that.

I watched him getting ready to go out at The Oval recently and marvelled at his meticulous preparation. It was like the ritual before he went out to bat – groomed, looking his best, feeling up to it, the lover to his lass. Speaking of which I wish he would settle down and get married; otherwise we'll all worry too much about what might happen when he finally retires. It is the one subject I have never discussed with Dickie. Our other mutual friend, John Hampshire, formerly of Yorkshire and England and now a fellow umpire, once did. It was during the tea interval when they were both standing at Worcester. John told Dickie it was time he was wed. They continued their discussion through tea and were still at it as they walked out to resume play. Dickie was still chuntering as the two men separated, Dickie to the Cathedral End, Hampshire to the Pavilion End. As Dickie arrived at his post he shouted across at his friend: 'Anyway, I'll nivver get married.'

'Why not?' Hampshire asked.

'Because I'm frightened everyone's got Aids,' Dickie bellowed.

'What, even me and our lass?' Hampshire replied. By this time the players who were waiting on the umpires to start play were convinced they had strayed into the middle of a Monty Python sketch.

There is for all his Yorkshire common sense a surreal streak in Dickie which makes him irreplaceable. Invited to Chequers he arrived early but was accommodated by the then Prime Minister John Major who took time off to talk cricket with him for two or three hours. When an interviewer asked if the Prime Minister didn't have better things to do that day, like run the country, Dickie said: 'Normally he would but you see it was a Sunday.'

When you think about it, only Shakespeare could have invented a character so full of life's rich juices as Dickie Bird. Cricket's genius has been to accommodate his foibles and celebrate his humour. My delight has been in knowing him for all these years.

Michael Parkinson
June 1997

1

EARLY DAYS

I WAS born on 19 April 1933, in a terraced house in Church Lane, near the centre of Barnsley, the son of a coalminer. We had no bathroom in those days, and the only toilet was outside, but it was a good place to go to read the sports pages without being interrupted.

I was christened Harold Dennis Bird, after my father, James Harold. The nickname 'Dickie' was given to me at school. All the Whites were 'Chalkie', all the Clarks were 'Nobby' and all the Birds were 'Dickie'. Tommy Taylor, my schoolfriend and later an international footballer, became 'Tucker' – Little Tommy Tucker.

Tommy's father, Charlie, and my father were very close friends, and both worked at the same coal face at Monk Bretton Colliery. When I look back I think also of Dorothy Hyman, the great Olympic athlete from Cudworth, whose father worked down the mine, as did the father of journalist and broadcaster Michael Parkinson. His father was a deputy at Grimethorpe Colliery. It is quite remarkable that such a small area should produce four sons and daughters of coalminers who were to become household names in their chosen professions.

When Tommy left school he went to work at Wharncliffe Woodmoor, and Dorothy became a tracer at Woolley Colliery.

But Parky went straight into journalism. My father was adamant that I wasn't going to go down the pit to suffer as he had to do, and wanted something better for his lad, but there was little other local employment, and I ended up working on the pit top in the fitting shop at Monk Bretton.

Geoffrey Boycott is also the son of a coalminer, although he is not from Barnsley, as a lot of people think, but from Fitzwilliam, near Pontefract. When he left Hemsworth Grammar School he worked at the National Insurance Offices in Barnsley and played cricket for Barnsley. He was not long at Shaw Lane before moving to Leeds in the Yorkshire League.

Many other cricketers have mining backgrounds – Harold Larwood, Freddie Trueman, Bill Voce and Les Jackson to name but a few of the great fast bowlers. Indeed, it was said in those days that you had only to shout down a pit shaft and up would pop a fast bowler – or a centre-forward like Tommy Taylor.

Lord Mason, of Barnsley, is another with colliery connections. He worked down the pit himself as a young man before going on to hold government office, becoming one of the best Northern Ireland ministers we have ever had.

My father worked down the pit, in the bowels of the earth, from the age of thirteen to sixty-five. He lived only five years after retiring, with nothing left in him. He was worn out after working all those years, sometimes in an eighteen-inch seam, crawling on his stomach, sometimes waist deep in water. It was all hand work – pick and shovel, no machinery – and when he arrived home each night he was so tired. Bath, a meal, bed, and then off to work again. Days, afternoons and nights. Three different shifts in rotation. What a life!

I would have given anything for him to have seen me umpire a Test match, but he never did. That is one of the saddest things in my life. Today I would be able to give both my parents comfort and wealth, all the things they were never able to enjoy in those long-ago days, but they are both gone. The only consolation I have is that their reward, the only one they ever sought, was probably seeing me gain success by following their advice and keeping on the straight and narrow.

My parents were poor in terms of money, but rich in other ways. They always made sure there was good food on the table, we had good clothes to wear, and we were well cared for. I have a lot to be thankful for to both my parents, and I respected them so much. Children today do not respect their parents enough, and that is where a lot of the trouble lies when youngsters go off the rails.

In those early days my parents taught my two sisters and me the right way to live. The difference between right and wrong was instilled into us. It was a good, happy family life, and I will always treasure the memory of it.

My sisters, Marjorie and Sylvia, were good church people. Sylvia was a lay preacher and went all over the country. She died of a brain haemorrhage in her early forties, and my mother and I always wondered why that should have to happen to her. She had given her life to the Lord, and was a wonderful, wonderful woman, yet she had her life taken away.

Mother used to say, 'Dickie, the good Lord must have wanted her for some reason,' but she never did get over Sylvia's death. It was a terrible blow for her. The Church has always remained an important part of my life. My parents took me and my two sisters to the Elim Pentecostal church in Barnsley every Sunday, and it is still there today. I still go whenever I can to a little Methodist church in the village of Staincross, just a few miles from Barnsley, where I now live in a cottage in which the great preacher John Wesley stayed during one of his visits. He actually slept in the bedroom I now occupy. It is documented in a biography, *Hudson Taylor in Early Years*, which opens with a chapter describing Wesley's stay in the cottage, which belonged to the Shaw family.

According to the *Barnsley Chronicle* of 30 September 1905, Wesley's visit was on 27 July 1761. The entry in the book reads, 'Had not John Wesley himself appeared one Mapplewell Feast Monday boldly addressing the crowds in the Market Place while the Midsummer Fair was going on? It was a courageous thing to do in that Yorkshire Town, where baiting the Methodists had become a favourite pastime with those of the rougher sort.'

The book, by Dr and Mrs Hudson Taylor, first published in 1911, goes on, 'The Shaws' cottage still stands on the ridge which divides it from the neighbouring parish of Royston. Substantially built of stone, it hardly shows the wear and tear of two centuries, and it is the best preserved of the few remaining dwellings that form the oldest part of the town.'

I could hardly believe it at first. I knew the cottage had a lot of historical interest and was one of the first, if not the first, building in the village. But I didn't expect to find that John Wesley actually slept there.

During my travels abroad I always look for a place to go to worship. On one occasion I went into a Methodist church in Barbados just before the start of the service and sat right at the back. It was jam-packed with smartly dressed women in their Sunday best, the chaps in their suits. The preacher stood up.

'Brothers and sisters,' he said, 'we have a great surprise for you today.'

There was an 'ooooh' round the church.

'Yes, brothers and sisters, we have in our midst Mr Dickie Bird, the Test umpire from England.'

The church erupted, and the congregation stood and clapped and cheered. After the service I just couldn't get away. Everybody wanted to talk to me. It was a great feeling: all those thousands of miles away from home, yet among so many friends.

That is what belonging to a Church family means, and I believe that my faith has helped me through many dark times.

If my mother was instrumental in introducing me to the Church, it was my father who was always there to bowl to me, play football with me, and help develop my love for both sports. He was not a bad footballer himself, and had played for the Barnsley YMCA when they had a really good side. During his time they won the Yorkshire Trophy for the only time, beating Ripon 1–0 at Oakwell, the home of Barnsley Football Club. Dad also won medals in the Barnsley League with the YMCA team.

It was hardly surprising that my father should also encourage me to join the YMCA, another big factor in my development, and of other youngsters like me. It kept us off the streets, and we were able to enjoy table tennis, snooker, and, of course, football.

My father offered some sound advice: 'Keep off cigs,' he said, although he was a smoker himself, 'and don't drink.' I took that advice. I have never smoked, and only drink in moderation, usually red wine which my doctor assures me is good for the circulation.

'If you want to be a successful sportsman,' Dad warned me, 'steer clear of women in nightclubs.' He was right. How many top sportsmen's careers have been ruined by one, or even all, these 'vices'?

I have to admit, though, that one day I was a bit naughty, and played truant from school, along with several other boys. We went to watch England play Australia at Headingley. It was 1948 and I remember Ray Lindwall bowling Len Hutton in the first over of the day. I was so disappointed. I had wanted to see the great man bat all day. He told me many years later that he never picked the ball up, and I was to learn the hard way that it was, indeed, very difficult to see the ball when facing the football stand in those days before sightscreens were introduced. That trip also cost me six of the best when I reported back to school next day and admitted where I had been.

I suppose it is the dream of most sports-mad youngsters to become an England international at either football or cricket. I was different. My big aim in life at the age of fifteen was to play for my country at both football *and* cricket.

Although the smallest player, I was made captain of both the football and cricket teams at Raley School in Barnsley and earned a place in the Barnsley Boys team. Our two teachers during those days – Arthur 'Pop' Hudson and Harold Rushforth – both loved their sport, and passed on their infectious enthusiasm to us.

I remember my headmaster at Raley, a chap called Henry Bird – yes, that really was his name – sending for me one day, just before I left, and saying to me, 'Just one word of advice, lad. If I were you I'd stick to sport. You're not much good at anything else, but I think you might do rather well at that.'

Two of my friends at Raley were Tommy Taylor, who went on to play football for Barnsley, Manchester United and England, and Arthur Rowe, who represented England in the shot putt at the Rome Olympics of 1960.

Tommy and I used to practise for hours and hours together on very rough ground in a field near our home in the Smithies area of Barnsley. I would float the ball across and he would head it. Tommy became the finest header of a ball I have ever seen, and I like to think that I played a small part in that development, with all those crosses I sent over for him. He had the gift of being able to rise in the air and hang there, waiting for the ball to come to him, and then he would head it with incredible power and accuracy. Nor was it like heading those plastic-coated balls of today. This was a heavy leather thing, with the bladder sticking out in a large blob where the stitching had burst. We couldn't afford a new one.

I have seen some of the best centre-forwards, from Tommy Lawton to Alan Shearer, and for me Tommy was the best of them all. He played nineteen times for England, scoring eighteen goals for his country before losing his life so tragically in the Munich air disaster of February 1958, a tremendous strike rate at international level.

When we played with the rest of the lads, it was usually about thirty a side on a strip barely thirty yards long. When it got dark it would be a case of 'next goal wins', and then we would go home.

Tommy and I signed amateur forms with Barnsley Football Club and played in the Northern Intermediate League. Jock Steele, a former player who was later to become manager, was the youth team coach at that time. We used to go down to Oakwell every Tuesday and Thursday night, and I really enjoyed those training sessions.

I was determined then to pursue my ambition to become a double international, but at the age of fifteen I had to have a cartilage operation, and I haven't kicked a ball since.

It happened one day when Barnsley's Northern Intermediate League game at Hull was postponed because of a waterlogged pitch. Jock Steele said I could go and play for the YMCA in a Barnsley League game away to Dodworth if I liked. I did, and crocked my knee. There was no keyhole surgery in those days, and I was bedbound for four weeks. Even then it was not a complete success. I have had five operations since, and it has always been a handicap.

That was the end of my football career, the end of my double international dream, and I was devastated.

I had always thought that my best chance was in football. My dad and other good judges always said that I was a better footballer than a cricketer, despite the fact that I was so small. My height was no handicap as far as I was concerned: Tom

Finney was small – he could not even get into his school team because of his size – yet he went on to become one of the greatest of them all. However, there is nothing you can do about an injury. Fate had dealt me a cruel blow and there was nothing for it but to concentrate all my efforts on cricket.

I first became interested in the sport at Raley Secondary School. The sports master, 'Pop' Hudson was very keen, and he encouraged me as much as anybody. He would organise cricket for us, and we would practise in the playground during the morning and afternoon breaks. We would chalk wickets on the school wall and make bats out of pieces of old wood, tying flattened sardine or cocoa tins round the bottom to strengthen them. We went to local fairs and begged some of the hard balls they used for throwing at coconuts. At other times we stuffed rags and all sorts into an outer cover and used that as a ball. We could not afford proper equipment. We had to make the best of the raw materials around us. They were hard times, no doubt about that, but happy times, too. To be honest, I think youngsters today are missing out. They have so many other things outside of sport to occupy their minds, and fewer of them are taking the opportunity to know the pleasure that can be gained from playing cricket.

Fewer youngsters play cricket on any waste ground they can find, as we used to do, but walk down any street in India and Pakistan and you will find hundreds of youngsters either side of you playing the game anywhere available to them. They are all hungry to succeed. They all want to play for India, or Pakistan, which is why these countries produce such good young players while we are struggling.

One day after I had left school I went to Barnsley Cricket Club to try to get a game. I had to catch two buses to get there, and then there was quite a long walk from the bus station to the ground. When I arrived I went up to a chap called Don Wollerton in the nets and asked if I could have a bat. He took one look at this skinny young lad and told me to go away. I was heart-broken, and turned to walk back down Shaw Lane to catch the bus home. As I walked a man on his way up to the ground stopped me and asked why I was crying.

'I've been to ask for a trial at the cricket club, but they just told me to go away,' I explained.

'Come with me, lad,' he said, and he took me to the nets. He bowled to me all night, then told me to come back – and I kept going back. But for him I could have been lost to cricket.

His name was Alf Broadhead, and he bowled not only to me, but Geoff Boycott and Michael Parkinson for hours and hours on end to give us batting practice.

Alf had had a great loss in his life. His son, Harry, was a tremendous prospect, having played with Barnsley and Yorkshire Boys, but he died from double pneumonia at the age of fourteen. I always believed that Alf took me under his wing because he could see some of Harry in me.

Alf is dead now, although I'll never forget him. I owe him so much. When I was featured on *This Is Your Life*, many stars from the world of cricket came to pay tribute to me, but I was so pleased that the last man they introduced was Alf. They brought him into the studio in his wheelchair, and I cried. Who knows what might have happened had he not stopped me on my way home from Shaw Lane that night . . .

I went on to open the innings for Barnsley while I was still only fifteen years old. Parky was the other opener. Boycs arrived at the club a little later, batting at number six in those days.

Those two always tell the story of how they used to have to put my pads and gloves on for me because I was so nervous, and claim that one day they tied my left and right pads together, so that when I got up to walk out to the middle I fell straight back down again. They also claim that I chewed right through the end of my gloves and then started on my nails. The truth is I have never bitten my nails in my life – twiddled my hair and left it standing up on end like chapel hat pegs, yes; but bitten my nails, no. Hubert Padgett usually opened with me, but there was one game at Hull when he was unable to play. Hull had batted first and scored 186, and our captain, Norman Umbers, said to Boycott at the tea interval, 'I want you to open the innings with Dickie.'

Geoff said, 'I'm not opening. I'll bat at number three. Let someone else see if they can knock a bit of the shine off the ball, then I'll go in and bat through to finish them off.'

Norman insisted, 'I want you to go in first with Dickie,' but Boycs was adamant.

'I've told you I'm batting at number three. No way am I going in first.'

In the end Eddie Legard, who went on to keep wicket for Warwickshire, volunteered to go in first with me, and we knocked off all 186 runs!

As we walked off the field and into the dressing room to celebrate our ten-wicket win, Boycott threw his bat. It whistled over our heads and smashed into the door.

'Why didn't one of you get out and give me a chance to bat?' he stormed.

I remember on another occasion batting with Parky at Shaw Lane when I decided that the pitch needed patting down. I gave it a hard thwack, and one wag on the boundary edge shouted, ''Ere, don't thee 'it it too 'ard, Birdy, there's men working under there.' He was right: Dodworth Colliery ran right under the square.

In another Yorkshire League game Parky and I put on 200 for the first wicket. Parky made 100 and I was 92 not out. It was form like that which earned us an invitation to attend the Yorkshire nets, and Parky's father John Willie was delighted. Parky was a fine club cricketer, and John Willie's big ambition was to see him playing for Yorkshire. If Parky was playing now, I reckon he would have been good enough, but not in those days. Yorkshire had such a strong side. League cricket in those days was better than it is today. The Barnsley team that played in the Yorkshire League while I was at Shaw Lane included Geoffrey Boycott, Eddie Legard, Michael Parkinson, Eric Butcher and Graham Pearce – to name but a few. All very good players. Three of us went on to play county cricket, and Boycott, of course, played for England. In more recent years Martyn Moxon, Arnie Sidebottom, Graham Stevenson and Darren Gough have all progressed from playing for Barnsley in the Yorkshire League to win international honours, although I have seen a gradual and worrying decline in the standard of cricket being played in the Yorkshire League and similar competitions.

However, the thrill remains the same when you are invited to county headquarters for a trial, and I remember that first day, when Parky and I went to the Headingley nets, as if it were yesterday.

I stood there at the side watching as Parky was put through his paces. Arthur Mitchell, the coach, a former Yorkshire and England player, sidled over to me. 'Is this bloke wi' thee?' he asked.

'Yes, Mr Mitchell.'

'Mm, what's 'e do, then?'

'He's an opening batsman, Mr Mitchell.'

'Is 'e now?' he said, stroking his chin. ''As 'e got a job?'

'Oh, aye, he's a journalist, Mr Mitchell.'

'I see. Well, from what I've just witnessed 'ere, would you pass on a bit of advice from me? Tell 'im ter stick ter journalism.'

It turned out to be good advice, and Parky has not done too

badly for himself in that sphere. He is probably the best feature writer in the world, and I also thought he was the best television chat show host. I am a tremendous admirer of Terry Wogan, a true professional, but Parky was the best.

I remember Parky telling me about his two most famous interviews, including the one in which he was given a bit of a rough time by Cassius Clay, as he then was. Mike's father was so upset at the treatment handed out by the man who went on to become a heavyweight champion legend as Muhammad Ali, that he went round to the dressing room afterwards and said to Mike, 'Tha shouldn't 'ave put up wi' that, lad. Tha should 'ave put one on 'im and flattened 'im.'

It was Mike who was flattened during that never-to-be-forgotten episode with Rod Hull, when Emu attacked him and dragged him off his chair and on to the floor of the studio. Parky didn't like that one little bit, but we still have a good laugh about it, even now.

Mike and I have kept our friendship to this very day, and we still talk about that first Headingley net. When Parky had finished, it was my turn.

Mitchell turned to me and queried, 'Where are you from, son?'

'Barnsley,' I answered proudly.

'Oh no, not another one! Which club?'

'Barnsley Cricket Club, Mr Mitchell.'

'Batsman?'

'Yes, Mr Mitchell.'

'Then put pads on, and them three theer will send thee a few balls down.' I looked across to where he was pointing. 'Them three' were Freddie Trueman, one of the finest fast bowlers in the world, Bob Appleyard, a marvellous off-cutter, and Johnny Wardle, a slow left-arm spin bowler who had also played for England. It would have been a daunting enough ordeal in perfect batting conditions, but I was being asked to face them on a rain-affected strip!

I was in the nets fifteen minutes and never laid bat on ball. All I did was keep sticking the stumps back in and replacing the bails. I was totally dejected. I couldn't have been more upset, or so I thought, until Mitchell came up to me and said, 'Well, lad, if tha's gooin' ter play like that, better not bother ter cum back.'

I did go back, however, because I was determined to show the old so-and-so that I *could* bat. It was the old coalminer's son spirit shining through again, and Mitchell liked that response. He appreciated the character and determination that I had shown. It was what he had been looking for. His method sorted out the men from the boys. Some youngsters went home crying and never did go back. Maurice Leyland, the other coach, was totally different. He would have a quiet, fatherly word in your ear, using the softly-softly approach. The two of them working in tandem proved a great success. I am proud to say that I ended up playing in the same team as all three of those great bowlers who bowled to me in the nets that day. Trueman, Appleyard and Wardle became my colleagues in the Yorkshire side.

Years later, Fred told me of his first experience in the Yorkshire nets. It could not have been a greater contrast to mine. The great Yorkshire coach then was George Hirst. He watched this raw young lad of fifteen or sixteen send down five balls, then stopped him. ''Oo 'ave you come wi', lad?' he asked.

'My dad brought me,' replied Fred.

George said, 'Right. Tell thy dad ter tek thee 'ome.'

'But I've only bowled five balls,' protested Fred.

'Aye, lad, and that's good enough for me. Tha'll be coming back, don't thee worry about that.' George Hirst knew straight-away that he'd unearthed a rare diamond from the mines in Frederick Sewards Trueman.

I made my own journey to the Yorkshire nets from Barnsley every Tuesday and Thursday through the winter months of January and February, and it was not easy. I had to get up at four thirty in the morning to go to work in the fitting shop. When I finished I would have a bath, get changed and grab a quick bite to eat. I would get my gear together – bat, pads and all the rest – hoist my bag on my shoulder, and go to catch the bus from Barnsley to Leeds. Cyril Turner, who also played for Yorkshire, was often on the same bus.

Arriving in Leeds I took the tram to Headingley. Very often it was lashing it down with rain, and the wind was howling around. Sometimes it would be snowing and bitterly cold.

I can picture Maurice Leyland now, wrapped up in an overcoat, cap on head, warming his hands in front of the dressing-room fire. I would sit and chat to him before we went off to the draughty indoor nets to practise on the old wooden boards, with no heating to keep fingers warm and supple.

Afterwards it was back on the tram into Leeds, then the bus home to dear old Barnsley. I would arrive home at about eleven thirty, catch five hours of sleep, and then clamber bleary-eyed out of bed for work in the early freezing hours of the following day.

I did that two nights a week every January and February until I finally signed for Yorkshire, and it strengthened my resolve to succeed. I thought to myself, Dickie lad, don't waste all this. Don't go through all this for nothing.

Would youngsters of today put up with all I had to go through? I doubt it.

2

YORKSHIRE GLORY – AND WHY I LEFT

I SIGNED for Yorkshire when I was nineteen years of age. My contract was not a written one. It was a gentleman's agreement. I merely shook hands with the chairman of the club, Mr Brian Sellers, and that was it.

Things went well at first. I scored a lot of runs in the second eleven and eventually earned my place in the first team for a three-day match against Scotland at Hull. In that side were Willie Watson, Freddie Trueman, Bob Appleyard, Raymond Illingworth, Johnny Wardle, Frank Lowson and Jimmy Binks, all of them internationals.

There are some players from whom you can learn an awful lot. Wardle, who I rate as one of the greatest slow left-arm bowlers of his type, was one such player. He was a fountain of knowledge and taught me more about cricket in half an hour than others did in a lifetime. He was a very hard and self-centred man, however. I occasionally travelled in the car with him and he used to put the radio on for the cricket scores. The announcer would go through the county games and Johnny's ears pricked up when it came to Yorkshire. 'And at The Oval, a good day for Yorkshire, who won by an innings, with Wardle taking 6 for 41.'

Then Johnny would turn the radio off. That's all he wanted to hear. He wasn't bothered about what other people had done.

Like most Yorkshiremen, Johnny was a bit tight with his brass, too. I was twelfth man for one match and he sent me for a packet of cigarettes. I stood waiting for him to give me the money, but he didn't. So off I went and bought the cigarettes myself, hoping that he would pay me when I handed them over. But no. As a young lad I was rather in awe of him, so I was too scared to ask, and I never did get my money for those cigs.

That hard edge was reflected in his attitude to the game. He was a tremendous competitor who really did play to win. That showed when he was selected for a tour of South Africa, when Peter May was captain. Before the start of the first Test he said to May, 'Do you want to win this series?'

May looked at him quizzically. 'Of course I do,' he answered. 'That goes without saying.'

'Right, then,' said Johnny. 'Let me bowl my googlies and chinamen.' He knew that on the good batting pitches of South Africa he would be able to get more turn bowling that way, and it was the best chance England had of success. He always maintained that the South Africans were unable to pick his wrong 'un, and he was right. I have talked to South African players from that series and they admit as much.

May was not keen on the idea. He wanted Wardle to bowl his orthodox leg spin. It led to a lot of arguing, but in the end it was decided to let Johnny have his way, and he won that Test series for England bowling his nonsense stuff. He really was a great bowler.

So, too, was Bob Appleyard. He typified the way all the Yorkshire bowlers went about their job. If he was bowling to me in the nets he would say, 'Right, Birdy, I want you to bat as if you were playing in a Test match. I'll tell you how my field is set, and I want you to take that into account when you are playing your shots. If you are not prepared to play that way, then I'll get someone who is.'

He even said the same to Colin Cowdrey in the England nets. Appleyard was so keen to get it exactly right that he had one of the country's best-ever batsmen helping him.

This attitude was ingrained into all the Yorkshire players at that time, bowlers and batsmen alike. It was part of the secret of the team's success. I do not think that modern-day players practise with such attention to detail, nor do I think they have the right attitude to training.

We all built up gradually over the months before the beginning of the season by playing cricket and using the muscles that we needed. We did all our work out there in the middle, where it mattered.

The proof of the pudding is always in the eating. Freddie Trueman bowled a thousand overs in a season, yet never once was he on the physio's table during his entire playing career.

Nowadays circuit training is the thing, and players are picking up more injuries than ever. Too much stress is being put upon the knees, ankles and base of the spine by the type of fitness work they are being asked to do.

We planned our cricket in the nets in those days. The younger players talked to the senior professionals and learned from them. We chatted about the game all the time, and it helped to develop a team spirit, as well as making us better cricketers.

Of course, there are certain things that can never be taught. How to take catches like Phil Sharpe, for example. Sharpey was one of the best slip fielders I have ever seen, if not the best. I would certainly put him up there with Bobby Simpson and Ian Chappell of Australia, England's Ian Botham and Eddie Barlow of South Africa. He had a gift of catching the ball when it had gone past him. It was remarkable to watch him. I've never seen anyone else take catches quite like that. But throw a tennis ball to him and it would spill out of his hands every time. Don't ask me why.

When you think about it we had a great side at Yorkshire in those days, and all the touring teams – Australia, West Indies and Pakistan – tasted defeat at the hands of the White Rose. You could run through the line-up and there would be ten internationals. It was the best Yorkshire side in all my time as a player and umpire, although the one from the Sellers' captaincy era, which included Verity, Rhodes, Leyland and Hutton, must also have been a great side.

There were also superb captains in Vic Wilson, Ronnie Burnet and Brian Close, and a great senior professional in Raymond Illingworth, whom I considered the brains behind it all. I rate Illingworth as one of the greatest captains of all time, along with Richie Benaud and Ian Chappell of Australia, and Michael Brearley and Peter May of England, but it was as a senior professional that he masterminded the success at Yorkshire.

I felt very privileged to have played with Close, who went on to become the kind of captain who led by example. He would never ask his players to do anything that he was not prepared to do himself. He led from the front. You have only to look at the success he had with Yorkshire, and later with Somerset, to see what a superb captain he was.

He was as hard as nails, too. He used to field as close to the wicket as possible to try to intimidate the batsmen. Brian himself tells the story of when a batsman pulled a long hop and hit Closey smack on the forehead. The ball ricochetted to a colleague and the batsman was caught out at cover first bounce off Closey's head. Everyone ran to him, concerned for his safety, and there was blood all over the place. But all he could think of was, 'Did you catch it?'

There was a similar occasion when I was umpiring a match in which Close captained Somerset. What he was doing there I'll never know. He should have carried on with Yorkshire. Brian Sellers was chairman of the committee which sacked him as captain and I do not think they treated him fairly, not after all the success he had. As if to prove a point he did a fabulous job at Somerset. They were a very mediocre side when he went there and he turned them into a force with which to be reckoned. They moved right up the championship table and reached the final of the Gillette Cup.

Anyway, I was umpiring this particular match between Somerset and Australia at Bath when Greg Chappell received a half-volley in line with the leg stump, and hit it with tremendous power towards Close at short leg. The ball hit him smack on the shin, and he just stood there as if nothing had happened. He did not do or say anything. He didn't even rub the spot where he had been hit. I thought, surely he must be in a lot of pain from that, it went with such force.

Later, when he thought no one was looking, he pulled up his trouser leg to view the damage, and his shin was twice its normal size. It looked like a rotten tomato, with blood oozing out. I said to him, 'Don't you want to go off, Brian? You ought to let someone have a look at that. It needs treatment.'

'Nowt ter worry about, lad,' was all he said. 'I'm alreight.' He always called me lad, did Brian.

There is another story about Closey, although he denies it, which came about when Yorkshire were playing Worcestershire at Worcester. We stayed in the Diglis Hotel, which is right beside the River Severn. After dinner we were all having a quiet drink before going to bed when Closey said, 'Will anyone bet me that I won't swim across to the other side of the river and back?'

Now the thing is, Closey always liked to have a bet on the gee-gees. I've seen him in the Yorkshire dressing room on a summer's day, mug of tea in one hand – he could drink tea for England – *Sporting Life* in the other, looking down the list of runners and riders to see which nag he could lose his money on.

On this particular occasion he must have felt a sudden urge for a flutter, and, in the absence of anything worthwhile, decided to shout the odds himself. It was pitch dark at the time, which made his dare even more bizarre. I can't recall if there were any takers, but Closey was undeterred. He dived into the river, swam across to the other side, then back again. Absolutely crazy! He might have done himself an injury, but he never gave a thought to the possible dangers. That was Closey all over.

Brian was the youngest player ever to represent England when he toured Australia in 1948 at the age of eighteen. He was also a very good golfer, with a very low handicap playing either right-handed or left-handed. He would have made a top-class golfer, but chose cricket as his profession. He also played football for Arsenal and Leeds United, which some people forget. A bad knee injury influenced his decision to concentrate on cricket. He was a magnificent all-round sportsman and one of cricket's truly great characters.

I have always been a great believer in a strong captain and a strong senior professional. I don't see any need for a manager. Good captain, good senior pro, and a good coach in the background – that was the Yorkshire system, and it worked. People will argue that times have changed, and maybe they have, but if I was captain of Yorkshire, or any other team, I would not want a manager interfering. I would live or die by my own decisions; I wouldn't want a manager putting his spoke in.

In 1996 Yorkshire returned to having a strong captain, David Byas, with a strong senior professional in Michael Bevan – and they had one of their most successful seasons for years. It is a system I am convinced would also work at international level. Too many cooks spoil the broth, so keep the structure as simple as possible.

My first experience of playing under this system with the Yorkshire first team came against Scotland at Hull. I had sat there in the dressing room as twelfth man on quite a few occasions, but now I really felt part of the county championship scene. It came as a bit of a surprise to be drafted into such a great side at the tender age of nineteen, but I was absolutely delighted.

I played my first county championship game against Derbyshire at Leeds in August, 1958, but I was subsequently in and out of the team, unable to command a regular place. I did, however, think I had done enough to stay in after one particular fixture.

I was recalled for a game against Glamorgan at Bradford Park Avenue in May 1959, because Ken Taylor was playing for England. At that time Glamorgan had some of the best spin bowlers in the country: England Test player Jim McConnon, an off-spinner; Don Shepherd, who bowled off-cutters and took stacks of wickets in county cricket; a slow left-arm bowler called Peter Walker, and Jimmy Presdee.

It was a poor wicket, which should have suited them, but we beat them by an innings – and I scored 181 not out. I remember looking up to the balcony where the thirty-odd members of the Yorkshire selection committee were gathering for a meeting to choose the team for the next three matches. When I finally came off the field having made my 181 not out I thought to myself, surely they must have picked me again after that.

The chairman, Brian Sellers, walked into the dressing room as I was taking my pads off. He came up to me and said, 'Well played, Birdy, that were a reight good knock. Tha's certainly played well, there.' Then he paused. 'But,' he went on, 'we've decided to drop you. You're in t' second team for t' next match.'

'Thank you very much, Mr Sellers,' I said to him. 'I'm just so proud to be part of a great Yorkshire side.' Those were my very words, and I meant them. I would have played for Yorkshire for nothing. When I walked through those gates at Headingley my chest used to swell with pride.

People have said that I never played for Yorkshire again, but I did. In fact, I was back in the side just a few weeks later for the game against Hampshire at Bournemouth. I was with Yorkshire Colts at Hull when the call came from Headingley for Jack Birkenshaw and myself to go straight down to Bournemouth to join the first team for the county championship fixture.

The situation at Hull was that Cheshire had set us 221 to win. Ted Lester, who was then the Colts' captain and went on to become Yorkshire's scorer, sent Jack and myself in first.

'Better get on with it,' said Ted. 'As soon as you're out, off you go to Bournemouth.' Jack soon gave a catch as he hit out, but I didn't fancy giving my wicket away, so I 'retired hurt' on 13.

Even so, we were cutting it fine. We had to run from the ground, still in our whites, with our clothes tucked underneath our arms and our spikes sending sparks cascading from the pavement as we dashed to the station. We just managed to scramble aboard the London train in the nick of time. The line runs past the ground and we were able to look out of the window and wave to our team-mates as they were busily chasing the runs.

That game finished with Yorkshire on 211 for 8, but with me on the train it was really for 9, and Freddy Millett, the Cheshire captain, always used to pull my leg about the incident, claiming that I almost gave his side victory.

Although we lost at Bournemouth, I top-scored in the second innings with 68. It may hardly come as a surprise to learn that I was dropped for the following game.

We had a bit of a hiccup after that, losing to Somerset at Bath by 16 runs and then suffering a disaster against Gloucestershire at Bristol. They scored 294 for 8 declared and beat us by an innings and 77 runs. We were bowled out for a meagre 35 in the first innings, and I was one of six batsmen to get a duck.

Brian Close was playing hell in the dressing room. 'Play forward, play forward!' he kept screaming as one batsman followed another. Then he went in, played back and was bowled first ball by one that kept low. We did a bit better in the second innings, making 182, to which I contributed 5 before being run out.

Tony Brown, now the administrative secretary at the England & Wales Cricket Board, did most of the damage.

Thankfully, we put a stop to the rot by beating Worcestershire by six wickets, Trueman and Illingworth returning after missing the two defeats because they were on Test duty, and from there we went on to clinch the championship at Hove, thus ending Surrey's remarkable run of seven successive title wins.

It was an extraordinary achievement by Yorkshire. In 1958 the first team had finished near the bottom of the table, which was hardly surprising in view of the fact that in the two or three preceding years they had parted company with some of their great players – Appleyard, Watson, Wardle and Lowson.

While we had won the minor counties championship that same year, it was not thought that even the richly talented younger players would be ready to make a championship challenge twelve months later.

I did not play in the match at Hove when the team made certain of the title by beating Sussex, but I was there as twelfth man. And what an occasion that was.

We scored 218 in ninety-eight minutes to win the match, and I still have a newspaper cutting which describes the scenes of jubilation immediately afterwards:

Yorkshire were the heroes even of Sussex folk, who gathered outside the pavilion calling for the players. Led out by Ronnie Burnet the team received thunderous applause. Surrey's vice-captain, Alec Bedser, who had led the reigning champions so often in the absence of Peter May, took Yorkshire's success in his usual sporting fashion. He said, 'I think a lot of the credit for Yorkshire's success must go to their skipper Ronnie Burnet, who has moulded all the youngsters into a first-rate team.'

Yet seldom has there been such criticism of a county cricket captain than of Burnet. He had never played first-class cricket when he took over, a fact that was held against him by his critics, but he never pretended to be a first-class cricketer. He was called upon to do a job and he did it to the best of his ability. It wasn't bad to win the county championship in only his second year.

After the Sussex match we travelled up from Hove to Scarborough, where we were due to play in the annual cricket festival. There were no motorways then, so it was a long journey, and we didn't arrive in Scarborough until four a.m.

We tried to snatch a few hours' sleep before going to the ground on the Saturday morning to find thousands and thousands of people lining the roads. The ground itself was absolutely chock-a-block, and they had to close the gates. At eleven thirty, when the game should have started, we were still sitting out on the pitch having our photographs taken.

The fêted championship-winning team comprised Bryan Stott, Ken Taylor, Doug Padgett, Brian Close, Raymond Illingworth, Ronnie Burnet, Jimmy Binks, Jack Birkenshaw, Don Wilson, Fred Trueman and Bob Platt. I was twelfth man

I had occupied that position fairly regular for most of the season. There is more to it than meets the eye. For example, it was part of my job, as twelfth man, to get all the players' bags together after a match, say at Headingley, load them on to a van, accompany them to the railway station and see them into the guard's van in preparation for the trip to somewhere like Southampton for the next match the following day. Then I would have to unload them at the other end and make sure they arrived safely at the hotel.

I became so proficient at this task that I am sure the selectors used to say, 'Hey, Dickie's brilliant at seeing to all the baggage, fellas, let's make him twelfth man again.'

We travelled a lot by train in those days. It was much more relaxing than travelling by car. With no motorways it meant taking what amounted to country lanes from Leeds to Bristol, Southampton, Hove, Canterbury and all those places. Players had to take it in turns to drive, which was very tiring. There was often barely time for a late-night drink before we were snuggling up in bed trying to get some sleep before turning out for another hard day's slog the following day.

One of my very close friends in those days was Don Wilson. He loved his cricket and enjoyed every single moment of his career. He was a very good slow left-arm bowler who reminded me of Bishen Bedi in many ways. He was not a great spinner of the ball, but he had superb variation of flight. He was also a brilliant fielder in the mid-wicket and cover point areas. He was a lot like me. We were so proud to be part of that Yorkshire squad.

I remember the first day he came to the county nets. He never laid bat on ball for twenty minutes.

Arthur Mitchell came over to me and asked, 'What does this lad do for a living, Birdy?'

'He's a joiner from Settle, Mr Mitchell,' I told him.

'A joiner is 'e? Then tell 'im from me, the next time 'e comes, 'e'd better bring an 'ammer, some nails an' a few planks o' wood to board that end up. 'E needs summat ter protect his stumps, 'cos that bat's neether use nor ornament.'

However, although Don may not have been the best batsman in the world he was good enough with the ball to go on to play for

England. He was head coach at Lord's for a time and is now doing a wonderful job as coach at Ampleforth College, near York.

While he was at Lord's he tells me that he was looking out of his office window at the Nursery End one winter's morning and spotted me out in the middle practising my signals. He immediately called all the young lads over and said to them, 'Look there, that's my old pal Dickie Bird. He is to become a Test umpire. He'll practise his art at every opportunity, and I'm asking you all to do the same. What's good enough for him is good enough for you. You have to practise if you want to get to the top. But take a good look, because I don't think you'll see anything quite like it again.'

I spent many happy hours in Settle with Don and his parents. He and I also used to travel together with Yorkshire, along with Phil Sharpe. The three of us were big fans of the Black and White Minstrels. We would go all over to watch them. After the show, usually at the Victoria Palace in London, we would go to the dressing room to chat with the lead singers, Tony Mercer, Dai Francis and John Boulter – they had beautiful voices – Reg Thompson the resident comedian, and the compere Leslie Crowther. All were cricket fanatics and we got on famously.

They used to appear at Scarborough for the summer season, so we were regular visitors during the cricket festival there in September. I do miss those days. We used to go through the Black and White Minstrels' routine with them from start to finish. One of my favourites was 'Abba Dabba'. Don said I was quite brilliant at it. Leslie Crowther became a Lord's Taverner, like me, so we saw a lot of each other through the years. I was devastated when he died.

Don first made his mark in the county side after the controversial sacking of Johnny Wardle in 1958. Wardle always said what he thought and had often been in trouble with the Yorkshire committee. Things came to a head when he made some comments about his colleagues in an article in the *Daily Mail*. Shortly afterwards the Yorkshire committee issued a statement which read as follows:

> The Yorkshire County Cricket Club Committee regret the unpleasant publicity given to their decision to dispense with the services of J.H. Wardle after the present season. In past years Wardle has been warned on several occasions that his general behaviour on the field and in the dressing rooms left much to be desired. As no improvement was shown this year, the decision to dispense with his services was made, as it was unanimously considered that it was essential to have discipline and a happy and loyal team before any lasting improvement could be expected in the play of the Yorkshire XI. It was felt that the recent articles published in the *Daily Mail* fully justify the committee's decision. Wardle broke his contract when he wrote these articles without first obtaining permission, and the committee are therefore terminating his engagement forthwith.

His dismissal came just three days after he had been chosen by the MCC to go to Australia, and the MCC subsequently withdrew their invitation.

Wardle had always had a chip on his shoulder with regard to the captain, Ronnie Burnet. He had no respect for him because of the fact that he had come straight out of league cricket, playing for Baildon, when there were others far better qualified to lead the side. Wardle also criticised the committee and the players.

It did not surprise me. He always had that ruthless streak in him, both on and off the field. He was too outspoken and he paid dearly for it.

I thought it was harsh that he should have been given the sack and we were all shocked. The dressing room was in a state of sheer disbelief. The entire cricket world was stunned. They say that a bowler of his type, left-arm slow, does not learn his trade until his early thirties, so Wardle was really very much at his peak. One moment he was about to tour with the MCC and suddenly he was out in the wilderness, on the scrap heap at thirty-five.

He never thought Yorkshire would sack him, but the committee wanted to show that no one player was bigger than the club. It could be said that the committee was proved right, because the year after he had been so severely criticised by Wardle, Burnet led Yorkshire to the county championship.

I still felt sorry for Wardle. He was a great bowler who really knew the game – I learned a lot from him – and he was an entertainer. The crowds loved him. He sometimes used to pretend to lose the ball, slipping it into his pocket and having everyone search for it. At other times he would pretend to throw the ball in to the wicket-keeper after it had gone past him. The batsmen would stop dead in their tracks, not quite knowing what was going on. It was fun for the fans, but the committee did not always appreciate it.

He once told me that what upset him more than anything in life was that Tony Lock was preferred to him in the England side. Johnny always thought that Lock threw the ball.

The saddest thing was that Wardle died shortly after the current committee had asked him to return to the fold as a bowling coach, a task he was looking forward to immensely. He still had a lot to offer and the job would have given him a lot of pleasure and satisfaction.

When his sacking was announced back in 1958, Don Wilson and I were with the second team at Scarborough. We received a telegram from the Yorkshire secretary, John Nash, telling us to report the next day to Middlesbrough, where the first team were playing Essex. Wilson played, took five wickets, and that was the start of his career. Needless to say, I was twelfth man. Again.

While it was remarkable that we won the championship the

following year with such a young team, we had three very experienced players in Trueman, Illingworth and Close, all well-established internationals, and there is no doubt that they played a significant part in the success.

Burnet also proved a very strong captain. Although an amateur, he fought for his professional players. He had nothing to lose, you see. He had his business. He was not reliant on cricket. He probably summed it up best when he said, 'It has been a team job. All the season it has been team spirit that has counted. I am very proud that Yorkshire have taken the title from Surrey after such a long run.'

I played in the last match of the season, against the MCC at Scarborough, and scored 60-odd despite facing up to the fastest bowler I have ever known – Frank Tyson. They called him 'Typhoon', and through the air I honestly believe he was quicker than any of the great bowlers.

I opened the innings against him and hit his first three deliveries through the off side for four. With supreme confidence I went on to the front foot for the fourth ball. Tyson dropped one short. It reared up and hit me on the chin. I went down as if I'd just been on the receiving end of a right hook from Tyson's namesake Mike.

Former Yorkshire captain Norman Yardley was one of those who had no sympathy with my plight.

'Thought you had more sense,' he muttered to me. 'After those first three deliveries you should have been on the back foot waiting for the short-pitched one.'

I still carry the scar to show for my folly that day. There was blood all over and I saw stars. I could hear bells ringing in my head, although they told me afterwards that was the ambulance on its way to pick me up and cart me off to hospital. I had several stitches inserted in the wound and returned to resume my innings.

Tyson was immediately reintroduced to the attack, but I hit the first delivery straight back over his head for four, remembering the words of Maurice Leyland: 'You know, Dickie,' he had once told me, 'none of us likes playing against fast bowlers, but some of us don't let on.'

Leyland was a real gentleman. Michael Parkinson once told the great Australian leg-spin bowler, Bill O'Reilly, that Leyland was one of the kindest, gentlest men he had ever met.

O'Reilly studied Parky for a while. 'That's good to know,' he said. 'But then, you didn't have to bowl at the little bugger.'

In those days the county champions played a team selected from the rest of the counties to bring down the curtain on the season, and we were due to fulfil that fixture at The Oval immediately after the Scarborough festival finished. I thought I would surely be in the squad, so you can imagine my feelings when I was left out again. Even the rest of the Yorkshire players were so disgusted at the way I had been treated that they clubbed together to take me down to The Oval with them.

Afterwards I had a long clear-the-air chat with Brian Sellers, who said to me, 'Tha's been in and out o' t' side all summer, Birdy. And tha's played some good innings. So tha's a good chance o' startin' next season in t' first team. We feel that Vic Wilson is at end of 'is career, an' 'is place is likely to go to you.'

'Thank you very much, Mr Sellers, that's given me a lot of hope and confidence,' I replied.

Then, in January, I had a phone call from Burnet. He was crying down the phone.

'Why are you crying, Skipper?' I said.

'Dickie, I've been sacked as the Yorkshire captain.'

'You're joking,' I said. 'They can't sack you. You've just won the county championship.'

'That's what I thought,' he wept. 'I was certain they would

give me at least another season. What's more, do you know who they've made captain in my place?'

'No, Skipper,' I said.

'Vic Wilson.'

'Well, that's it for me as well. There goes my chance of getting into the side. And after all Sellers said to me.'

Years later Freddie Trueman told me, 'Burnet shouldn't have been the captain in the first place. I should have been the bloody captain.'

However, Burnet had done a tremendous job, and I could not believe what had happened.

It was with a sense of unease that I reported back in the nets that April. However, I was determined not to let things upset me and I had a good month, making some big scores in the practice matches, and was confident of making the party for the southern tour, which preceded the county championship season in those days. Both Arthur Mitchell and Maurice Leyland told me that because of the way I had played throughout April they had recommended that I should be in the side.

At the pre-season lunch Mr Sellers got to his feet to announce a squad of fourteen for the southern tour. He read out those fourteen names, and mine wasn't among them. I could not believe what I had just heard. I sat there with the other Yorkshire players and cried.

When I got home I told my father that I had been left out again and that I was bitterly disappointed.

He said, 'Fight it out, son. You've got to fight it out.'

'Dad, I don't think I can. I just can't take any more of this. I've made up my mind. I'm going to ask for my release from Yorkshire.'

Dad was against it, but I was determined, and I wrote a letter to the Yorkshire committee asking them to release me. Mr Nash, who was secretary at the time and a wonderful man, wrote back on their behalf, telling me that, after some discussion, they had decided not to release me.

So I banged in another letter. The reply was the same. They were not prepared to let me go.

In went a third letter. This time they wrote back saying that, with great reluctance, they agreed to my release, but only, they stated, because I was so insistent.

Their reply said that even then the committee had been split, and Mr Nash wanted me to know that Herbert Sutcliffe had stood up for me. 'No way,' Sutcliffe had said, 'can you afford to let Dickie Bird go,' which, coming from a great man like Herbert, was marvellous. He averaged more than 60 in his Test career and was one of the best batsmen of all time, and his comment meant so much to me. However, I was still adamant that I would leave.

Meanwhile, Willie Watson, who had left Yorkshire and was now captain of Leicestershire, had approached me, saying that if I ever decided to leave Headingley, there would be a place for me at Grace Road. So that's where I went, and it was the biggest mistake of my career.

When Yorkshire released me, nearly every county made an approach, but Watson had got in first and he was very persuasive. I gave in to that persuasion without really thinking things through, without talking to other people in the game who might have advised me. I was too upset. The result was that, at twenty-six years old, I was joining a side at the bottom of the county championship table after being with a side that had just won the title. It was a big step down the ladder.

To play in a team struggling at the foot of the table is a very hard job, particularly as the Leicestershire public were looking to me as some sort of a saviour: the man to pull the side round, to get stacks and stacks of runs. The Press also built me up, and it put a lot of pressure on me. While I have always been able to handle pressure, sadly I was never the player at Leicestershire that I had been at Yorkshire. Possibly the expectations were too great, yet I still scored more than a thousand runs in my first season, was always in the side, and was awarded my county cap. Then they made Maurice Hallam, a Leicestershire man, the captain in place of Watson. Hallam had it in for Yorkshiremen, simply because the England selectors had picked Ken Taylor, of Yorkshire, before him. Now, I am the first to admit that Hallam should have played for England instead of Taylor at that time – he had scored a thousand runs at the end of May, while Taylor had managed about 450 – but it was so unfair that Hallam should choose to take it out on the four Yorkshiremen at Leicestershire: Jack Birkenshaw, Jack Van Geloven, Peter Broughton and me. It was not as though we had selected the England side, was it? But Hallam stated publicly that he would make it very difficult for the Yorkshiremen in his side, and he certainly did just that.

It was not all gloom and doom, however. For instance, Hallam and I put on 277 runs for the first wicket against South Africa in July, 1960, the county's best opening stand since the war. It is said that a late arrival at Grace Road that day blinked at the scoreboard, shrugged his shoulders and muttered, 'South Africa 200 for none? Ah, well, what could we expect?' He then moved nearer the play and could hardly believe his eyes when he realised that the tourists were, in fact, the fielding side. Surely it could not be Maurice Hallam at one end? It certainly was. And Dickie Bird at the other? Right again.

On another occasion I was 98 against Sussex at Grace Road and confident of completing my century. I hit the ball to mid-off and called to my partner for a single. He let me get right up to him, then sent me back. He never moved, and I did not have a snowball in a hot oven's chance of regaining my ground. My batting colleague that day was the aptly named Rodney Pratt.

I do, however, hold a record at Leicestershire. I bagged two noughts between tea and close of play on the first day of a match, and that will take some beating. Sussex batted first and scored well over 300 before their captain, Ted Dexter, decided to declare.

We went in after tea. I was dismissed for a duck, and the entire team was back in the pavilion with only 30-odd on the board. We had to follow on, with just time for one over before close of play. That was long enough to see me out again, in exactly the same way, caught by Doggart round the corner at leg slip off a Thompson inswinger for nought.

Willie Watson did not fare much better. He got nought and one. We were eventually bowled out for 40-something the following day.

I certainly did not enjoy my time at Leicestershire, I have to be honest about that, but the club changed dramatically when Michael Turner took over as chief executive and Raymond Illingworth was brought in. Illy led them to the county championship and he and Turner breathed new life and ambition into the club. It is now one of the best in the world, having won the Sunday League, the Benson & Hedges Cup and regained the championship crown in 1996. I am a life member and proud to be associated with what is now a tremendous set-up. To play for Leicestershire today would give me a great thrill.

One of the players in that first championship side under Illingworth was Chris Balderstone, who is now a first-class county umpire. He was an opening batsman and there was one famous occasion when he made an unbeaten century on the Friday, dashed off straight after close of play to turn out for Doncaster Rovers in their final football league fixture of the season, returned to his hotel for a good night's sleep, and continued his innings on the Saturday morning.

Yorkshire are also enjoying a resurgence under Sir Laurence Byford as president and Bob Platt as chairman of a good cricket committee. There is now a sound structure at the club and the future looks brighter than for some years. I believe it is only a matter of time before Yorkshire win the county championship again.

They have some magnificent young players, and, while I am not one for putting my head on the block, because so many youngsters with so much natural ability and flair fall by the wayside, I am convinced that in Anthony McGrath, Michael Vaughan and Chris Silverwood, Yorkshire have three outstanding prospects who could all go on to play for England.

The current crop of Yorkshire players are a credit to the club. They go to lunch in their blazers, not tracksuit tops, and there is a lot to be said for that kind of dress code. It shows a pride in the club and the White Rose.

I am thrilled to have been made an honorary life member of the Yorkshire County Cricket Club. It is a tremendous honour and I never dreamed, when I left Headingley, that one day I would be joining that list of such great names as Sir Donald Bradman, Sir Len Hutton, Brian Close, Raymond Illingworth, Geoffrey Boycott and Paul Getty.

If I could have my time over again I would not have left Yorkshire. I would have stuck it out like my father advised, even if it meant being in and out of the side. I do, however, feel that if Sir Laurence Byford had been in charge in my day, my career would have taken a different course. This fellow is good for the game. He has already done a lot for Yorkshire cricket, and I would like to think that Yorkshire will win something for him.

Still, having said all this, if I had stayed on at Yorkshire, I might not have ended up with so many wonderful memories and honours collected during my marvellous years on the international umpiring scene.

As my father always said, 'The good Lord moves in mysterious ways.'

3

GATEWAY TO
SOUTH AFRICA

I RETIRED from county cricket at the end of the 1964 season at the comparatively young age of thirty-two. I was not at all happy at Leicestershire and I was also having problems with my right knee, which had been a weakness throughout my career. There were one or two shots which really pained me, especially the sweep, which was a favourite of mine and one which I played particularly well. Twinges would shoot through my whole body, and the pain was excruciating at times. What with one thing and another, it all got too much for me, and I decided, reluctantly, to call it a day.

It was one of the biggest decisions I have had to make in my life, but, although it was a big wrench to leave county cricket, looking back it was the right one. So, at the same time as my old mate Geoffrey Boycott was making his maiden Test century against the Australians, I was turning my back on the first-class game – or so I thought.

I had, however, one or two other irons in the fire. Some very good opportunities had been offered me, and I gave them serious thought. One of the offers came from Plymouth College, the public school in Devon, who wanted me to go there as a cricket coach. I have always enjoyed coaching, and the idea appealed, so for the next three seasons I coached at Plymouth College while playing professionally for Paignton Cricket Club on Saturday afternoons. I enjoyed the new challenge and was happily soon back among the runs.

In my first season for Paignton I scored 2,000 runs, including 30 half centuries, in 40 innings at an average of 81.2; the following season I did even better, with 2,520 runs, including three centuries and 23 half centuries, in 47 innings for an average of 90.12; and in 1967 I topped the 2,000 mark for the third successive time at an average of 79.12. Another 2,000 runs flowed from the Bird bat in 1968, but I am sad to say I slipped up in 1969 when I managed only 1,900 runs, although in fewer innings.

Those were happy, relaxed times for me, and I also enjoyed working with the schoolboys at Plymouth College, so much so that I went in for the advanced coaching certificate. Receiving that award in January 1966 was almost as thrilling as first playing for Yorkshire, and winning my Leicestershire cap. Only those who had played county or minor counties cricket could take the advanced examination, which meant there were only about 350 of us worldwide and a mere half-dozen in Yorkshire.

The advanced coaching certificate provided the opportunity to go to South Africa. That winter my former Yorkshire colleague Don Wilson invited me to Johannesburg along with Geoff Boycott, Phil Sharpe and Tony Nicholson, to coach in schools there. All the schoolboys were cricket mad and the standard was far ahead of anything I had seen in schools in England. The climate helped, of course, and the pitches were first class.

I was determined from the start not to coach natural ability out of young players, and I hope I never did. It is, perhaps, a mistake that is made too often by over-enthusiastic coaches. My aim was always to encourage a player's strengths while at the same time working on any weakness. A lad might come up to me and say, 'I'm getting out like this, Dickie, what do you think I'm doing wrong?' I'd try to help cure the problem without getting too complicated and technical.

Take a bowler, for example. I've seen young bowlers going wide of the return crease, yet I have made no attempt to rectify what might be seen as a fault, because they also had a natural gift of being able to pitch on the line of middle stump and make the ball leave the batsman. Those kinds of skills need developing, not curbing.

Malcolm Marshall is a prime example of this. He always bowled wide of the crease with an open-chested action, yet he was a truly magnificent bowler. The West Indies will be eternally grateful that no one coached that out of him, although one or two English batsmen might wish they had! Natural talent should be allowed to blossom and flourish. It should be nurtured.

While on the subject of coaching in schools, it occurs to me that one of the reasons why England have struggled to produce world-class players in recent years is that there is now an alarming lack of cricket being played in schools, particularly the comprehensives. They say teachers are no longer available to oversee practice sessions and matches, and facilities at most places are virtually non-existent.

Care should always be taken in coaching, not only at schoolboy and youth levels, but also with the senior players. We keep on about changing the structure of county cricket, and more and more coaches are being wheeled in all over the country. There are coaches here, coaches there, coaches everywhere, for this, that and the other, telling players all kinds of different things and inventing all kinds of theories, filling young heads with contrasting opinions and ideas so that most of them end up in a whirl of confusion.

I am convinced that is what happened to Darren Gough for a time after his early Test success for England in Australia. Too many people were offering their 'help and advice' with regard to his action and technique and, as the Aussies themselves believed, he became over-coached to such an extent that he was no longer sure what he was supposed to do.

In 1968 South African cricket suffered a terrible blow with the cancellation of the MCC tour and all the political implications that followed. There was an objection to the inclusion in the MCC team of a Cape Coloured South African, Basil D'Oliveira. The cancellation of that tour brought the problems of apartheid more forcibly before the British public and there was a great deal of controversy surrounding it.

The cricket-loving public of South Africa were upset because they felt they had a chance to prove that their players were the best in the world. The players wanted to play, the fans wanted to watch, but they were all denied the opportunity because of the apartheid question which had been brought dramatically to the fore by D'Oliveira's selection for the tour. If that tour had gone ahead I honestly believe that South Africa would have triumphed in a great series.

For me it continued to be a successful time. Having been selected as manager and coach to the Transvaal Cricket Union's Under-15 touring team to Rhodesia, I was delighted when the lads won all eight matches. They were also unbeaten the following year on a ten-day tour of Cape Town and the Western Province.

Meanwhile, one of the most satisfying aspects of my coaching was that we had begun to take the game to the black kids as well as the whites. I was proud and privileged to be one of the first coaches to go to Soweto, the African township outside

Johannesburg, to coach children from the schools there. There was tremendous excitement when Don Wilson started his Soweto coaching clinic in January 1973. More than thirty schools were involved. For the first time the black schoolchildren began to talk about wickets, slips, byes, bowlers, batsmen and boundaries, instead of centre-forwards, right-wingers, full-backs, goalkeepers and goals. The average daily attendance was about 120 students, although one day there was a record 515.

When I first went there it was so dangerous that I had a police escort. When I arrived at the venue where I was supposed to be coaching there was not a soul to be seen. Then all of a sudden, they came over the top of the hill, a bit like the natives in that old Michael Caine film, *Zulu*. Most of them had ragged, patched-up pants, no shoes, although a few had sandals, and certainly there was not a single one of them dressed for cricket; nor did they have any gear. I had never experienced anything like it before, and it really saddened me to see children in that state.

It was very different from the magnificent playing facilities enjoyed by their white counterparts. Even the practice pitches in Johannesburg were out of this world, and here were these black lads with not a cricket stump, a bat or a ball between them, turning up to play on a bit of waste ground.

I remember a teenager who wore a bowler hat and carried a brolly – he had obviously picked them up after they had been thrown away – but had no shoes or sandals on his feet. He asked me, 'Excuse me, but are you Mr Dickie Bird, the Professor of Cricket?'

'That's me, man,' I answered.

'We're here for the cricket coaching,' he said.

'Right then,' I told him. 'Let's make a start.'

However, as I looked round I thought, 'What am I going to do? There simply isn't enough equipment to go round.' It was a bit like Jesus trying to share out the five loaves and two small fishes amongst the multitude. Eventually I decided to split them into small groups, give each group a bat and ball, which our sponsors had provided, and get them playing little games of cricket.

They had no idea how to start. I went to each group in turn trying to explain the rudiments of the game to them, but as soon as my back was turned they started playing football. I could not believe it. There they were, bare-footed, kicking a cricket ball around, flicking it up in the air and controlling it on their thighs and instep as it came down. After a while I gave up. I just let them carry on. Just so long as they don't start heading it, I thought. Then I really could have a problem!

They were football daft, you see. They loved sport that was quick and exciting – football, rugby, cycling and boxing. They talked about Pelé, Eusebio and Cassius Clay. They knew of Bobby Charlton and Stanley Matthews from England. In fact Sir Stanley was doing a marvellous job coaching football in Soweto. They were much more interested in him and his sport than in me and mine.

I did my best and gradually the youngsters responded. Given time one or two cricketers will come through from the black community, but it will be a very long and tough road for them. I saw one or two with talent, but it was very raw. It will take years of patient coaching to bring them up to the standard of the white lads, although Paul Adams is already making a huge contribution. The black South African footballers, however, are already emerging on the world stage. Some are playing in the English leagues. There are some magnificent football stadiums in Soweto, capable of seating up to 80,000 people, and now they have their own Football League, in which the standard is improving by leaps and bounds.

Seeing those children play football and cricket on that rough ground brought back memories for me because it was not unlike the area I used to play on around my Smithies home with 'Tucker' Taylor and the lads. One thing we never experienced, though, was the presence of a girls' team, who played against the boys with such enthusiasm and determination that it was difficult to spot the difference.

I wanted to take a party from Soweto into the Wanderers Club in Johannesburg so that they could see first-class cricket for themselves. I thought it would be a good idea for them to watch the game between Transvaal and Natal, but my request was met with consternation. On no account could black children be allowed into the ground.

Undaunted, I said, 'Well, what about bringing them in at a time when there is no game being played, just so they can have a look round?'

Jack Cheetham, a former South African cricket captain, who was then president of the Transvaal Cricket Union, said, 'You don't know what you're asking, Dickie. In our country this is just not possible.'

The only blacks who were allowed into any of the cricket or sports grounds were those who were employed as workers under a white head groundsman. I was most upset. It doesn't matter to me whether a person is white, black, yellow, or sky-blue with yellow dots on, if someone wants to watch or play cricket he or she should be allowed to do so. To be fair, most of the cricket-loving South Africans felt the same. They would have loved to see the blacks and whites playing together, and, thankfully, that is now happening due to the efforts of President Nelson Mandela and Dr Ali Bacher, who is the managing director of the United Cricket Board of South Africa.

Because of this I anticipate South Africa becoming strong again as a cricketing force. Another five years or so and you just watch, they will have some great players and a very good team. Remember, they trounced England at Lord's in 1995 not long after being re-admitted to the Test scene – I umpired that match – and they will continue to improve.

It is just so very sad that because of the apartheid troubles such great players as Barry Richards, Michael Proctor and Graeme Pollock, to name but three, were lost to Test cricket. They played only a handful of matches for their country and you can only wonder at what they might have achieved had they played more.

When I returned for my fifth winter it was as the official head coach in charge of a group of English professionals, one of whom was Bob Woolmer who is a national coach in South Africa. Also with me were Jack Simmons, who played for Lancashire; Clive Radley (Middlesex and England); Kevin Lyons, of Glamorgan, who went on to become coach at Worcester and a first-class umpire; Mike Taylor (Nottinghamshire), and his brother Derek (Surrey).

I have to admit that I am not a good sailor, so the times I have sailed out to South Africa have left me looking a bit green around the gills. I have always had to take sea sickness tablets to try to ease the situation. I'm fine on the train, the bus is no problem; I'm all right driving the car although I'm not too happy if someone else is driving; but I dread going on boats and planes.

Don Wilson was with me on one of my trips and I started feeling sick while the *Windsor Castle* was still in the harbour at Southampton. Don sent for the nurse and told her, 'Look, my mate here is a bad traveller. He is going to be sick. You've got to give him something.' She gave me an injection which caused me almost as much distress as the sickness. On top of that it cost me a guinea.

I am so bad on water that I even felt queazy one afternoon when Don and I decided to take one of the rowing boats out on the lake at Peasholm Park in Scarborough – and it's only eighteen inches deep. Just as well because I felt so ill that I had to get out of the boat in the middle of the lake, roll up my trousers and paddle my way to the bank. Goodness knows what all the holidaymakers thought.

In 1973 I accepted the post as coach at St John's College in Johannesburg. As in all white schools in South Africa they had classes in the mornings, and the afternoons were given over to sport, cricket, tennis, rugby and swimming being the major ones.

I had a wonderful non-cricketing experience when I spent an afternoon with the legendary former undefeated world heavyweight boxing champion Rocky Marciano. He was in South Africa for the welterweight championship fight between Willie Ludick, of South Africa, and Carmelo Bossie, the European champion from Italy.

Rocky told me all about the great fights he had with Joe Walcott, Ezzard Charles, Archie Moore and many others. He talked about Muhammad Ali, or Cassius Clay as he then was.

'A great fighter, lovely boxer, beautiful mover,' he told me. 'But if he had been around in my day I'd have knocked him out in the twelfth.'

In South Africa I lived like a millionaire. The food, fresh fruit and wine were simply wonderful. I made many friends, all of them with beautiful homes and swimming pools in their gardens. There I was, sun on my back, doing something I enjoyed and getting paid for it. What could be better? But I was aware of the way the kids in the townships lived. The difference between the living standards of whites and blacks had to be seen to be believed. That is why it gave me more pleasure than anything to coach cricket in Soweto.

It was a tough decision in many ways to stop going to South Africa, which, for all its problems, I always think of with great fondness, but when the Gleneagles Agreement came into force banning South Africa from all international sport, there was only one course of action to take. Something had to be done about apartheid and if the ban would help, then so be it.

In the early nineties I returned to South Africa on a speaking tour, along with Freddie Trueman and his wife Veronica, and Ian Botham and his wife Kathy. We were held up and arrived late for a flight from Johannesburg to Durban, but when we finally arrived at the airport we found the plane still on the runway. It meant, however, that we had to clear the formalities pretty quickly. The other four went through with no problem. But not me.

The buzzer went as I passed through the magic eye and I had to go back to be frisked. I kept telling them, 'Look, I've got nowt in my pockets. I've no idea what's causing the blooming thing to go off, but my plane'll be off if I don't get through here sharpish.' So I had another go and again the buzzer went off. Fred, Ian and their wives were by this time getting almost as agitated as me.

'For goodness sake, Dickie,' they said. 'Get a move on.'

Finally, a third search solved the mystery. They discovered an old half-crown just visible in the lining of my blazer. They didn't bother getting it out, though, and it's still there to this day. We just caught the plane.

Now South Africa has been welcomed back into the international arena and it was heart-warming for me, when I returned there, to see blacks and whites beginning to come together. Nelson Mandela has done a marvellous job in that respect. When I met him I found him to be a very charming man, keenly interested in all sport and totally committed to the integration of blacks and whites in his country.

They now play sport together, go to school together, travel on the same buses and trains. There is still a long way to go and difficulties remain, but I believe they will overcome them. Mandela is a very brave, wise man and he deserves, after all he has been through, to see his dream fulfilled.

4

THE SURPRISE DECISION

AFTER retiring from first-class cricket and taking up the coaching position at Plymouth College, I continued to play at the weekends for Paignton Cricket Club.

It was during one of Paignton's games against a touring team called Heffle Cuckoos that the visitors' captain, J.J. Warr, the former Middlesex and England fast bowler, who is now on the MCC committee, asked me if I had ever thought about becoming an umpire. I just laughed at him.

'What, me?' I said. 'You've got to be joking.'

However, it set me thinking. It had never entered my mind that my career might take off in that particular direction, but some of my old Yorkshire colleagues thought it was a good idea when I mentioned it to them. Could there be something in it?

The more I thought about it, the more I liked the idea. After all, I said to myself, being an umpire was the next best thing to actually playing the game. And I would still be involved in first-class cricket, which I had missed. Umpiring, I eventually convinced myself, would be a good substitute for playing, so why not give it a shot?

Of course, people who knew me well, such as Ray Illingworth,

Michael Parkinson and Geoffrey Boycott, all said I had such a nervous nature that never in a million years would I make a good umpire.

The amazing thing is that I changed completely. I lost all those nerves. I told myself that I was going to make a success of it, and that I was going to relax and enjoy it at the same time. I was going to smile, have a good laugh. That is what sport should be all about. Enjoyment. Once you lose that you might as well pack it in because it isn't sport any more. That was partly why I retired from county cricket when I did. As well as enjoying myself as an umpire, I was determined to earn the respect of the players. I would be willing to share a joke with them on the field, but not allow it to go too far.

I worried much more as a player. If I got three low scores I could not sleep at night, worrying where the next run was going to come from. With umpiring it was different.

The late Syd Buller said to me, 'The most important thing in umpiring is, when you make a mistake – and we all make one from time to time – put it out of your mind straightaway and concentrate on the next ball.'

I never forget those words. That is the way I have umpired throughout my career. If an umpire gets a decision wrong he should not think about it. Another golden rule is never try to even it up. If you do, that is two mistakes you've made.

If I could give any advice to someone setting out to be an umpire, it would be to take note of these three things: enjoy yourself; don't dwell on mistakes; and earn the respect of the players. Then three-quarters of the battle is won.

Those thoughts were flitting through my mind in the summer of 1969 as I toyed with the idea of applying to become a first-class umpire. As always, I wanted to talk things over with my father, who had advised me throughout my career, right from my schoolboy days. Sadly, he was ill in hospital in Barnsley. I will never forget that day in June when I told him that I was thinking seriously of becoming an umpire. He said nothing at all, but just looked at me, which was most unlike him.

When I left the hospital I realised it was the first time in my life that Dad hadn't offered me some encouragement or advice in anything I had decided to do. He just didn't seem to take it in. It hit me that he must have been really ill. He was. The next day he died.

He never saw me umpire, which I find very, very sad. I would have given anything if he had been able to live to see what I have achieved.

I did not seek advice or help from anyone else. It was my decision, and mine alone. My mind was made up. Somehow I knew it was what my father would have wanted.

In August of that year I applied to Lord's to become a first-class umpire, and three months later I heard that I had been accepted.

Every October or November the most experienced captains sit down with the hierarchy at Lord's to decide on the county panel for the coming season. If any umpire's marks are not up to standard he can be sacked if his contract is at an end. When that happens a list of applicants is studied and a suitable replacement is chosen. I was one of the lucky ones.

A new umpire will initially go on to a reserve list and stand at either Varsity matches, or possibly the odd tourist match. His marks are then studied, and if they are up to scratch he will be considered a worthy replacement for an official who has come off the list, either because of low marks or retirement. There are many people applying now to become first-class umpires, most of them former England players.

At the moment there are twenty-six full-time professional umpires, paid monthly by the TCCB, with Test matches, one-day internationals, quarter-finals semi-finals and finals bringing in extra money. All umpires are on a contract, from one to three years. That contract is binding on both parties, but if, at the end of it, an umpire's marks are not good enough, his contract will not be renewed.

If an umpire is seen to be slipping he will get a letter from the TCCB advising him and helping him to try to improve areas in which he has been criticised in the captains' reports. If he is a bit weak here or there he will be told to work on those failings. If there is no improvement he will be off the list as soon as his contract expires. There is no appeal. That's why all our chaps argue for a three-year contract. The only judgement is provided by the report from the captains. That is the system, and I believe it is the only way. All kinds of other ideas have been considered, including the use of assessors, as in football, but I do not think that would work in cricket, because assessors would be too far away from the action.

As a matter of fact, I do not think they should have assessors in football, either. The system is one of the worst ideas to be introduced into the game. If a referee knows that an assessor is in the stands watching him, he cannot possibly be relaxed and go out there and be his natural self. I do not think he can do his job properly in such circumstances.

There was a referee from Wales, Keith Cooper, in his last season on the football league list in the 1995–96 campaign, who obviously enjoyed every minute of every game. All the lads told me that he was the best referee there had been in the last few years, but he never received a top honour. The assessors were obviously not as keen on the way he controlled matches, yet surely it was the right one. We umpires did not want to go down that particular path, so assessors were ruled out.

It was also suggested that umpires do away with marks altogether, which is not as daft as it may sound, at least in the restricted way it would operate. My colleagues felt that we could dispense with marks for those umpires who had been on the list for five years. The argument was that if they could not umpire by that time, they never would be able to umpire. If they had proved they could, then fine. Allow them to do so without worrying about their marks.

However, having considered numerous other possibilities, the captains' marking system is still probably the best and fairest of them all.

When I first went on the umpires' list we were marked out of ten. Then it was reduced to five. Then back to ten. In 1997 it has gone down to five again. I prefer the ten-point system. It is more flexible, has greater scope, and gives a better idea of who the best umpires are. We are not told what our marks have been until the end of the season, and even then we are only given an overall average, not match by match.

In my first season on the county championship circuit I finished fifth, and I received a letter from Billy Griffith, who was then secretary of the TCCB, congratulating me on my excellent umpiring.

In 1995, the year before I announced my retirement from the Test arena, my mark was eight out of ten, which I thought was pretty good for someone who had reached the venerable age of sixty-two, especially when you consider that put me in the top three in the country. One year my mark was 3.95 – out of five, I should add – and I finished top. They must have been marking low that year. In another season someone might well have got the sack for that.

Portrait of a young cricketer, in my days with Yorkshire.

Captain of the Raley Secondary Modern School fooball team (*front row, centre*) in 1948, before a final at Barnsley FC's Oakwell ground.

My father (*extreme left, front row*) with the YMCA team which won the Yorkshire Trophy at Oakwell in the 1921-22 season.

Father helping me to pack my bags for another season with Leicestershire.

My mother, who was instrumental in introducing me to the Church and sowed the seeds of my christian faith.

Walking out to bat with Vic Wilson at the Scarborough Festival after Yorkshire had clinched the championship in 1959.

Executing my favourite sweep shot on the way to 181 not out against Glamorgan. I was dropped for the next match.

With Maurice Hallam at Leicester and a couple of crates of sherry presented to us after we had put on 277 for the first wicket against the touring South Africans in July 1960.

My Yorkshire first-team debut against Scotland at Hull in 1956, and what a line-up! *Left to right:* Vic Wilson, Ray Illingworth, Billy Sutcliffe (captain), Fred Trueman, Johnny Wardle, Ted Lester, Bob Appleyard, me and Frank Lowson.

The Yorkshire team which played Warwickshire at Edgbaston in their 1959 county championship winning year. *Back row (left to right):* Doug Padgett, Phil Sharpe, Don Wilson, Mel Ryan, David Pickles, Brian Bolus and me. *Front row:* Ray Illingworth, Vic Wilson, Ronnie Burnet (captain), Brian Close, Jimmy Binks.

Being introduced to her Majesty The Queen during the England v New Zealand Test at Lord's in June 1986. She was obviously amused – and so was Richard Hadlee! England captain Mike Gatting is to my left.

Sister Majorie (*left*) and niece Rachel (*right*) give me moral support as I wait to receive the MBE at Buckingham Palace.

David Lloyd, now the England coach, gingerly tests the surface after snow has stopped play in the match between Derbyshire and Lancashire at Buxton in 1976. Peter Lever, Clive Lloyd, Frank Hayes and myself all loook rather glum.

Relaxing at home in the garden of White Rose Cottage at Staincross.

The doyen of them all, Richie Benaud, the best cricket commentator in the world.

The best all-rounder I have ever seen, Sir Garfield Sobers. My former colleague Tommy Spencer is the umpire.

Another of the all-time greats, Keith Miller, who is also a very good friend.

Sir Leonard Hutton, arguably the best opening batsman, certainly the best on bad pitches.

One thing I was not prepared for, when I first started out, was the tremendous increase in paperwork through the ensuing years. We played to times in those days: an eleven-thirty a.m. start; lunch from one-thirty to two-ten; afternoon session until fifteen minutes past four; tea break until five-and-twenty minutes to five. Close of play was six-thirty, and that was it. Now there are so many other things to take into consideration. For example, just take a look at the following sections in an umpire's report sheet:

1. Report any breaches of the playing conditions or laws of cricket or advertising insignia regulations. If necessary, report in detail overleaf.
2. Light meter readings: please state which end facing when reading taken; the time the reading was taken; whether play was stopped; time of restart; meter reading at restart.
3. Britannic Assurance Championship matches only: based on the information on your record card, please enter the net duration (in minutes) for each innings in the match. Any time lost due to weather interruptions, bad light etc., resulting in the players having to leave or remain off the field should be deducted from the total innings time in each case. Details of all other suspensions of play due to injuries etc. should be entered in section 4 below.
4. Details of any time lost through injury or due to circumstances beyond the control of the cricketers.
5. Cricket balls: state make used. Were the balls satisfactory? Number of balls changed under first-class playing conditions 13 or 32. Standard of replacement balls provided.
6. Any comments on conduct of players or any other general matters.
7. Law 24 – no ball. In accordance with the playing conditions, I certify that the actions of all bowlers in the above match were fair, with the following exceptions. Details of unfair actions should be specified if possible.

Then we have also to make a report on the pitch, answering the following questions:

1. How would you rate this pitch as providing the right conditions for a first-class match of 3/4/5 days' duration, bearing in mind the importance of (a) good consistent bounce; (b) producing a reasonable balance between bat and ball? Very good/Good/Above average/Below average/Poor/Unfit. If below average please give your reasons.
2. How would you assess the bounce of the pitch, e.g., high, medium, low, consistent, variable etc.? 1st day . . . 2nd day . . . 3rd day . . . 4th day . . . 5th day . . .
3. (a) Was a heavy roller used during the match? State yes or no each day. (b) Do you think that it affected the pace of the pitch? State yes or no each day.
4. How would you assess the pace of the pitch on each day, with marks out of 5 (5 very fast, 1 very slow)?
5. Did the pitch appear to be completely dry at the commencement of the match? Comments if any.
6. Did the pitch have a uniform covering of grass along its entire length? If so, was the grass cover (i) heavy (ii) medium (iii) light? If the covering of grass was not uniform, please give details.
7. Were spin bowlers used to a reasonable extent during the match? If so, at what stage, if any, did the pitch take spin?
8. Did the covering of the pitch and ground conform to the minimum requirements as laid down in the playing conditions? If not, specify how deficient.
9. General comments on the pitch and its effect on the quality of play in the match.

In addition to all this, after each session on each day we have to fill in a card stating the total length of the session; the total suspension of play; the actual time spent on the field; time lost through injury. In assessing these, we have to take into consideration time lost through such details as the moving of sightscreens, a player changing his bat or gloves, and injuries. The cards have to be filled in immediately each session finishes, otherwise we would forget something. People do not realise just how much of this form-filling there is and how time consuming it can be. Not much of the interval left for lunch or tea, is there?

Then, of course, there are all the different playing conditions for all the different competitions to think about – NatWest, Benson & Hedges, Sunday League, county championship, Tests, one-day internationals. For one-day cricket we also have to keep a record of the overs bowled by each bowler. So many things to consider.

It is not just a case, therefore, of standing there and giving a player out, or not out, as the case might be. Umpires all have briefcases and calculators now, and it will be computers next.

There was none of this when I first started out early in May 1970, with a county championship fixture between Nottinghamshire and Warwickshire at Trent Bridge. Included in the line-ups were seven Test stars, including the world's greatest all-rounder, Sir Garfield Sobers – or still plain Gary Sobers as he was then – playing for Nottinghamshire. The very strong Warwickshire side included Rohan Kanhai, Lance Gibbs, Mike Smith, Alan Smith, David Brown and Dennis Amiss. David Constant was my umpiring colleague, just as he was for the Sunday League clash between the two counties, sandwiched in between the championship fixture.

My next match was Surrey versus Yorkshire at The Oval the following Saturday. To my consternation I discovered that I was unable to book a hotel near to the ground because they were all full. What I had failed to realise was that it was also the rugby league Challenge Cup final at Wembley that Saturday, and thousands of fans were coming down from the north to stay overnight on the Friday.

Eventually I had to settle for a hotel at Swiss Cottage on the other side of the river, and I began to worry that I might be caught up in the heavy traffic on the morning of the first day. I had nightmare visions of arriving late for only my second county game as an umpire.

I decided, therefore, to set off early, so I asked for an early-morning call – at four thirty!

The night porter was aghast. 'What on earth do you want to get up at that time for?'

I told him I was umpiring Surrey versus Yorkshire at The Oval and didn't want to be late.

'What time does it start?' he asked.

'Half past eleven,' I told him.

'Good grief,' he replied. 'Get up at that time and you could walk it to The Oval and still be there a couple of hours before it was due to start.'

'That's as maybe,' I said. 'I'm taking no chances. Just give me a call at half past four.'

So he did. I had a cup of tea, a bit of toast, and off I went. I sailed across London with no trouble at all and was at the ground before six o'clock. Needless to say, there was no one there and the ground was all locked up, so I threw my bag over the gate and started to climb over. I had just about made it to the top when I heard a voice saying, 'Oi, and what do you think you're doing?'

I looked down and saw a London bobby. I jumped down sharpish. 'Er, well, Officer, I, er, know you're not going to believe this, but I'm officiating at the cricket match here today, Surrey against Yorkshire.'

He looked at me, then at his watch. 'Come off it,' he said. 'It's only six o'clock in the morning. They don't start until half past eleven. Who are you trying to kid? Not even an umpire would come that early.'

Eventually I managed to convince him that I was genuine, and I sat down with him outside the gate and had a good natter and a laugh about it until the groundstaff arrived at just before half past seven and opened the gates.

Standing with me on that occasion was an Australian called Cec Pepper, who arrived at the ground a little bit later than me. I was told that he had been a great all-round cricketer but never played for his country because he had upset Sir Donald Bradman. Whether that was true or not, I don't know, but some of the top men, such as Garfield Sobers and Keith Miller, told me what a good player he was. He bowled leg-spin and googlies and was also a top-class batsman. He came over here to play in the Lancashire League and went on to become an umpire.

It really was a classic case of poacher turned gamekeeper, for when he played in the Lancashire League Cec used to frighten the poor umpires half to death, kidding them into giving him lbw decisions. He would say things like, 'Ooh, that was close, Umpire, but you're right; just missing leg stump. Good decision.' Next time he hit the batsman on the pad he would panic the umpire into sending the batsman on his way. 'Owzaaaaaaat!' he would shriek. 'Must be out this time. Plumb.' And up would shoot the finger. As an umpire himself, Cec found he had to make those decisions, and a good job he made of it, too.

On this particular occasion at The Oval we had been forced off by bad light. Nothing changes, does it? I was sitting in the corner of the umpires' room thinking to myself that the light seemed pretty good to me, and we ought to be out there. I looked across the ground from the window and I could see Big Ben in the distance. Clear as a bell.

So I said, in the respectful manner of a young umpiring whippersnapper in his first season, to a senior and respected colleague, 'Excuse me, Mr Pepper, but don't you think we ought at least to go out and make an inspection?'

He replied, 'Sit down in that corner, lad. I'll tell you when we're going out to inspect the light.'

I argued, tentatively, 'But I can see Big Ben quite clearly.'

He glared at me dismissively. 'Just leave it to me. I'm in charge.'

This went on and on. We were off for an awfully long time. I kept urging him to have another look, but he would not budge.

Eventually all the Press came knocking at the door wanting to know what was happening – or what was not happening might be more accurate – and Cec gave them a few salty Aussie oaths for their trouble, telling them in no uncertain terms where to get off. Where they could go, as well, if I remember rightly.

The next day the Press was full of the bad light controversy at The Oval, and the papers really set about Cec as the senior umpire. He glanced through one or two of the reports, getting redder and redder until I thought he was going to explode, then he raced round to the Press box and gave the newspaper lads another verbal volley that must have melted all the typewriters.

Yet Cec was a good-hearted man, really. From there we went on to Fenners together for the Cambridge game, and he took me out for a delightful evening meal. But what a character!

Other experienced umpires around at the time included Syd Buller, Arthur Fagg and Charlie Elliott, and I sought their advice because they were such fine Test officials. They all gave me a lot of encouragement. One umpire, however, another great character in the game, did try to dissuade me. He was Jack Crapp, who had played for Gloucestershire and was on the umpires' list when I started out. I asked if he could give me any advice and he said, 'Yes, young man, pack it up.' I had barely started! I found out later that he gave the same advice to all the new umpires, and I am glad I did not take it.

I learned a great deal from my fellow umpires in those days, and I treasure the chats I had with them when they talked about their own experiences and the great players they had seen down the years. I particularly enjoyed the tales of Sam Cooke, a former Gloucestershire player with one England cap, who had actually played with the legendary Walter Hammond. Like all the other good judges of that period, Sam insisted that Hammond was the best player there had ever been on all pitches.

Sam used to love to tell the tale of one particular game when he went in to bat at number eleven. Hammond, who had gone in at three, was still at the other end. Sam strode to the crease, took guard from the umpire for the last ball of the over, and then paused as he saw Hammond walking down the wicket towards him.

'Sam,' Hammond said, 'I just want you to block this last ball of the over. That's all. Just block it. Leave the rest to me.'

Sam did as he was told, and he and Hammond went on to share a last-wicket stand of 100, with Sam never having to face another ball. It just shows what a remarkable player Hammond was.

I saw Hammond when my father took me as a schoolboy to watch him play in a Victory Test in the early forties at Old Trafford. He made 50-odd, a magnificent knock which still stands out in my mind today, but I never saw him in his pomp.

There is another story about Hammond when Gloucestershire played Somerset at Bristol. In those days Gloucestershire had a very good off-spinner called Tom Goddard, who bowled Somerset out twice after Hammond had scored a big century in a Gloucestershire total of well over 300 in their opening knock.

When the innings victory had been duly completed, Hammond took the Gloucestershire players out on to the field, instructed Goddard to bowl to him on a pitch where he had twice run through the Somerset line-up, and he played the spinner with the edge of his bat.

Another fine umpire, Arthur Jepson, was also on the list when I started. He had played for Nottinghamshire in a match against Gloucestershire at Bristol, and he told me that Hammond had instructed Charlie Barnett to open the innings. Charlie refused, and Hammond insisted, 'I'm captain of this team. I'm telling you to go in first, Charlie.'

After a lot of argument, Barnett put his pads on, went out and scored 99. When he was dismissed in the last over before lunch, he strode into the dressing room, and said to Hammond, 'That's the way to play.'

Hammond said nothing, but he went out after the interval and scored more than 200. Jepson knew all about that innings: he bowled to Hammond most of the afternoon.

Alec Skelding was an umpire who won and retained the affection of everyone in cricket. Like me, he liked to inject a touch of humour. In charge at Lord's during a game between Middlesex and Northants, he saw Denis Brookes pad up to a delivery which pitched, came back up the hill from the Nursery End, and knocked out the off stump.

Denis departed, shaking his head sadly, as the next man, the tough Aussie Jock Livingston, walked in to replace him. Livingston took his guard, looked round, twirled his bat and asked, 'How many balls to go, Alec?'

'Two,' came the reply, 'but if the first is as good as the last, one will be enough as far as you are concerned.'

They were great guys, those old-time characters in the white coats. I have seen so many umpires come and go and I can honestly say it has been a pleasure to work with all of them. I have had marvellous support from my colleagues right the way through my career over so many years. We are all members of the Association of Cricket Umpires and Scorers which is known throughout the world and I will certainly be keeping up my membership in my retirement – if only so that I can keep on receiving their excellent magazine, *How's That*.

After a while I had my own stories to tell of things that had happened to me in my first two seasons as an umpire, including the time I stopped a county fixture between Lancashire and Middlesex at Old Trafford to allow a VC10 to fly over. The players could not believe it when I announced, 'I'm sorry, gentlemen, but I must stop the game until that jet goes over, because with that row going on, if anybody gets a nick, I won't be able to hear it.'

Everyone knows that I like to make my decisions clear, and whenever there is a no-ball I really let rip so that everyone hears it, including the chap who has nodded off in the back row of the stand.

On one occasion I was umpiring a game between Derbyshire and Middlesex at Burton-on-Trent. There was also a local match taking place just down the road from us, and the batsman there heard a no-ball called, tried a tremendous heave, and was clean bowled. He naturally stood his ground.

The umpire raised his finger and said, 'You're out.'

The irate batsman argued, 'But you shouted no-ball.'

'I never said a word,' rejoined the umpire. 'I'm telling you, that's out.' And so it was. The no-ball shout the batsman heard was one of mine in the county game up the road.

In another of my early matches Surrey were playing Hampshire at Guildford and the Hampshire captain, Richard Gilliat, was batting. A short ball from my end was lofted miles high into the air, so I ran from my position behind the stumps and followed the ball right to the boundary's edge, where

I tried to catch it. I had momentarily forgotten that I was no longer a player, but an umpire. The ball just cleared the boundary ropes and, as it did so, realising what had happened, I turned and signalled a six to the scorers. Talk about keeping up with play!

That reminded me of the time when I was fielding down at third man for Leicestershire, right under the pavilion. The grass there was very lush, and I had rubber-soled shoes on. I raced round to field the ball when I suddenly slipped. I flew straight into the pavilion railings and my head became stuck fast. I couldn't move. The ground was in uproar. The players couldn't do anything for laughing. In the end the game had to be held up until they found a joiner to get my head out.

There was another incident when I was umpiring at square leg during Hampshire's championship match with Lancashire at Southampton. Keith Goodwin, the Lancashire wicketkeeper, set off for what I considered to be an impossible second run. I was so involved with the game that I forgot I was umpiring, and shouted to him, 'No Goody, get back, get back.' He took no notice, carried on running, and I had to give him out. The Hampshire fielders just fell about laughing.

The fun came thick and fast. On another occasion I was standing at a match between Yorkshire and Kent at Headingley when Richard Hutton was about to bowl to Stuart Leary, Kent's South African batsman. Leary was quite a character, and as he waited for Richard to bowl he said, 'Just watch out, Dickie, I'm going to hit his first and fifth balls over mid-wicket for six.'

'Bet you won't,' I answered, quick as a flash.

Richard bowled the first delivery; Stuart swung his bat and the ball soared many a mile over the leg-side boundary for six. I raised both arms in half surrender. The next three were dot balls, and as Richard prepared to send down the fifth I kept saying to myself, 'Nah, he'll not do it again – he can't do it again.' Hutton bowled, Stuart swung and the ball sailed over the boundary for another six. I couldn't help but jump up and down in excitement.

'Eh, look at that,' I cried out. 'He's bloody done it.'

Richard, mind you, could more than hold his own. There was the time, for example, when he was bowling for Yorkshire against Kent, who had Graham Johnson at the crease. Johnson kept playing and missing, playing and missing, and this irritated Richard. Finally, totally exasperated, he strode down the wicket to the batsman and enquired, 'Excuse me, young man, what are you in the side for? Can you bowl?'

'Er, well, no, not really,' Johnson replied.

'Well, come on then, tell me, what are you in the side for?' Hutton persisted. 'Your fielding perhaps?'

'Well, no, not just for that,' Johnson muttered. Then came the bumper delivery from a dismissive Hutton.

'Well, what on earth are you in the team for then, because you can't bloody well bat.'

This is what cricket is about: comradeship, friendship, and a fund of remarkable stories to while away the winter hours – or even those many stoppages for bad light and rain.

'Hey,' someone will say, 'do you remember when . . .'

5

BAPTISM OF FIRE

AFTER just two years on the county circuit I received a letter in November 1972, saying that I had been appointed to the Test match panel. I could hardly believe it. I knew my marks had been good, but I was only thirty-nine with limited first-class experience. If I was surprised, I was also thrilled and delighted. Looking back, it is amazing to think that I remained on the Test panel right up to my retirement from international cricket in 1996.

Shortly afterwards, I received another letter, this time from the Mayor of Barnsley, Councillor Fred Lunn, which stated, 'Dear Mr Bird, on behalf of all the cricket enthusiasts of Barnsley and district I am delighted to send you our congratulations on being appointed to the Panel of Test Umpires. This is a great honour which I am sure will greatly further your cricketing career.' To receive the appreciation of my home town was a bit special.

I was proud to find that my first Test, between England and New Zealand in the summer of 1973, would be at my home ground of Headingley, where I had played county cricket for Yorkshire, and in fact made my county championship debut against Derbyshire in 1957.

As usual, I arrived very early at the ground – seven o'clock

– and, of course, I could not get in. I had to wait until the groundstaff arrived to open up the gates.

Once inside I went to sit at the back of the football stand, and looked out over the empty ground. All sorts of thoughts went through my mind, but I never dreamed, as I sat there, that I would have such a long and distinguished career at international level. I then went to the dressing rooms, had a cup of tea and a biscuit, wittered, and invented all kinds of things to worry about. I also went to the toilet quite a few times.

When I decided to become an umpire I always hoped and prayed that one day I would be able to stand in a Test match, and now here I was, the third youngest Test umpire in the history of the English game.

I will remember that morning as long as I live. It was completely different from the county matches I had umpired. Everyone was there, TV, Press, radio, all buzzing round the changing rooms. The cameras didn't bother me, however, and I wasn't really conscious of all those millions watching on television. I wasn't going to start thinking about them. Once you do that, you've no chance, I told myself. If you make a mistake, you make a mistake. That's all there is to it.

It was a tremendous thrill when I walked out at Headingley, and I got a marvellous reception from a full house. A tingling sensation went through me that is difficult to describe. I had to loosen my top button because it felt like I was going into a hot oven. Even the most experienced players were tense. It was nerve-racking, yet exciting at the same time.

An incident just after my colleague Charlie Elliott and I had reached the middle helped take some of the tension away. I was just putting the bails on the stumps when I looked up and saw a familiar face. Who should be standing at my side but Stan

Bulmer, a photographer from my local newspaper, the *Barnsley Chronicle*.

'Mind if I take a picture, Dickie?' he asked.

'Well, I don't mind, Stan,' I told him, 'but someone else might. You're not supposed to be out here, you know. We're just about to start a Test match.'

All the world's Press and TV were there, but not one of them dared stray on to the middle at that stage of the proceedings – except Stan. How he did it I'll never know. I keep asking him, but he won't tell me. He got his picture, however, which appeared in the *Chronicle* the following week.

Another *Chronicle* photographer, Don Oakes, has been taking various pictures of me for the last thirty-four years, and there have been quite a few unusual ones amongst them. There was one with a camel, another with some peacocks that were pestering me by keeping me awake with their love calls, one in a turban and flowing robes prior to a Sharjah visit, and one with Old Father Time in my garden, as well as all the more orthodox shots to mark a particular period of my career. Thanks to Stan, Don and my many other friends behind the lens I have been able to build up a vast pictorial record of my days as an umpire.

I felt even better after making my first lbw decision. I knew it was the right one, but it still gave me a funny feeling to see all the players on the balcony vanish into the dressing room as if by magic, so that they could watch the playback on television, to make sure I had got it right.

The game itself passed off without incident: no bad light, no rain, no controversy. Overall things could not have gone better, and I began to enjoy myself.

I had developed a habit of offering my white coat to any barracker who thought he could do better, but never imagined I would dare do so in front of all those televiewers and the game's dignitaries. When the opportunity arose on the first morning, however, I could not resist it.

A lively character by the name of Ronald Griffiths, who had brought some West Indian gaiety and wit to the Test scene, saw fit to criticise my decision to signal for a wide by Yorkshire's Chris Old. 'Give the lad a chance,' he yelled out.

Quick as a flash, without pausing to think what I was doing, I took off my umpire's jacket and invited Ronald to put it on. The crowd howled, and that helped reduce the tension even more. Now I really did begin to feel at home.

Mr Griffiths was also a big fan of Boycs and always addressed him as Sir Geoffrey. I became 'my son'. 'Good decision, my son,' he would bawl out, or 'Come on, my son, get that finger up, he's got to be out.'

However, during that particular Test, Ronald ventured to offer an opinion on my ability on only one further occasion, when a ball from Geoff Arnold struck the batsman's pad. 'Come on, Mr Arnold, appeal occasionally. You never know what this umpire might do.'

A magnificent century by Boycott and some fine bowling by John Snow stood out during that Test as England chalked up a win. Snow, incidentally, paid me a great compliment in a newspaper article after that game. He wrote:

There is nothing like a Test match at Headingley for bringing out the best in a Yorkshire-born cricketer. They obviously feel they can do no wrong in front of their own supporters. Geoff Boycott's great century, Ray Illingworth's highest score of the series, Chris Old's performance with bat and ball. All great stuff. Don't overlook the performance of another Yorkshireman, either – Harold 'Dickie' Bird, from Barnsley, making his debut as a Test umpire. Dickie was so keen to get going, he was at Headingley on the first day while the rest of us were still tucked up in bed. He is easily recognisable with his white flat hat, his elaborate signals, and his speed off the mark getting into positions for run-outs. I am sure he will be around the Test scene for some time to come.

I bet Snowy didn't imagine it would be for twenty-four years!

Snow was one of the finest fast bowlers England has produced, but he was also a crafty blighter. Three years later I was standing at a Test between England and the West Indies at Trent Bridge, and England were in a spot of bother. Snow felt that he ought to try to slow the game down a bit, thus putting the West Indian batsmen out of their fluent rhythm. So, after lunch, he went out with his pockets stuffed with breadcrumbs. He proceeded to sprinkle these all over the ground, and within seconds we were invaded by more pigeons than I've seen in one place in my life – including Trafalgar Square. I just don't know where they all suddenly appeared from. You could hardly see a blade of grass for them all. It certainly did the trick, though, as play was slowed down so much that it came to a full stop.

As one Bird to another I suppose I ought to have had some influence on our feathered friends, but I just stood there and flapped, I was so flabbergasted.

I had been appointed to two Tests in that summer of seventy-three. The second, in a split tour, was between England and the West Indies at Edgbaston in August, and, from an umpiring point of view, it turned out to be one of the most eventful Tests ever played in this country.

For the first time in the history of Test cricket an umpire said he was packing up and going home in the middle of a game. Arthur Fagg was so incensed about the behaviour of the West Indies captain, Rohan Kanhai, that he refused to take his position on the third morning of that second Test. Only a few weeks earlier I had made my Test debut after just two years on the county list, and now here I was in the middle of a cricketing sensation.

What sparked it all off was an appeal for a catch behind the wicket. Early in his innings Geoff Boycott played forward to Keith Boyce and there was a tremendous shout. They all went up, but Arthur Fagg was unimpressed. 'Not out,' he said.

Kanhai took the decision badly. He raised his arms in protest, much like a footballer when a referee turns down a penalty appeal. He stamped and stormed around, and generally caused quite a scene. What made it worse was that Boycott and Dennis Amiss went on to share a first-wicket stand of 96.

I could see Arthur was upset by Kanhai's reaction. He hardly spoke a word in the dressing room at the end of the day's play, and showered and changed clearly in a state of distress.

'Don't let it get to you, Arthur,' I said to him. 'You'll feel a lot better when you've had a good night's sleep.' He just shook my hand, and we went our separate ways, he to his hotel, me to mine.

It was only when I came down to breakfast the following morning and saw all the headlines in the Press that I realised just how serious the situation was. One of them screamed, 'TEST UMPIRE IN I'LL QUIT THREAT'. When Arthur had walked away from the dressing room to the car park the previous evening he had been surrounded by the national Press, and because he was so upset he had probably said things he should not have said.

When I met Arthur back at the ground on that third day he said to me, 'Dickie, lad, I'm going to take no further part in this game unless I get an apology from Rohan Kanhai for his behaviour yesterday. If he doesn't apologise, then they can get someone else.

'If they won't accept decisions there is no point carrying on. Why should I? I'm nearly sixty. I don't have to live with this kind of pressure. I had to live with it for two and a half hours out there. People don't realise how bad it has become.

'I just don't enjoy umpiring Test matches any more, nor Sunday League matches, come to that. There is too much at stake. The players shout for things, and when they don't get the decisions, they react in the way Kanhai reacted yesterday. The game has changed. And not for the better, I'm telling you. Umpires are under terrific pressure these days. Players will have to learn to accept decisions, otherwise there is no point in people like me continuing.

'We make mistakes, but so do the players. We are all human. It shouldn't matter whether Boycott was out or not. It was an umpire's decision, honestly given. Boycott signalled with his arm that the ball had brushed his leg and looked at me for the decision. You know that when players are trying it on, they don't look at you. I didn't see any deviation. What could I do but give him not out?'

As I listened, it was clear that Arthur was in a very emotional state. He was one of England's leading umpires, and here was I, a mere novice at that level, trying to console him, to lift him. He had helped me so much since I had become an umpire, and now I wanted to help him, but there seemed so little I could do.

When no apology was forthcoming Arthur said, 'Right, that's it. I'm packing my bags. I'm off.'

By this time all the television and Press people were trying to crowd their way into the room, eager to know what was happening. It was sheer bedlam.

I took Arthur to a corner, sat with him, and tried to persuade him to change his mind. I respected him as a great player – the only man to get two double centuries in a county championship match – and a fine umpire, and I realised that he could be bringing a very sad end to a wonderful career.

'Look here, Arthur,' I reasoned, 'I do know how you must feel, but you've got to go out there.'

He was adamant. 'No way. Not unless I get an apology.'

I was staggered. I hardly knew what to do at first. It was like being in the middle of a very bad dream, but time was marching on, and it suddenly struck me that I would have to go out there and stand at both ends. I could not believe that all this was happening to me in only my second Test.

I went to see Leslie Deakins, the Secretary of Warwickshire County Cricket Club, and Alec Bedser, the Chairman of Selectors, told them what the situation was, and asked for someone to stand at square leg. They decided to call on Warwickshire coach Alan Oakman, the former Sussex and England player, who had also been a first-class umpire.

'Alan,' they said to him, 'we've got a little bit of a problem and we want you to go out with Dickie and stand at square leg.'

He looked at them in amazement. 'Oh, no, no, no, no,' he protested vigorously. 'I don't fancy that. Not in a Test match. I can't do it.'

Leslie Deakins reminded him, 'I employ you at Warwickshire County Cricket Club and I am telling you that you must go out there.'

So Alan did, while Arthur prepared to go home.

When Alan and I eventually walked out there was a terrific roar, but when we reached the middle Alan turned to me and said, 'Er, Dickie, I don't quite know how to tell you this.'

'Come on, man, spit it out, what's the problem?' I asked.

'I've forgotten the bails,' he stammered.

'That's all I need. You'd better go and fetch them, then.'

So off trotted poor old Alan, with the crowd all jeering and shouting, not quite knowing what on earth was going on.

Eventually the game got underway, with Alan at square leg, and me taking both ends.

After a short while, to Alan's relief there was suddenly another tremendous roar, and Arthur came walking out into the middle, booed by the large West Indian contingent in the packed house, and cheered by the England supporters.

That was not the only problem during the match. We also had trouble dealing with timewasting and intimidatory bowling. Arthur and I had a chat in the middle and decided that we were not going to stand for it any longer. There was far too much short-pitched bowling and the West Indies were constantly, and it seemed deliberately, slowing down the over rate. It was getting close to lunch, so we arranged that, during the interval, we would call a meeting for both captains, Kanhai and Raymond Illingworth, West Indian tour manager Esmond Kentish, and England's Chairman of Selectors, Alec Bedser.

We met in the umpires' room and told the West Indies representatives that if their team did not quicken up the over rate after lunch and cut out the intimidatory bowling, then we would come down hard on them. Thousands of people had paid a lot to watch the game and they were entitled to good value for their money. We really read the riot act, telling both parties that we wanted them to play the rest of the Test match in a good spirit, and they did. It was a wonderful game of cricket after that.

When the game was over Kanhai was the first man to shake Arthur Fagg by the hand. Whether he actually apologised I don't know, but, in any case, the damage had been done. Arthur was never the same man, and never really recovered. He became ill soon afterwards and never umpired another Test match. It was all very sad. On the other hand, that trouble-torn Test did me nothing but good. Because I had stood up to them I must have earned the West Indies' respect; on returning home from a rain-abandoned county match between Lancashire and Somerset at Old Trafford shortly afterwards, I received a telegram from Lord's telling me that I had been appointed to stand at the final match of the England v West Indies series.

Again, I found it hard to believe, so I rang Donald Carr, the Secretary of the Test and County Cricket Board, for an explanation. He confirmed that Dusty Rhodes had originally been appointed to the game, but I was to take his place. A Press statement was released saying that Dusty had an eye infection, but the real reason for the change was that the West Indies had asked for me to stand at the decisive match of the series. It was staggering news. It meant the realisation of a cherished ambition to umpire a Test at Lord's, the headquarters of English cricket, and it would make a wonderful climax to my first season on the international panel. I felt very sorry for Dusty, however. I could imagine his disappointment. Little did I know what I was letting myself in for. Play has been stopped for many things, but never a bomb scare – until I umpired that game at a full-house Lord's.

About an hour and a quarter after lunch on the Saturday, MCC secretary Billy Griffith, a man I admired, announced on the public address system that there had been a warning from the IRA that a bomb had been planted in the ground. It was a very frightening experience. I got this cold feeling, and shivers shot through my whole body when a bomb was mentioned. The police wanted all twenty-six thousand spectators to leave, and requested that they make for the exits in as orderly a manner as possible. Instead, thousands surged across the playing area to join me, colleague Charlie Elliott, and the players, in the middle. It was quite frightening for a while as they swarmed towards us like a great incoming tide.

The covers had been brought out to protect the playing area, and I thought the safest place would be sitting on them. I knew there was no bomb under there. We didn't really know what to do, and I just sat there, with my head in my hands, worrying about what might happen if a bomb did go off.

The West Indian supporters did not seem in the least bit concerned. 'Don't you worry about the bomb, Mr Dickie Bird,' they said to me. 'Just look at that total on the scoreboard and worry about that.' I glanced across: West Indies 652 for 8. England, in fact, followed on and lost by an innings and 226 runs, the second biggest defeat ever suffered by an England side, the worst having come in Brisbane during the 1946–47 tour of Australia.

Half an hour or so after the original warning Billy Griffith came on the Tannoy again to say that the police wanted both teams off the field immediately. We were taken to the big marquee on the lawn at the back of the pavilion while the search went on elsewhere.

After a break of eighty-five minutes it was announced that play could resume. There was no bomb, but, of course, the authorities could take no risks, especially in view of the fact that a bomb had gone off in Baker Street that same morning.

It was difficult to concentrate on the game after that, but, of course, we had to get on with it, players and umpires alike.

That was the Test when Garfield Sobers made 150 not out, one of his greatest innings. It also signalled the end of Ray Illingworth's reign as England captain, and he lost his job after the heavy defeat. At forty-one the authorities probably thought that he was too old to be able to turn things round and that the England team needed an injection of new, younger, blood.

The bomb scare brought me an additional disappointment. I had been so looking forward to meeting Her Majesty The Queen, who was scheduled to be introduced to the teams and umpires on the Monday. Because of the continuing IRA threat the visit was cancelled for security reasons, and it came as a great blow to me. It had always been one of my ambitions to shake hands with the Queen, but there were to be other opportunities.

It was certainly an eventful first season on the Test panel, but, looking back, I gained a lot of satisfaction from it. When I was first appointed I thought that just possibly my nerves might let me down; the pressures might prove too much. After the Arthur Fagg ordeal and then the bomb scare, however, not to mention the intimidatory bowling and the timewasting tactics, I knew that if I could handle all this, I could handle anything. I had satisfied myself that I had the temperament needed for the international arena.

6

WORLD CUP
HAT-TRICK

People often ask me which is the best international match
I ever umpired. As far as the one-day variety is concerned,
the game that stands out above all others is the first World Cup
final at Lord's in 1975, when the great West Indian side beat
the never-say-die Australians.

There has never been another day quite like it. Not only
was it a unique occasion, but the match itself had everything
– one of the best individual one-day innings I have ever seen,
fine bowling, magnificent fielding, a wonderful fight-back, and
a dramatic finale. I had officiated at Test matches before, but
I was not prepared for that Saturday. It was different from
anything I had previously experienced.

My legs had been like jelly all week just thinking about it, and
when I walked out into the middle there were tears in my eyes.
I could hardly believe what was happening to me. I had to keep
reminding myself, 'You've done it, Dickie, you've done it. The
World Cup final. The first ever. And you're in charge.'

Quite honestly, if I had not been given the final I would have
been very disappointed. I had not said anything to anybody,
and I kept trying to convince myself that I wouldn't get it so

that the let-down would not be as great if it went to someone else. But really, deep down, I wanted it very badly. And what a magnificent game it turned out to be.

Clive Lloyd produced one of the great one-day knocks, rescuing the West Indians after they had slipped to 50 for 3, having been put in to bat. First to go was Roy Fredericks. Along with thousands of ecstatic countrymen, he was celebrating a spectacular six off Dennis Lillee when it was noted that he had lost his balance making the stroke and by a cruel piece of misfortune, had knocked off a bail.

Whether that upset them or not, I don't know. What I do know is that they struggled after that against some accurate Australian bowling, and when the third wicket went down with only 50 runs on the board, their captain, Rohan Kanhai, said to me, 'We are in a very bad position, Dickie. It will be very hard to win this one from here.'

I must confess I secretly agreed with him, although I did not tell him that. It was then, however, that Clive Lloyd slouched to the wicket in that familiar shambling style of his, and suddenly the game changed. He took the bowling by the scruff of the neck – and you have to remember we are talking about those great bowlers Lillee and Thomson – to score 102 in only 82 balls. It was a remarkable effort. By the time he was out, caught down the leg side off the persistent Gary Gilmour, the West Indies were in control. They went on to make 291 for 8, which left Australia needing five an over off the 60 overs in order to win, a formidable task against the battery of West Indian quick bowlers.

John Arlott, the man who turned cricket commentary into an art form, described the action for radio listeners, and I have kept a cutting which was part of a tribute to him at the time of his death. It quoted from his broadcast on that first World Cup final, as follows:

And they've scored off the last 15 balls: it's now difficult not only to bowl a maiden over, but apparently to bowl a maiden ball . . . Gilmour comes in, bowls, and Lloyd hits him high over hill and dale and mid-wicket, the stroke of a man knocking a thistle-top off with a walking stick. No trouble at all, and it takes Lloyd to 99. Lloyd 99 and 189 for three. Umpire Bird's having a wonderful time, signalling everything in the world, including stop to the traffic coming on from behind. But he lets Gilmour in now and he comes in, bowls, and Lloyd hits him into the covers; it's half fielded there on the cover boundary, and the century's up and the whole ground seething with West Indian delight.

Brilliant! Arlott once said, 'For me it was a sort of seventh heaven to be watching cricket and talking about it.' I know what he meant.

Lloyd's magnificent innings had ensured that the odds were heavily stacked against the Australians, but they were convinced that they had a chance of pulling off a shock win. They might well have done so, but for five suicidal run-outs – an incredible number of self-inflicted dismissals. Those run-outs cost them the game.

First to go was Alan Turner, run out by a brilliant underarm throw by a youngster who was just beginning to make a name for himself – Vivian Richards. He was just like a cat in the field, pouncing and throwing in one graceful movement that had the purists purring. If there was even the tiniest doubt in a batsman's mind, he was better off not attempting a run, but the Aussies did not learn by their mistakes and lived to regret it. From the same mid-wicket position, Richards accounted for Greg Chappell after he and brother Ian had put on 34. Ian Chappell provided Viv with his hat-trick of run-out victims, a bullet-like return leaving the batsman stranded well out of his ground. Ian played the ball wide to mid-on, began to run, hesitated, then started to run again as Richards appeared to fumble. That was a big mistake. The ball zipped in to Lloyd, who was at the bowler's end, and he whipped off the bails like lightning.

Richards scored only five runs in that game, but he almost won the match with his fielding alone.

So it was that Dennis Lillee came to the crease as the last man, with the score on 233 for 9 and the Aussies still needing 59 for victory. He took guard, winked at me, and said, 'Don't worry, Dickie, we'll get these.'

I looked at him, smiled, and thought to myself, 'Dream on, Dennis, my old mate, you've no chance.' I couldn't see Australia doing it, not in a million years. But slowly the runs started to accumulate and the crowd became more and more excited as the gap closed. I began to wonder if miracles did, indeed, happen. Could Dennis the menace be right after all?

It was obvious that the West Indians were having doubts as well. They had decided to allow the last pair a diet of singles in order to save the boundaries which Australia needed if they were to reach their target, but both Lillee and Thomson played very sensibly, taking the occasional risk of a big swing, and making it pay.

But then Thomson took one chance too many, failed to connect cleanly with one almighty heave, and saw the ball describe a graceful arc before falling into the safe and grateful hands of Roy Fredericks. The crowd immediately went wild. They thought it was all over – just like football's World Cup final at Wembley nine years earlier. But here thousands, not just the odd one or two, swarmed on to the pitch. We were completely engulfed. I felt my white cap snatched from my head, along with three sweaters that had been draped round my waist, and a spare ball from my pocket.

For a moment or two I felt dizzy, but recovered my senses

when I saw that Thomson and Lillee were still running between the wickets. You see, what they and the rest of us on the field had heard, but the crowd obviously had not, was Tommy Spencer's shout of 'No-ball'.

'Keep going, keep going,' panted Lillee. 'We'll soon have won it at this rate.'

'How many is that you've run?' I asked him.

'You should be keeping count,' he grumbled. 'But I make it about 17.'

When order was eventually restored thanks to some friendly police persuasion, and it finally dawned on the crowd that it was not all over after all, I had to disappoint Lillee by telling him that I was giving him only 4 out of 17 for his gallant running exploits. Fredericks, after catching the ball, had hurled it at the stumps in a bid to pull off yet another run-out off the no-ball. It missed and disappeared into the middle of the onrushing tidal wave of spectators. According to the laws we had, therefore, to award 4 runs and call the ball 'dead' due to 'interference with the ball' – much to Lillee's breathless disgust.

Inevitably, though, it was a fifth run-out which ended the brave Australian last-wicket resistance, Thomson being the final victim, and that left the West Indians victors by 17 runs. It was a close-run thing.

For the second time that day the ground was invaded. There was simply no stopping the fans who were keen to pick up a memento from that unforgettable game. Thomson lost his bat, his pads were ripped off him, and they even had poor old Keith Boyce on the floor as they took the boots from off his feet. The stumps disappeared, but what the people who took them did not realise was that we had removed the good set at tea and replaced them with some old ones, anticipating such an eventuality. Those scenes were some of the most amazing I have ever experienced. It was sheer bedlam.

By the time the game finished it was five minutes to nine. Play had started at eleven o'clock that morning so you can imagine how shattered Tommy Spencer and I were. Tommy, incidentally, did well to stay out there. He took a nasty blow on the shin from a Doug Walters drive and there was quite a lot of blood about. But the doctor patched him up and Tommy said, through clenched teeth, 'I'm all right; I'll manage. The game has to go on.'

Before the World Cup started, all the teams and umpires attended a buffet lunch at Buckingham Palace where we met the Queen and the rest of the Royal Family – Prince Philip, Charles, Andrew, Edward, Princess Anne and the Queen Mother. Prince Philip handed out the awards at the end of the game, and when I went up for my medal he asked me what time I had arrived at the ground.

'Eight o'clock, sir,' I told him.

'My goodness,' he said. 'That's a very long day for you. You must be very tired. Just look at the time, it's turned nine o'clock now. I'll be in trouble when I get home, I can tell you!'

But the fact that we had still been able to play to a finish after such a long day showed the advantage of staging the World Cup in England. It is the ideal place because of the long daylight hours in the middle of summer. It is also ideal because of the motorway network, making it easy to get to the different grounds, unlike in India and Pakistan, for example, where you have to travel thousands of miles from one ground to another using transport that is not always too reliable.

Prince Philip also remarked on the fact that my white cap had been stolen.

'Yes sir,' I said. 'That's another one gone.'

I had got so used to it happening that, whenever I was involved in a series with the West Indians, I would have a full box of caps sent to me from my suppliers in Luton, Richards and Thirkell Ltd. I also use some for charity auctions and a tremendous amount of money has been raised that way.

I actually found out where that particular cap ended up. The following year I was back at Lord's umpiring the county championship match between Middlesex and Surrey. My car was off the road at the time, so I travelled down to London by train. Arriving at the station, I hopped on to a bus to get to my hotel.

This big West Indian bus conductor came up to take my fare. He was wearing a white cap and I thought, 'Funny, I'd know that style of white cap anywhere. It looks remarkably like one of mine.'

So I said to him, 'Excuse me, but where did you get that white cap?'

He immediately became agitated. 'Man, haven't you heard of Mr Dickie Bird, the great Test match umpire? This is one of his famous white caps, and I am so proud of it. I took it off his head in the 1975 World Cup final when we beat the Australians at Lord's. We all ran on to the field and I won the race for Dickie Bird's white cap.'

I never let on who I was; he is still probably wearing the cap. It had certainly gone to his head, I can tell you.

In the days after the match I received two letters which I treasure to this day. The first came from the Australian team and was signed by their tour manager, Fred Bennett. It said, 'On behalf of Ian [Chappell], myself, and the team, I would like to say how much we appreciated your efforts in the World Cup final at Lord's last Saturday.'

The other was from former England captain, Colin Cowdrey, who wrote, 'Many congratulations on your superb handling of the World Cup final. It contributed much to the success of everything, and it is nice to be able to say that England has the best umpires in the world.'

After reading those letters, and looking back over the game in the days which followed, I thought to myself, 'If I never umpire again, I can always say that I've done the big one. The first World Cup final. The greatest match ever played. They can never take that away. It's mine. I did it.'

In fact I had the honour of completing a hat-trick of World Cup final appearances – the only umpire to achieve that distinction – but when I was given the 1975 final I thought it was the pinnacle of my career. It never occurred to me that I might be given the honour twice more. I thought I might get a semi-final in 1979, but I was stunned when I was told that I was going to stand in the final again. I had always said that there was nothing to beat the Test match atmosphere, but the final of the World Cup is extra special.

I was delighted to learn that standing with me would be former Gloucestershire player Barrie Meyer, who once scored four goals playing football for Bristol Rovers against my beloved Barnsley at Oakwell – a fact he never allows me to forget.

After the preliminary group matches and semi-finals England had won through to take on the mighty West Indies in the final, and this was a confrontation which gripped the whole nation. Could England beat the holders and wrest the World Cup from their grasp?

It seemed more of a nightmare than a dream when the West Indies rattled up 286 for 9 in their 60 overs, especially with their battery of speed merchants – Andy Roberts, Michael Holding, Colin Croft and Joel Garner – ready to fire their bullets at the English batsmen.

But there was a moment in that opening knock when man-of-the-match Viv Richards thought that his team were heading for defeat. When they lost their fourth wicket with only 99 runs on the board, Viv turned to me and said, 'We're really struggling,

Dickie. This is serious. If they get another wicket now, we've had it.'

It is history now that England did not get another wicket for some considerable time. Instead, Collis King marched in to set a capacity crowd alight with one of the greatest one-day knocks I have seen, very reminiscent of Clive Lloyd's in the first World Cup final four years earlier.

Suddenly the game swung the West Indies' way. King and Richards put on 139 for the fifth wicket, with Richards not out at the close on 138, and King finally falling on 89, caught on the boundary by Derek Randall, going for another mighty six. King hit the ball so hard and so high on occasions that it looked just like a pea flying through the air. What a magnificent innings it was, yet it was Richards, defiant to the last, who earned the man-of-the-match award.

Despite the onslaught from these two, there was some excellent fielding by the England side. This was one of the finest fielding sides England has ever had, and Derek Randall confirmed that he was one of the best fielders in the world, worth his place in the side for that alone. In fact, he was responsible for giving me my only close decision of the day, judging the run-out of Gordon Greenidge.

When England replied, everyone in the home camp was quite happy at tea with a score of 79 without loss from 25 overs, but Clive Lloyd showed no concern at all over the situation. Shrugging off the failure of the West Indian bowlers to achieve the breakthrough he commented, 'I thought England would have opened with Gooch. As it is they are scoring at only three an over, and that's not bad from our point of view.'

England captain Mike Brearley, who had elected to open the innings with Geoff Boycott, claimed that England were in a good position, but he and Boycs had pushed Richards for a lot of singles when critics thought they should have been going for the boundaries, and there were grave doubts about the scoring rate. That opening stand of an eventual 129 became a topic of fierce debate. In reaching that score without loss the two openers had fallen well behind the clock, and I have often wondered if Clive Lloyd deliberately dropped Boycott early on in his innings at mid-on, a comfortable catch for as gifted a fielder as the West Indian skipper, in order to keep him in.

Boycott, incidentally, wore a protective helmet for the first time and it did cross my mind that it might be restricting him.

The runs had come so slowly that England went into the last phase of the game needing to score at a rate of eight an over, which was an impossible task against the West Indian attack, particularly Joel Garner. At six feet eight inches he was so tall, and his arm so high at the point of delivery, that the ball came out of the trees at the nursery end, above the line of the sightscreen. When he pitched the ball well it was almost impossible to pick it up. 'Big Bird' took five of the last seven wickets, firing fast and straight yorkers at leg and middle, and the England batsmen went down like skittles as the West Indies completed a comfortable 92 run victory.

In the end, after that mid-innings scare, the West Indies proved much too powerful for England, and they confirmed their status as the best team in the world at that time. Some people claimed that they used to allow their heads to drop when they were in trouble, and start to panic. But they were in trouble in this game, as Richards admitted to me, yet they still found the right man at the right time to lead a great fight-back.

It was a magnificent game, played in a great spirit, and the only worrying moment for me was when the excitable West Indian fans swarmed on to the field at the end. I just won the race back to the safety of the pavilion, white cap still intact, but I pulled a muscle in doing so.

The West Indies' first World Cup defeat came at the hands

of India in a Group B match of the 1983 competition, which was once again staged in England. Yashpal Sharma made 89 out of his side's 262 for 8 and left-arm spinner Ravi Shastri gave a hint of things to come as he took three wickets in India's 34 run success, but it was the all-round teamwork of the side that was so impressive.

It was not impressive enough, however, for anyone to make the Indians favourites when, after dismissing England in the semi-finals, they came up against the West Indians for a second time in the final at Lord's. Everyone thought that the holders would win easily and thus claim a hat-trick of World Cup successes. When the Indians contrived to get themselves out for only 183 on a perfect batting pitch it seemed that all those predictions were going to be fully justified.

The West Indians bowled well, as usual, but the Indians did not do themselves justice, and I felt sorry for them. Srikkanth got them off to a good start, but there was too much carelessness throughout the rest of the innings, and the usually brilliant Kapil Dev had to take some responsibility, as captain. He foolishly threw the bat in much too cavalier a fashion and paid the penalty, being dismissed by the gentle medium pace of Larry Gomes. It was hardly a good example to set, but he could not complain if his colleagues followed suit.

When they began their reply, I sensed there was a distinct change of mood in the West Indian camp. The players were too relaxed. It struck me that they were suffering from a drastic case of over-confidence, convinced that the title was theirs for the taking.

As the Indian medium-pace bowlers began to swing the ball far more than the quicker West Indian bowlers had done, I thought, 'What a pity they did not get around 240. Then we really would have had a great game on our hands. That would have given them a fighting chance.' As it was, the task seemed to be way beyond them. The West Indies obviously suspected the same.

Gordon Greenidge uncharacteristically gave his wicket away, padding up and being bowled by Sadhu, but when the West Indies reached 50 without further alarms they looked well set. Then came another lapse of concentration, Desmond Haynes barely moving his feet when driving far too casually off the bowling of Madan Lal and being caught.

It was at that point that Kapil Dev strode up to me and said, 'Do you know, Dickie, we will win after all. They think it is too easy. They will get themselves out if we just keep the ball up to them and bowl straight.'

I was still not convinced. Seeing Clive Lloyd ambling to the crease to join Viv Richards I dismissed it as wishful thinking. The turning point came as the West Indies suffered two major blows.

Richards had so much time to play his shots that sometimes he was accused of being lazy or careless when getting out. I always thought that was terribly unfair, because the margin between success and failure is so slender. But at Lord's on that fateful day in 1983, Richards was definitely more than a little annoyed with himself at losing his wicket. He had no need to force the pace, or indulge in any extravagant stroke-making; he had simply to get on with the job in a straightforward manner. However, he could not contain his natural impulses, went for the hook off Madan Lal, and was caught by Kapil Dev running back at mid-off and judging it to perfection.

Worse followed for the West Indies as Lloyd pulled a groin muscle. He stayed at the crease, batting with the aid of a runner, but that was a mistake. In his position I would have retired hurt with the option of returning later if necessary. Richards said afterwards that he agreed with me but, of course, it is easy to judge these situations with the benefit of hindsight. Had Lloyd gone on to make a big, brave score, despite his handicap, we would all have hailed him as a matchwinning hero.

Lloyd had to make the decision there and then and he got it wrong; simple as that. He did not last long, and there is no doubt in my mind that his injury played a big part in his dismissal. He went to drive Roger Binny, but grimaced as he tried to get to the pitch of the ball. A fully fit Lloyd would have hit it a lot harder. As it was the ball went straight to Kapil Dev, still coolly supervising the changing events from mid-off, who took a simple catch.

The West Indies literally limped into tea at 76 for 5 from 25 overs. From that point they managed to hit only one more boundary, a defiant hook for six by Jeff Dujon, which emphasised how difficult it became for the holders as they saw their crown slipping away from them. I am not sure that they were right to abandon their usual cavalier, attacking style, even when Kapil Dev, sensing a memorable victory, turned the screw tighter and tighter. He had no room for error. Just one mistake and it might all have gone horribly wrong but he never lost his sense of purpose, nor his judgement. It was a brilliant piece of captaincy, more than compensating for his indiscretion with the bat.

Several times he said to me, 'We've got them now, Dickie, we've got them.' He may have been trying to reassure himself rather than me but he was right. As the drama built up the West Indies were unable to shake off the stranglehold that the Indians had imposed on them. They became uncertain, hesitant, totally out of character, and their opponents gradually grew in confidence.

It fell to me to put the West Indies out of their misery. Michael Holding shuffled into a position which left him plumb lbw – and even I had to give him out. As I lifted the finger that effectively pushed the crown from off the heads of the champions, I said, 'That's out, and thank you for a wonderful game, gentlemen.'

No sooner had I uttered those words than I was off as fast as I could go to the safety of the pavilion as the over-joyed Indian supporters raced on to the field. I made no attempt to prevent them taking the stumps. I wasn't going to get involved in any violence. I just let them get on with it. In any event, after previous experiences I had learned my lesson. Once again I had switched one of the stumps for an old one during the tea interval – only this time the original was safely in my dressing room as a memento of the occasion.

There was little controversy in that game, although some critics did think they had caught me out when a television replay made it appear that I had made a mistake. I had to concede that it seemed clear enough in slow motion that one West Indian batsman had failed to ground his bat before a throw from a fielder hit the stumps. Yet I was still happy enough with my 'not out' decision.

I knew that the batsman had just failed to make his ground, but he had been obstructed by Indian bowler Madan Lal as he attempted to complete his run, so I ruled 'unfair play'. There was no dispute from Madan Lal, who agreed that he had stepped into the batsman's path.

Most people, before hearing of the reason behind the decision, thought I had made a mistake, and were only too happy to point it out, but Richie Benaud, that doyen of Test match captains and television commentators, spotted what had happened and was quick to back me up.

There was a stack of telegrams from all over the world afterwards congratulating me on my hat-trick of finals, but the one which possibly gave me most pleasure came from the Mayor of Barnsley, Councillor Keith Borrett. I thought that was a wonderful gesture. I really appreciated it. It made me proud to come from Barnsley.

I have always found it difficult to come back down to earth after a big game, particularly after the excitement and tension of a World Cup final, but I was certainly given the opportunity on the following Wednesday, when I was one of the umpires at a first-round NatWest Trophy tie between Lincolnshire and Surrey at Sleaford. I might have done three World Cup finals, but I was not going to be allowed to let that go to my head. The game did, however, provide me with another first. I had never umpired at Sleaford before. In fact, I had to get a map out to find out where it was.

7

INTIMIDATORY BOWLING

INTIMIDATION was one of the main problems while I was umpiring, particularly at Test match level. Of that there is no doubt.

Through the years fast bowlers had gradually become fitter and stronger than they had ever been, and they also started to hunt in packs of three or four rather than in pairs. They began to dominate the game at international level to a point at which too many batsmen were putting the emphasis on physical safety rather than making runs, and that cannot be good for the game.

The original law dealing with the bowling of fast, short-pitched balls said that the bowling was unfair if the umpire at the bowler's end considered that 'by their repetition, and taking into account their length, height and direction, they are likely to inflict physical injury on the striker, irrespective of the protective clothing and equipment he may be wearing. The relative skill of the striker shall also be taken into consideration.'

In the event of such unfair bowling, I, as an umpire, was then duty bound to call and signal 'no-ball' and caution the bowler. I had to inform the other umpire at square leg, the captain of the fielding side, and the batsman, of what had occurred. If the caution was ineffective, then it was up to me to repeat that procedure and indicate to the bowler that this was a final warning. Should the warning also prove ineffective, then I, as the umpire at the bowler's end, was empowered to call and signal 'no-ball', and when the ball was dead, direct the captain to take the bowler off immediately and to complete the over with another bowler. The bowler who had been taken off would then not be allowed to bowl again in the same innings.

The occurrence would be reported to the captain of the fielding side as soon as the players left the field for an interval, and would also be reported to the executive of the fielding side and to any governing body responsible for the match, who would then take any further action that was considered appropriate against the bowler concerned. To me, this was a good ruling, relying on the discretion and strength of the umpire.

Although we all have our faults, and we all make mistakes, the one thing I have always been very strong on is unfair, or intimidatory, bowling, however you want to describe it, and it was one of my strengths as an umpire. I have never run away from my responsibility in that direction.

However, in October, 1994, experimental conditions were brought in for a three-year period, with regard to the bowling of fast, short-pitched balls in Test matches, one-day internationals and other tourist matches. These stated that:

(a) A bowler shall be limited to two fast, short-pitched deliveries per over.

(b) A fast, short-pitched ball is defined as a ball which passes, or would have passed, above the shoulder height of the batsman standing upright at the crease.

(c) In the event of a bowler bowling more than two fast, short-pitched deliveries in one over, the umpire shall call and signal 'no-ball' on each occasion.

(d) The penalty for a fast, short-pitched 'no-ball' shall be two runs, plus any runs scored from the delivery.

(e) A differential signal shall be used to signify a fast, short-pitched delivery. The umpire shall call and signal 'no-ball' and then raise the other arm across his chest.

(f) If the bowler delivers a third fast, short-pitched ball in one over not only must the umpire call 'no-ball' but he must also invoke the procedures of Law 42.8 (a) in regard to cautioning the bowler.

What some people may not realise is that this experimental ruling was slightly different for championship matches, where a bowler was limited to only one fast, short-pitched ball per over per batsman. Confusing? I'll say so. But then we umpires have had to get used to all the different rules for different competitions.

Let us consider the Test ruling which now says that a bowler is allowed two balls per over above shoulder height, with the batsman in a standing position. I do not think that such a ball is dangerous. When it comes at shoulder height or above, a good player can just sway inside the delivery and let it go.

As far as I am concerned, intimidatory bowling is the fast, short-pitched ball into the region of the batsman's ribcage. When such a ball is fired in it is then that I feel an umpire must be firm. I would pounce on any delivery at shoulder height, and say to the bowler, 'That's your one,' and 'That's your two.' However, I would immediately come down hard on the ball into the ribcage, and tell the bowler to cut it out. Such a ball is intimidatory and dangerous. Bowlers would, of course, argue that it was not above shoulder height and that, under the rules, they were entitled to bowl that way, but I believe a ball like that is aimed at the batsman with the intention of hitting him. That's the killer ball, and that is when I always step in.

Bowlers will bend the law, however it is phrased, as people do in any sport. Make any law and they find a way round it, which is why I preferred the old ruling where an umpire could use his discretion and step in if and when he thought that a bowler was sending down too many dangerous deliveries, never mind two an over.

If I ever thought things were getting out of hand I used to have a quiet word with the bowler concerned, saying, 'Now look here, there are too many of these short balls going down and I'm not happy. Will you please space them out or I will be forced to take further action.' Sometimes a bowler has persisted and I have had to issue a warning, but I have never had to ask for a bowler to be removed from the attack. I have always found I was able to nip it in the bud, which is possible if you handle the situation in a proper manner. I was never officious and was always polite and courteous, but at the same time I left the bowler in no doubt that I was not going to stand for any more, and players respected that.

I have had to warn the West Indians on numerous occasions. For example, I gave them an official warning at Old Trafford in the summer of 1995, and there was a good deal of misunderstanding about that. Courtney Walsh was not sure whether I had given him a warning or not, but after I had a word with him he accepted it and got on with the game. I have found that if you tell Courtney to space out the short-pitched balls he will. West Indies coach Andy Roberts took it badly, however. He did not complain directly to me, but I know he was unhappy about the situation. What he did not realise was that I had already spoken to England's Dominic Cork about the same thing. Consistency is important.

In another Test at Headingley I warned Kenneth Benjamin for bowling a couple of short balls to Devon Malcolm. I told him, 'Look, I'm stepping in here because I do not think that Devon Malcolm can defend himself against bowling like that.

He is not a good enough player. He is going to get hurt, so I don't want any more of it.'

Benjamin pitched the next ball right up to the batsman – and knocked Devon's stumps all the way into Cornwall!

Roberts, again, was unhappy, but I knew it was without good cause, because, as at Old Trafford, I had also given an official warning to an England bowler about short-pitched bowling – Malcolm himself.

Standing in another series at Edgbaston in 1984, I watched Malcolm Marshall bowl three short-pitched deliveries to Paul Downton in one over, all of them rearing unpleasantly. Worse still, he went round the wicket, which indicated to me that he intended to attack the body, a tactic the West Indies have often employed. Colin Croft, for one, gave Geoff Boycott a really hard time that way.

I asked Marshall to space out the short balls, but he took no notice, and tested Ian Botham with three more lifters in an over. Botham, of course, was always well able to look after himself, and relished the opportunity to chance his arm against any type of bowling. The law makes a fine distinction with regard to the ability of the batsman, but I still decided to step in. Six short-pitched balls in two overs was more than enough, so I called a no-ball, gave Marshall an official warning in accordance with the procedure, and informed my square-leg colleague Barrie Meyer and West Indies captain Clive Lloyd.

Marshall appeared to be very upset and childishly kicked the ball towards the boundary. I could not let him get away with that. 'Malcolm,' I said to him, 'while I am having a word with your captain, I would like you to fetch that ball back.'

I then told Lloyd that I was giving Marshall an official warning. He challenged my judgement, protesting 'This is ridiculous. We are bowling half-volleys.'

I suggested he must be joking, and judging by the resigned smile that crept across his face, he was.

Marshall duly retrieved the ball and from that moment on kept a very good length, being rewarded with a five-wicket haul. As we were coming off at the end of play he thanked me. 'It probably did me a lot of good, Dickie.'

'Course it did, Malcolm,' I said. 'A bowler of your class will always take a lot of wickets by keeping the ball pitched up. There's just no point in banging it in short.' It was good advice, but, perhaps, from England's point of view, I ought to have kept quiet.

One man who did not agree with my handling of the situation was John Woodcock, of *The Times*. He had previously had a go at umpires for not being strict enough in clamping down on intimidatory or unfair bowling, yet, after all his earlier criticisms, on this occasion he claimed that I should not have stepped in. He argued that Botham was quite capable of looking after himself and had been hooking some and missing some.

That's as maybe. But I was more concerned that Marshall had been launching short-pitched deliveries at the England wicketkeeper, and had taken no notice of my warning to space them out.

The other Press lads asked why it always had to be me who put his head on the block. But I could not have lived with my conscience if I had allowed intimidation to get out of hand. I would have felt that I was not doing my job properly.

The sequel came when I arrived at Old Trafford for the fourth Test. I bumped into Jackie Hendricks, the West Indies tour manager, who said, 'Oh, by the way, Dickie, we're leaving Marshall out because you're umpiring. We don't want him warned again.' I looked at him in amazement before I realised he was having me on. The truth was that Marshall was injured, having broken a bone in his hand at Headingley, and I am sure he would have played in Manchester had he been fit.

I also had cause to warn Keith Boyce during the bomb scare Test at Lord's in 1973. He took no notice and I was forced to give him a stern final warning. Captain Rohan Kanhai did not take too kindly to that, but I had again been consistent in my interpretation, having also warned England's Bob Willis that I was not at all happy with the short stuff he had been sending down right from the start.

However, Gary Sobers, who was batting at the time, whispered in my ear, 'Please don't stop him, Dickie. Let him keep bouncing them down at me. I can play this stuff all day.' Being such a great hooker of the ball, he was revelling in it.

From what I hear, those two great Yorkshire batsmen of old, Percy Holmes and Herbert Sutcliffe, would also have given a shilling of their money for the sort of bowling that modern batsmen complain about. Like Sobers they would have taken it in their immaculate stride and benefited from it – and with no protective headgear in those days.

Another West Indian paceman, Wayne Daniel, is one of the nicest men I have ever come across on a cricket field, but I had to step in quickly and give him a piece of my mind when he tried to intimidate English batsmen with a stream of bouncers at Hove during the West Indies tour of 1976.

In one explosive over to Sussex wicketkeeper Arnold Long, Daniel hurled down four short-pitched deliveries, three of which hummed past the little lefthander's ears, the fourth hitting him in the chest. It was a wild response to a lecture I had given him on no-balls and running on to the pitch with his follow-through: I had no-balled him twelve times and he was obviously upset and annoyed. There was no way I was going to let him get away with those persistent bouncers, though, so

I read the riot act to him – in the nicest possible way, of course.

Daniel continued to have problems on that tour, but whenever I met up with him I talked to him about it and tried to help him find a solution. When he came back afterwards to play county cricket for Middlesex, he never ran on to the pitch, bowled few no-balls and rarely hurled down a bouncer, so I feel that, in some small way, I may have helped him.

I was due to take over from the unfit Arthur Fagg for the Test match at Trent Bridge immediately after that game at Hove, and it was thought that there may have been some reaction from the West Indian camp, but they took my stand against Daniel in good spirit. They accepted my authority and got on with it. I believe that my being firm through the years has not only made for better games of cricket, but has helped quite a few people to be better bowlers as well. They have learned that it is a waste of time bowling short against really good players. If a bowler keeps the ball pitched up he is always far more likely to take wickets.

When I was umpiring I never came across any persistent intimidation by fast bowlers of any side. Any threat of it and I would pounce, and that was enough. I am fully aware that the short-pitched ball is an important part of a bowler's armoury, and every established batsman must accept that he will have to contend with that type of delivery from time to time. I am, however, very much opposed to bouncers being bowled with the intention of hitting the batsman, and to any such delivery to tail-end batsmen who are not capable of fending it off. Under no circumstances will I allow that kind of bowling.

The Australians at one time had two of the most formidable fast bowlers in the world, Dennis Lillee and Jeff Thomson, and I had to call them together in the quarter-final of the Prudential World Cup when they were playing the West Indies at The

Oval in June, 1975. Lillee had just bowled two consecutive short-pitched balls and, in my most friendly manner, I told them that I did not think it was necessary for such great bowlers to have to resort to persistent bouncers. From then on neither of them gave me any trouble whatsoever. As far as Thomson was concerned, the greater problem was with regard to the no-ball rule. In May, 1977, I no-balled him fifteen times in seven overs against Somerset at Bath in only his second spell of the tour. His first bowl, against Kent at Canterbury, had been restricted to just three overs after Bill Alley, another member of the six-man Test umpires panel, had no-balled him four times in his third over. I called him for overstepping in all but one of his seven overs. He had to bowl eleven balls before completing his second over after I had called him five times, including three in a row. His third over cost twenty-three runs – three from no-balls, four from byes and the remainder in boundaries struck by Somerset opener Peter Denning.

When skipper Greg Chappell took him off after almost an hour, Tommo was left with figures of seven overs, one maiden, forty runs, no wickets. So it was that, in ten overs of the tour at that stage, he had been no-balled nineteen times, conceded forty-seven runs and had still to take a wicket. Things could only get better, and they did, but it was a problem with Thomson throughout his career.

There was one incident during an England versus Pakistan test at The Oval in 1974 that probably caused more controversy than any single delivery that has been sent down from my end. What sparked off the rumpus was the hotheaded frustration of Pakistan bowler Sarfraz Nawaz. Essex batsman Keith Fletcher, who had batted for 350 minutes to make an undefeated 76 out of England's 438 for 6, justifiably stepped away from the crease as Sarfraz strode up to bowl, because a spectator had moved behind the bowler's arm. Sarfraz hurled the ball petulantly to the grass and followed this with a hip-high full toss which Fletcher knocked to square leg for a single.

I allowed that ball to go without comment, but the next delivery was a vicious beamer which singed the eyebrows of England's Tony Greig, who stands well over six feet tall, and he was not at all amused. Greig just managed to duck out of the way, a considerable feat for a man of his height, and, after recovering from his astonishment, his shock turned to fury. He marched down the pitch to Sarfraz and threatened, 'I'm going to wrap this bat round your head.'

Sarfraz just stood there, hands on hips like some old Wild West gunfighter. 'I'm waiting for you,' he said.

I realised we were facing an explosive situation, so I whipped off the bails, stepped in between them, and said, 'That's tea, gentlemen, thank you very much.'

As we all walked off I sidled up to Sarfraz and warned him, 'I want no more of this nonsense. I want you to cut it out completely. And I won't tolerate another beamer.' On this occasion, for once, I was in no mood to add my usual 'please'.

'So sorry, Dickie,' he replied. 'You're quite right. No more. I promise.'

I also spoke to the Pakistan captain, Intikhab, asking him to have a word with the bowler, while Greig told me, 'Thanks for the way you handled that situation. It could have been very nasty.'

I was probably lucky, looking back on it. As it was tea I was able to get the players off the field and give them an opportunity to cool down. Had it been in the middle of an over halfway through a session of play I might have had more problems, because both men were clearly very, very angry.

I've spoken to Tony about the incident many times since and he always says, 'You saved my career, you know, Dickie. The way I felt, I was really going to hit him over the head with my bat.' Had he done so, of course, it would have been the last time he played for England and, possibly, anyone else for that matter.

Eight years later Sarfraz was still at it, and I had to step in and warn him again for unfair bowling. He was playing for the Pakistan touring team against Leicestershire at Grace Road and when one delivery whistled past the nose of tail-ender Les Taylor I immediately issued an official warning.

Taylor was none too pleased, either. He pointed a threatening finger in the direction of the bowler, who began to argue with him, saying that it had been a fair delivery. Sarfraz seemed to be very upset, but while I was talking to him he cheekily rolled the ball back past the batsman into the stumps at the other end, and the bails dropped off.

Sarfraz said that the lawmakers were loading the game for the batsmen and the bumper ruling, as it stood – one short-pitched delivery on over – was a soft line. It was crazy, he insisted. If a recognised batsman could not handle bouncers he should not be out there. But this was a tail-ender who was involved and I was not standing for it.

'Huh,' he muttered. 'I can see the Test series is going to be played with kid gloves.'

But I had no more trouble with him after that.

Another Oval Test, this time between England and Australia, brought me into conflict with that great character Merv Hughes. He was operating from my end and I was getting just a little bit fed up with his constant short-pitched bowling. I said to him, 'Come on, Merv, you've sent a few of those down in succession, now give it a rest, will you? Space them out more, there's a good chap.'

He took no notice, so I warned him again. Still he persisted, so I no-balled him. 'Right,' I said, 'that's your first official warning,' and I called Aussie captain Allan Border over to tell him what had happened.

Border ambled across mumbling and grumbling. 'At least you could have told him to space them out first, Dickie,' he complained.

Merv chipped in, 'Oh, he did that all right, Skipper.'

Border rounded on him. 'It's your fault, then, you big daft bugger. Get on with the flamin' game.' Then he added, 'And by the way, Dickie's right. Space them out. Or else . . .'

As I have said, I have always taken great pride in being strict with regard to intimidatory bowling, so you can imagine how annoyed I was during the 1976 Test match between England and the West Indies at Old Trafford when Robin Marlar, writing in the *Sunday Times*, condemned me for 'standing at square leg and doing nothing about it' as Brian Close and John Edrich took a severe battering from the West Indies attack.

I was not even umpiring that match. I was standing at a county fixture down south. The two umpires at Old Trafford were Lloyd Budd and Bill Alley. I immediately contacted my solicitor, Duncan Mutch, who said, 'Leave it with me, Dickie. We'll fire a few shots across their bows for starters and see how they react.'

Marlar duly apologised, his excuse being that it had been a typing error. It should, of course, have been Budd, not Bird. That I could just about accept, but Dickie for Lloyd? Marlar had dropped a giant clanger and he knew it. I accepted his apologies and took the matter no further, but if that's good Press then I'm a Martian. I get blamed for a lot of things, but, please God, not when I'm not even there!

Intimidatory bowling has always been an issue of controversy, right the way back to the Bodyline tour of Australia in 1933, and possibly even further back than that. Harold Larwood gained some notoriety on that tour, of course, and, although

I never saw him bowl, they tell me he was fearsomely fast. Larwood opened the bowling for Nottinghamshire with Bill Voce, who also played for England. One day they were up against Northamptonshire, who had a quickie by the name of Nobby Clark. Nobby was letting the Notts batsmen have everything – beamers, bouncers, rib-ticklers, the lot. Nobby's colleagues became rather perturbed by all this and eventually one of them went up to Nobby and warned, 'Just cool it a bit, will you? Remember they have two of the world's fastest bowlers in Lol Larwood and Bill Voce. There will be some revenge-seeking after this, you mark my words.'

Nobby snorted, 'Huh, they don't worry me one little bit. When I go into bat, if Larwood pitches in my half I'll hit him straight back over his head, and if he bowls them short I'll hook him out of Northampton. What are you frightened of?'

By the time Larwood came in to bat Nobby had taken seven wickets. Larwood was to become his eighth. The first ball was a vicious bouncer, straight at Larwood's head. Lol looked down the pitch and threatened, 'Nobby, it will soon be my turn.'

Nobby really had his dander up, however. 'You don't worry me, Lol. When I come in to bat, if you pitch 'em in my half I'll hit you straight back over your head. If you bowl 'em short at me, I'll hit you straight out of Northampton.'

Larwood contented himself by saying, 'We'll see about that.'

Northants went in to bat in reply, and they tell me no one had ever seen bowling as quick on that ground as was seen that day from Larwood and Voce. The two of them ran through the batsmen until it was Nobby's turn to come in at number nine. As he was taking guard Larwood smiled menacingly at him. 'Now then, Nobby,' he said. 'It's my turn.'

Nobby displayed commendable bravado as he replied, 'Yes, and I'm ready for you, Lol. Remember what I said. Pitch it in my half and it'll go straight back over your head. Pitch it short and I'll hit you right out of the county.'

Said Larwood, 'Should be a good contest, then.'

Nobby settled to face his first ball. In came Larwood and bowled a short-pitched delivery which reared up at tremendous pace straight towards Nobby's head. He swayed out of the way of it in the nick of time, and as it flashed by he swung his bat, got a thick edge, and the ball flew first bounce to third slip.

Nobby tucked his bat underneath his arm and started walking back towards the pavilion.

'Hey, you're not out yet,' yelled Larwood. 'Come back and fight.'

But Nobby kept walking. 'Well bowled, Lol,' he said. 'Well bowled.'

Then the umpire intervened. 'Come back here, Mr Clark. The ball bounced two yards in front of slip before he caught it.'

Nobby did not so much as shorten his stride. 'I'm satisfied it was a fair catch, Mr Umpire,' he shouted over his shoulder, and disappeared into the sanctuary of the dressing room.

There is another story told of Larwood when he came face to face with Wilfred Rhodes, the former Yorkshire and England all-rounder, whom Freddie Trueman rates as the best all-rounder of all time, though how he can judge I don't know – he never saw him play! Fred argues that you only have to look at his figures.

However, on this particular occasion, Rhodes took a very painful blow on the left toe from Larwood, and off he went, hopping about on one foot and moaning with pain. Larwood, having appealed in the heat of the moment, but now concerned for his rival's well-being, rushed forward to apologise. 'Oh, Wilfred,' he said, 'I'm so sorry. I do hope you're going to be all right.'

The umpire, the great Frank Chester, was also very sympathetic, and eventually Rhodes showed signs of recovery, gingerly putting his foot to the floor and testing to see if it would support his weight.

'Good,' said Chester, 'it looks as if you can walk well enough.'

'Yes, I think I can, if you'll just give me another minute,' said Rhodes.

'You can have all the time you like when you get back to the pavilion,' replied Chester, 'but if I were you I'd set off now. You're out, lbw.'

It is not, however, always necessary for the bowling to be exceptionally quick for the batsmen to be afraid for their lives. Rain-affected pitches have caused havoc, and I have seen some strange conditions affect play in remarkable ways.

There was one freak incident at Buxton in 1975 when, in the middle of one of the hottest summers on record, snow stopped play on 1 June. We had six inches overnight and there was no play at all on the Monday, Lancashire having made 477 for 5 on the Saturday, which I believe is a record for the first day of a championship match.

In those days the pitches were uncovered, so it was not until Tuesday morning that we were able to resume. Lancashire had declared and the sun was shining brightly as the Derbyshire batsmen were caught on a very difficult pitch. I do not think I have ever experienced anything as bad. It really was virtually unplayable. A good-length ball would rear up head high, and Derbyshire were shot out twice, for 42 and 87.

However, the batsmen were not too bothered about the low scores, just so long as they escaped with their limbs and other bits and pieces intact. Ashley Harvey-Walker, for example, handed me his false teeth, wrapped in a handkerchief, when he came in to bat. 'Look after these, Dickie,' he said to me. 'I won't be long.' He was right. He was clean bowled, backing so far away from the wicket that he was nearly standing on my toes at square leg. At least he did not have far to go to collect his false teeth.

'I think that was out, Dickie,' he said. 'Thank goodness for that. I'm well out of it,' and he walked off, sliding his gnashers gently back into place.

There was another 'snow stopped play' headline early in the 1994 season when I umpired the game between Cambridge University and Nottinghamshire at Fenners. We started on time, but after about an hour the April day changed dramatically. Suddenly it started to snow and before we knew where we were there were several inches covering the ground. When it stopped I went out and built a snowman at the side of the stumps. They said it looked a bit like me, what with the white coat and all.

I was twelfth man for Yorkshire against India at Bramall Lane in 1959, when the captain of the touring side was Polly Umrigar, one of the finest players against spin and medium pace, but decidedly ill at ease when faced with anything quicker.

Umrigar's record of 59 Tests and 3,631 runs at an average of 42.22 shows just how good a player he was, but he didn't fancy facing Freddie Trueman and, on the morning of the match, suddenly developed a mysterious back strain. Then news reached the Indian camp that Fred had been ruled out with ankle trouble. Umrigar's back problem disappeared as quickly as it had developed. He did a couple of stretching exercises and decided that he might just make it after all.

Meanwhile, Fred was in the treatment room having his ankle strapped and it was agreed that he would give it a go, whereupon Umrigar suffered a relapse!

I was with Fred during the Indians' 1974 tour when we met Lt.-Col. Hemu Adhikari, the former Indian Test player who was then managing the side. He had been one of Fred's victims at Headingley when India lost their first four wickets without scoring a run. He had backed to square leg when Fred's first delivery whistled past, his face deathly white. Fred, introduced to him in the Old Trafford bar, enthused, 'Now then, Colonel, 'ow's things? Glad ter see you've got your colour back!'

No one could accuse Peter Broughton of being an intimidatory bowler, but I saw him bowl the beamer to end all beamers. Peter appeared briefly for Yorkshire in 1956 and did not do too badly by any means, taking 16 wickets at a cost of 22.81, and he went on to play with me at Leicestershire. In one Yorkshire game against Sussex at Bradford, our captain, Billy Sutcliffe, gave Peter the new ball in the absence of Freddie Trueman, who was playing for England. Very well aware of the honour, Peter decided to put everything into it. Operating from the old Football Stand End he tore up to the stumps, concentrating all his energy into his delivery stride. Neither he nor anyone else is exactly sure what happened next, and it would make a good teaser on *A Question of Sport*.

When he let go of the ball it whistled like a bullet past the amazed batsman, Don Smith, and over the wicketkeeper's head. Those who remember the Park Avenue ground will recall that the pavilion area was separated from the playing area by a substantial wall. Well, the ball cleared this, too, scattering the crowds immediately behind the wicket. It caused a good deal of consternation and someone waved a white handkerchief in mock surrender.

Peter had somehow bowled the ball straight into the members' enclosure. I doubt that he could have repeated the feat, even if he had wanted. It certainly could not have been easy to clear that wall with a proper bowling action. The general feeling was that the ball had slipped, but, even so, Peter might well have received a quiet word from the umpire.

It is quite possible for a bowler trying too hard to lose control, and the result can be quite spectacular. Not all hostile fast bowling is intentional, but a batsman has a better chance of dealing with a bouncer if he is at least half expecting it. When it comes about by accident he can be taken completely off guard and such situations can be very dangerous.

For example, I was standing at a very important championship match between Derbyshire and Nottinghamshire at Trent Bridge in 1987 when Devon Malcolm got himself into a spot of bother. Notts were pressing hard for the title and, with Derbyshire having made 339, and their captain, Kim Barnett, top-scoring with 130, Notts were well on their way to 389 in reply.

Devon is one of the nicest lads you could wish to meet, but he was really fired up as he desperately tried to get a wicket, and three bouncers went hurtling down in the space of seven balls.

'Come on, Devon,' I said. 'We can't have this. Pitch the ball further up. The odd bouncer is all right, but not all these.'

'I am very sorry,' said Dev. 'It won't happen again.'

A few overs later he hit Clive Rice on the arm with a wild full toss, and again he apologised profusely. 'It slipped,' he explained. 'I didn't mean to do it, honest.'

'That's as may be,' I replied, 'but you've had your sighters above and below the target. Now I'm giving you an official warning. Let's see if you can hit a decent length from now on,' and happily he did.

It does concern me, though, that there are bowlers who just go out with the intention of frightening batsmen to death right down the order instead of trying to bowl them out. It is up to all umpires to be strong in such instances and make sure that short-pitched deliveries are not used to excess.

Sparingly used, the bouncer can be a wicket-taking weapon. The top bowlers, including Dennis Lillee, Fred Trueman, Michael Holding, Andy Roberts and Ray Lindwall, used it to get the batsman on to the back foot, prepared to take evasive action. Then they would slip in the yorker – and bingo!

Intimidatory bowling has always been a contentious issue, and I guess it always will be, but it is no good to keep changing the law. It is almost impossible to legislate properly for it. I make no apologies for repeating that it should be down to the strength and discretion of the umpire.

As Clive Lloyd once said, 'When Dickie has applied the law we have accepted it. If he is strong and steps in, that is fine by us. We might not agree with him, but it is his decision. He is consistent in its application, and we respect him for it.'

8

INSIDE TRACK

THROUGH the years umpires and groundsmen have developed a special camaraderie because they have so much in common, the main thing being that they always find themselves in a no-win situation. Someone will always dispute decisions and someone will always criticise the pitch. Umpires and groundsmen have therefore learned not only to work together, but to stick together as well.

Groundsmen, I am sure, would agree with my definition of a good pitch as being one that has even bounce, pace, and, towards the end of the match, takes spin. That is the kind of pitch where all bowlers are brought into play and where all the great batsmen will tell you they were able to learn their trade. A youngster cannot develop his all-round skills on a pitch that seams all over the place from the first ball, or on one that turns square from the start.

Ray Illingworth argues that we prepare pitches which enable mediocre seam bowlers to win matches, and I agree with him. He has always been in favour of three-day county cricket and uncovered wickets, which, he argues, teaches batsmen to be adaptable, to cope with different challenges, or lose their place in the professional game. In his words, 'It helps cut away the dead wood.'

We are unlikely to go back to uncovered pitches, but Illingworth insists that we must tackle the vital problem of their preparation. He believes that groundsmen should be told that it is their duty to shape a wicket that is good for the game overall, not to suit the home side, because if things go on as they are there will be no game.

Those are strong words, but Illingworth has a point. Pitches should be firm and with bounce for the first part of the game, and then they should take spin. In that, Illingworth and I are in complete agreement. As he says, a cricket match should have a natural rhythm, one which offers challenges – and some encouragement – to all kinds of batsmen and bowlers. That is the glory of cricket: the range of the game, and the different skills it demands.

Illingworth believes that the 'short-sighted administrators of the county game have lost all grasp of those values. They are tied to the parish pump,' and cites the example of Lancashire, a team which has boasted international class talent over the last few years. Their record in one-day cricket is excellent, although in the 'real game', the cricket which shapes our Test players, their record is appalling.

Illy rounds off his argument by saying, 'Frankly, I sometimes despair that the message will ever get through. Groundsmen say they cannot cut the pitch to a spinner's length because it will spoil the look of a wicket. I say that we should be beyond cosmetics. The point is that we begin to play the game properly, and to do that we need the right kind of pitches.'

Groundsmen are not always free to provide 'the right kind' of pitch, however, and are always under pressure, from captain, club or country, to make a pitch that suits their own attack.

This state of affairs led to a certain disenchantment for former Trent Bridge groundsman, Ron Allsopp, when he retired from his duties with Nottinghamshire County Cricket Club. He is now employed in an advisory capacity with Warwickshire, and I asked him one day last year if he was missing Trent Bridge, because I knew it had been his life, just as cricket has been my life.

He told me, 'To be honest, Dickie, I'm not missing it at all. Funny that, isn't it, after all those years? But I was glad to get out in the end. You simply cannot win. You make a turning pitch, you're wrong. You leave grass on it and get bounce, you're wrong.'

It is perfectly true. If a groundsman prepares a pitch with lots of runs in it, the bowlers are less than happy, but when wickets tumble because the ball is leaping about and turning at ninety degrees, then the batsmen have it in for him. It's heads you lose, tails they win, because when conditions are spot on, it is the players who receive all the praise for producing such a good game, not the poor old groundsman. Generally the complaint is that the pitch is either too slow, too quick, too flat, too bouncy, too green, too bare, too wet or too dry, depending on the critic's point of view, and I have a lot of sympathy for Ron and his colleagues.

I have known Ron for many years, first when I was a player with Yorkshire and Leicestershire, and then as an umpire, and we soon developed a good friendship. He has always been ready with a laugh and a joke and is a good companion as well as an excellent groundsman. He started out in 1953 as a trainee at Trent Bridge under head groundsman Jim Fairbrother, who later left to take over at Lord's. Jim wanted Ron to go with him as his assistant, but Ron wouldn't, not for all the money in the world. A Nottingham man through and through, he did not want to leave his beloved Trent Bridge, and he stayed there until his retirement.

However, there was one period when he became so disillusioned with life that he applied for a job at a local hockey and cricket club in Nottinghamshire because the wages were more than he was getting at Trent Bridge.

When word came back that he had got the job, the Secretary of Nottinghamshire County Cricket Club, Mr Poulton, called Ron into his office. 'What's all this, Ron? Why are you thinking of leaving us? Have you a problem?'

Ron said, 'The problem is money. I've been offered more and I'm tempted to take it.'

Mr Poulton thought for a minute and then said, 'I see. Well, just leave it with me and I'll see what we can sort out.' He saw the committee, they came up with an extra four pounds a week and Ron stayed. Nottinghamshire will be glad he did, because he is one of the best groundsmen in the world.

A few years before he retired at the age of sixty-five the people at Lord's were engaged in a big campaign against counties doctoring their pitches. I was at Trent Bridge for a county championship match and gave the pitch a good mark. As I left I joked to Ron, 'Everything's fine, just don't do anything silly in future.'

I went back there later in the season for the Nottinghamshire v Middlesex game, by which time Ron had been told to liven the pitch up a bit because everybody was fed up with playing on completely docile tracks. As I walked up to have my usual pre-match chat with Ron on that first morning at about eight o'clock, I could not distinguish the pitch from the square, the grass was so long and green.

'Playing here, Ron?' I asked.

'No,' he replied. 'This is for a Bassetlaw League game at the weekend. That's today's pitch over there.'

I looked to where he was pointing, and I could not believe it. Both ends were very, very bare. It was all right for the quick bowlers on a seamer's length, but on a spinner's length it looked as if it would turn square. 'You must be joking,' I spluttered. 'You promised me that you wouldn't do anything daft, but you have.'

Then Middlesex captain Mike Gatting came up and started putting in his six penn'oth, and things became a little heated. However, Nottinghamshire suffered in the end, because the pitch suited Gatting and his side down to the ground. Middlesex won the toss, made 455, and, on the last day, routed the home team for 102 to gain an emphatic win, with John Emburey and Phil Tuffnell sharing seventeen wickets between them. In the end I took pity on Ron and still gave him a decent mark.

On another occasion Ron was preparing a pitch for the game between Nottinghamshire and Warwickshire in the days when Clive Rice was captain. Rice wanted a bouncy pitch because he felt that the Warwickshire players, used to playing on the featherbed at Edgbaston, would not be able to cope.

'I'm not too sure about that, Skipper,' Ron said. 'It doesn't seem quite right to me.'

Rice turned to him and said, 'What's the matter, have you gone religious or something?'

When Rice first took over as the Nottinghamshire captain, everyone will tell you that the pitches at Trent Bridge were renowned for being true, and were a batsman's paradise. One day Rice took Ron to one side and said, 'Look here, Ron, we'll never win the championship on pitches like this. I want you to start experimenting with the square to make pitches to suit myself, Richard Hadlee and Eddie Hemmings.'

Hemmings was an off-spin bowler who was not bothered whether the ball took spin or not, and thrived on a pitch where the ball bounced. He always maintained that you could have a pitch that turned square, but if the ball did not bounce you would not get the batsman out.

Rice wanted a pitch with pace and bounce, so Ron did as he was told, and in 1981 Nottinghamshire won the county championship under his captaincy. It was a deserved success, for Rice was a tremendous professional, a hard competitor, a matchwinner, a good captain and a fine all-round cricketer. On top of all that, we umpires thought the world of him because he was straight and honest. The tragedy was that, as a South African, he never played Test cricket because of the apartheid problem.

When Notts beat Glamorgan in the last match of the 1981 season to clinch the championship for the first time since 1929, the visitors complained about the pitch. In some ways they may have had good cause, for Ron tells me that Notts won every one of their home matches in that championship season. Rice had said he wanted result pitches and Ron provided them. The captain had told his groundsman, 'Don't you worry about those batsmen sitting in the dressing room thinking about their averages. I'm not bothered about them. I want to win matches. I want to win the championship,' and he did.

Ron had this gift of being able to prepare any pitch that was asked of him. If you wanted it bouncy with pace, he would make it; if you wanted a pitch to turn, he would make it. He was, and still is, a master of his craft.

Ron's Test pitches were always excellent. There is a different art in preparing a pitch for a five-day Test, and Ron had it off to a tee. Matches nearly always went the distance. He did, however, slip up once, when England were due to play Australia, and Ron thought that he would leave a lot more grass on the pitch to try to get more pace and bounce.

Unfortunately, he had not bargained for an Australian bowler called Terry Alderman, who was brilliant at making the ball swing in overcast conditions, or getting the most out of it if there was some moisture in the pitch. That pitch, with all that grass on it, was tailor-made for him, and he won the match for Australia. Ron was a sitting duck for the critics, one of whom was a very unhappy Geoff Boycott, who had not exactly revelled in the conditions.

When the match was over Boycs strolled out into the middle where Ron was tidying up and chided him, 'I'm not very pleased with that pitch, Ron. Whatever were you thinking of, preparing one like that?' Ron explained what he had tried to do, Boycott took it all in, appeared to accept the groundsman's point of view, and they parted on friendly terms. Boycs then went and criticised Ron in the papers the next day, and the latter was not amused. Despite that little altercation, they remained good friends, and Ron always said that, of all the batsmen he had seen play at Trent Bridge in Test matches, Boycott was one of the best.

Whenever it rained at Trent Bridge there was always a pantomime in getting the covers on. They are the heaviest covers in the world, and have to be pulled on with tractors. Once when England were playing New Zealand, a sprinkling of rain got on to the pitch, much to the consternation of New Zealand captain John Wright, who was batting at the time.

Wright urged Ron to cover the pitch as quickly as possible. 'Come on, Ron,' he implored. 'Hurry it up, there's a good chap.' But there is no hurrying those covers, and I didn't envy Ron his job. It is still the same at Trent Bridge today. Nothing has changed.

Arriving late in the afternoon the day before one county match was due to start I saw Ron working hard as usual out there in the middle, and I hid behind one of the seats in the stand. I kept peering out, shouting, 'What kind of pitch are you preparing for tomorrow, then, Ron?' and then ducking behind the seats again. Ron looked up each time, but could see nobody. After a while he began to get annoyed and I had to make myself known, otherwise his blood pressure would have shot off the scale. By the time I joined him on the square he had calmed down and we have always had a good laugh about it since.

Ron now advises head groundsman Steve Rouse at Edgbaston. Steve used to play for Warwickshire – he was a quick bowler, left-arm over the wicket – and when he retired he took up the job as head groundsman for all the grounds in the Birmingham area. He did a marvellous job, producing some magnificent pitches, so when there was a vacancy at Edgbaston Steve was the obvious choice. He declined at first, but eventually was persuaded to take it on, and he has done a superb job. Warwickshire have also made a shrewd move in bringing in Ron in an advisory capacity because of his vast experience. He knows pitches inside out, and it would have been a pity had such knowledge been lost to the game simply because he had reached retirement age.

Another fine groundsman who has now retired is Keith Boyce, the former head groundsman at Headingley. He started his career at Acklam Park, Middlesbrough, at a time when the ground was in danger of losing county matches because of the state of the pitch. One particularly low-scoring match between Yorkshire and Hampshire put its future in grave jeopardy. Keith turned things round in a comparatively short space of time, however, and in five years completely transformed the playing conditions. When he left, the pitch was in an excellent condition.

Keith enjoyed himself there and only left because he was offered the job at Headingley in 1978. 'It is every groundsman's ambition,' he told me, 'to prepare a Test match pitch, so when I had the opportunity it was a move I could not refuse. It was a great honour for me.'

It was not all plain sailing for him at Headingley, though, not by a long chalk. There was a lot of bickering down the years about his Headingley pitches, but he left on a high note in 1995. I umpired the Test against the West Indies that year on an excellent pitch which I marked very highly. Keith had got it right after a lot of aggravation.

I always had a lot of respect for Keith, even in the difficult times, when he was caught up in the middle of differing opinions. He always said, going back to the early 1980s, when he was getting most of the criticism, that he wanted to dig up the square completely and re-lay it, but his company would not listen to him. The main reason for them sticking their heads in the sand was Botham's Test in 1981, a magnificent match in which England beat the Australians against all the odds, thanks to Botham's brilliant century and Willis's inspirational bowling.

'What do you want to interfere with the pitch for, when we have just seen one of the most memorable matches in Test history being played on it?' was the question tossed at Keith. He realised there was little point in arguing, so he left the square as it was, continuing to do the best he could, but convinced in his own mind that he was right in wanting to start all over again.

He broached the subject again in 1985, but once more his timing could have been better. England had just scored more than 600 against the Australians, Nottinghamshire batsman Tim Robinson hitting 171 in the first innings, and had beaten the old enemy in another tremendous match which had gone into the fifth day.

'Dig it up? Dig it up?' they mocked him. 'What on earth for? We are getting exciting Test matches here. It is what the public wants to see. Why do you keep going on about digging it up?'

Then, in 1987, England were bowled out for 102 in the first innings against India and for less than 200 in the second innings. England captain Mike Gatting was far from happy with the pitch, despite the fact that England won a very low-scoring game. Keith told me that he had not been able to provide the pitch he wanted because he had been hindered in its preparation by the weather. However, it made him all the more determined to dig up the square, and this time he got his own way.

He eventually relaid twelve pitches on that Headingley square, going down eighteen inches deep, and that is when he started to produce such fine Test tracks. In the end he achieved what he had set out to do, and he said to me on his retirement, pride and satisfaction lighting up his eyes, 'Dickie, I realised my ambition in the end. I got the pitches I wanted. In my last year we got the best umpires' marks for pace and bounce of any pitch in the country, except for Edgbaston.'

He had, however, just one regret, and sighed, 'If only I had been allowed to dig up the square in the early 1980s, I would have got on top of it much sooner. The big problem was that there was so much in-fighting at Headingley. It put so much pressure on me and life was often very difficult.'

Sadly, just when Keith did get it right, he lost his wife, Margaret, through cancer. She died just before the Headingley Test of 1995 between England and the West Indies. I knew Margaret well. She was a great worker and a tremendous help to her husband. I'd seen her out there on the morning of matches, when the rain was lashing down, helping Keith pull the covers on, or assisting the groundstaff lads on the square. An amazing woman. We all miss her.

I felt very sorry for Keith. He took her death badly, and although he knew it was coming, it was still a great shock for him. At the end of that Test, when the players and umpires were presented with their medals, he felt he could not go up to receive his groundsman's award. There were tears in his eyes, and it would have been too upsetting. Sir Laurence Byford, the Yorkshire Chairman, went up to receive it on his behalf.

During Keith's time as head groundsman there were twelve

Tests in which outright results were obtained, and that is not a bad record. The Press never criticised Keith personally, because the Headingley pitches used to provide them with some excellent copy. There was always something exciting happening, some great drama, some controversy. Life was never dull at the home of Yorkshire cricket.

When Keith retired from Headingley he went to work on the Leeds rugby league pitch, although he still helps Yorkshire with their outgrounds. His place has been taken by Andrew Fogarty, who was second in command at Old Trafford when he was invited to succeed Keith. I've talked to Andrew and asked him why he wanted to leave a fine ground like Old Trafford. His reply echoed that of his predecessor.

'When you get the chance to be head groundsman at a Test ground you have got to take it, because it comes only once in a lifetime.'

At the Yorkshire CCC annual meeting in March, 1997, Bob Platt, the chairman of the cricket committee, and captain David Byas, said that Andy Fogarty was their twelfth man. Did they mean that he was providing pitches to suit the Yorkshire attack?

I am sure that Andy would have wanted to follow in the footsteps of Boyce and build on all the good work he had done at Headingley, but now, of course, he may have to start from scratch at the proposed new, custom-built county ground at Durkar, a move to which was approved by a seventy-five per cent majority at the annual meeting in March 1997.

Peter Marron, at Old Trafford, is one of the youngest head groundsmen at the age of forty-one, but he has already won the Groundsman of the Year award on two occasions. He started his career under Bert Flack, and he could not have had a better teacher. Bert was a great character, always with a smile on his face, and as knowledgeable on pitch preparation as anyone you

118

could wish to meet. He had been at Old Trafford for many years, where Test pitches have always been among the best in the world, and Peter has maintained that proud tradition. In his first year in the job, in 1983, he produced a track that saw Paul O'Shaughnessy beat Percy Fender's long-standing record for the fastest century in first-class cricket in the match between Lancashire and Leicestershire. Test pitches at Old Trafford always go the full distance and generally there is a result on the last day. In all the Tests I have umpired there I have never once seen a poor pitch.

There was a time when Peter was also a deputy pitch inspector for all the county grounds. If a pitch was reported as being below par he would be the one to go along, decide what was wrong, and advise on how to put it right. It was a part of his work that he thoroughly enjoyed, but he resigned on a point of principle after being docked twenty-five points for his own pitch which he had prepared for a game against Middlesex.

'Dickie,' he said to me, 'how could I possibly sit in judgement on other groundsmen and their pitches when I had been found guilty myself? I felt there was no way I could continue in that role. They complained about it being a damp pitch, yet it was an outstanding match which went the distance. The umpires, however, reported it as being damp, and the punishment was duly meted out. How could I go on after that?'

I asked him what he most enjoyed and he enthused, 'Oh, the Roses matches, without any doubt. They are special. They are always played in such a tremendous spirit, and there is a lot of fun between the teams, despite the competitive edge to all the meetings.' That is how all cricket should be, and I would back him up on that.

At the moment Peter is 'doing a Boyce' and re-laying his square because he says it has had its day and is quite worn out. It occurred to me that people could say the same about Dickie Bird. If only I could be relaid! Peter will do one pitch at a time, so the whole project could take quite a while, but he'll get there, and Old Trafford will be even better, if that is possible.

When I was a player, of course, I looked at pitches from a far different perspective, and I always remember the one at Ashby-de-la-Zouch in Derbyshire, which was not exactly renowned for being the best in the world to bat on. The Derbyshire attack of Les Jackson, Harold Rhodes, Derek Morgan and off-spinner Edwin Smith did not complain, however. That was a tremendous line-up and the pitches suited them admirably.

I once played there for Leicestershire on a very green pitch, and we were bowled out for 135 after Derbyshire had won the toss and put us in, Jackson getting most of the wickets. I made 79, and, having reached that total, I was beginning to think in terms of a headline-making century, which, on a pitch like that and against such good bowling, would have been a magnificent performance, even if I do say so myself.

Morgan was bowling round the wicket to me, and I tell you no lie when I say that this particular delivery pitched a good six inches outside the leg stump. I went to glance it, the ball hit my pad and there was a half-hearted appeal from the bowler. The umpire just happened to be Eddie Phillipson, who had played for Lancashire, and was now on the Test panel. He was renowned for giving lbw decisions, and sure enough, up shot Eddie's finger. I trudged off disconsolately. I had set my heart on a ton, and there was no way I should have been given out.

Afterwards, having a drink with Eddie, as we used to do in those days, I admonished him. 'Dear me, Eddie, what were you thinking of, man? I was struggling for runs, Eddie, and there I was, on seventy-nine, going for my century on a bad pitch, and what do you do? Give me out lbw yards outside the leg stump. That wasn't very nice, was it?'

All Eddie could say was, 'Never mind, Dickie lad. Look at it this way. That's another lbw victim I've chalked up.' You see, he kept a list of all the batsmen he had given out lbw during the season. It seems he was determined to add me to it. It's amazing to think that when he first started on the list he was regarded as a 'not-outer'. He certainly made up for it later on, and kept polishing everybody off. I was number whatever-it-was for that season yet we could still laugh and joke about it. There is no way you could do that today.

When Keith Boyce left Middlesbrough's Acklam Park for Headingley his place was taken by Tommy Flinthoff, who carried on the work there so well that I recommended him to Hampshire when they wanted a new man, and I was delighted to see him producing such fine pitches for them.

Then a vacancy came up at Durham's new ground at Chester-le-Street and Tommy successfully applied for it. He did not really want to leave Southampton because he had been so happy there, but he comes from the north east and this was an opportunity to 'return home'. They possibly played on the pitch at Chester-le-Street sooner that he would have liked, but he will get it right, because he is such a good groundsman.

Tommy had earlier applied for the job at Lord's when Jim Fairbrother died, but they decided it should go to Mike Hunt, who had been on the groundstaff there since he was a young boy. Tommy would have done a good job, I know that, but I had no argument with the appointment of Mike, whom I have known since he was a mere boy. He is very conscientious and a tremendous worker who does a marvellous job in preparing so many pitches. He has also been a great help to me through the years. He always says to me, 'Dickie, I am a very lucky man. This is *the* job in cricket.'

Another groundsman I have known for a long time is Brian Fitch, at Kent's Canterbury ground. He is so dedicated to the job that he virtually lives in the middle. He is there from first thing in the morning to last thing at night, but then, that's typical of all the top men.

Brian told me, 'Canterbury has given me the opportunity of being in charge of one of the most picturesque grounds in the country. They talk of it as being like New Road at Worcester, and it has always given me a great deal of satisfaction to work in such wonderful surroundings. It is not a concrete jungle. There is lots of character about the place. A few trees make all the difference. However,' he added, 'being a groundsman at such a delightful place does not mean that I do not need to have a thick skin. That still applies.'

For Brian cricket has always been full of memories, anecdotes and stories, and he recalls the time when Stuart Leary arrived at Canterbury for a Sunday League game, neck and neck with Clive Lloyd to win the competition for the most sixes in a season, with prizes given by the then sponsors John Player. Stuart asked Brian if he would move the boundary boards in, hoping to pip Lloyd for the first prize. Even then he didn't manage to clear the boards all day and his hopes of winning the prize were the only things to be hit for six.

Scarborough is another lovely setting for cricket and the head groundsman there, Mick Cawley, prepares some excellent pitches for county matches and the famous festival. Yet Yorkshire County Cricket Club, through the years, have complained about his pitches because they claim to struggle to get results there. What is the man supposed to do? He produces the best pitches possible, yet he is criticised. It is the same old story: groundsmen and umpires simply cannot win.

Mick, incidentally, is now an inspector of pitches, as is Peter Eaton, another fine groundsman at Hove, and they work under Harry Brind, the former Essex County Cricket Club groundsman, who is former Essex and Surrey groundsman and now ECB pitches consultant. Harry, too, has always produced great Test pitches, and it was he who helped Paul Getty with his new pitch at Wormsley. All the groundstaff at The Oval started there as young men under Harry and have stayed on to form a wonderful team.

I have seen a lot of groundsmen come and go, but one old-timer who is still plodding on is David Bridle, at Bristol, with whom I have spent many happy hours.

Last winter I was invited to Twickenham for the Five Nations rugby international between England and France. I took the opportunity to have a chat with the assistant groundsman there, a Yorkshireman by the name of John Richardson, and he opened my eyes as he recounted the different aspects of the art of preparing a rugby pitch.

At Twickenham they use a one-metre mower and cut the grass in two directions, thus leaving a striped effect which, John explained, helped the referee decide whether a pass was forward or not during the course of a game, and also helped him decide whether the opposition players were ten metres back for a penalty.

I was astounded that the grass was cut to help a referee in his decision-making, until I remembered it was not such a novelty after all. In New Zealand a few weeks earlier the groundsmen there had cut the grass in such a way that it clearly showed the umpire the inner fielding circle for the one-day internationals.

John also told me that he walked eight miles doing one cut of the pitch and it took him eight hours, a job that has to be done twice weekly during the summer. The grass is left at a height of two and a half inches for international matches.

Incidentally, John informed me that they have a terrible problem with female foxes. The ground is wick with them.

They come out of the cabbage patch at the back of the stands, urinate on the grass and do some dreadful damage as a result.

I also talked to Twickenham's security chap, Keith Webster, and the man who shows people round, Les Evans. According to these two, they employ twelve hundred stewards at matches, to control a seventy-five-thousand all-seater stadium, one hundred first-aiders and twelve ambulances. There is also a body of youths, all fit lads and mostly from university, who are there to pounce on any streakers.

Twickenham has been a bit wary of streakers ever since Michael O'Brien became the first one in April 1974. That streak was made in response to a ten-pound bet, but to win his money he had to reach the opposite touchline. PC Perry caught him yards short of his objective, but he was allowed to touch the fence while the bobby cautioned him. O'Brien now works as a computer software manager at the Australian Stock Exchange in Melbourne, and is the subject of the world-famous photo of a bobby holding his helmet over O'Brien's unmentionables.

Then, of course, there was Erica Roe, who became the first female streaker during an England v Australia match in January 1982. Personally, I don't really mind the odd streaker. It livens the job up a bit – especially if the streaker's female!

Incidentally, Boeings are not allowed to fly directly over Twickenham on their way to Heathrow in case some debris falls off into the crowd, or on to a player in the middle, and causes serious injury. Never mind the poor beggars walking around outside the ground, who might get dropped on from a great height!

Back to cricket, and it is appropriate that the final reflections on the subject of pitches should come from Dave Smith, one of the groundsmen at grass-roots level who has been with Hull Zingari Cricket Club for donkey's years.

As a club groundsman he has been asked to look at the

problems of poor pitches in league cricket, and one of the biggest mistakes clubs make, according to Dave, is pulling out the stumps after the last match of the summer and doing little or nothing to the pitch until the start of the following season. The quality of the pitch, he maintains, depends entirely on the work that is done in the autumn and through the winter. If the square is not renovated during that time it will almost certainly result in a poor pitch.

What kind of pitch is produced depends to a very great extent on the soil that is used. In recent years many grounds have been using a variety of soils to try to produce a good pitch, top dressing the square at the end of the season, and in many cases it has been quite successful. One of the drawbacks, however, is that it is very expensive and a lot of clubs find it beyond their limited means.

For the last four or five seasons Dave has used a soil from Essex which has produced good batting pitches. Unfortunately they have now become much slower, with the ball also coming through a lot lower, making the pitch virtually lifeless. Consequently pitches which have used this particular type of soil have had to be lifted and relaid, which is again very expensive, so the use of that type of soil is now being reviewed. Long-term drawbacks are outweighing the short-term benefits.

Possibly the biggest problem facing groundsmen these days is the amount of cricket being played on the square, sometimes as many as eighty matches a season. Consequently, old pitches are being played on before they have had time to recover from the previous fixture, and even on the best squares this is not conducive to producing good pitches.

Dave sums up the situation as follows: 'When I first started on a cricket ground more than forty years ago it was possible to repair pitches and have the ends grassed over again before you returned to that pitch. Nowadays you are back on it before it has fully recovered, and therefore we are not getting the quality of pitch that we would like. The quantity of cricket has increased tremendously, but I very much doubt that the quality of players has improved.' Therefore it is just as important that we provide good pitches at league and club level in order to give young players the right sort of grounding.

English cricket needs good groundsmen, and it needs to allow them to produce pitches that are not designed to suit their own team, but for the development of the game as a whole. I stress that pitches should be firm, with pace and bounce in the early stages, taking spin later on. Only when we get a conformity of pitches like that throughout the country will we get back on the right track as far as the quality of English cricket is concerned.

9

MONEY ISN'T EVERYTHING

ONE of the nicest letters I have ever received came from an old lady of eighty-nine from Sheffield shortly after I had turned down a mind-boggling offer to join Kerry Packer's so-called 'Cricket Circus' in 1977. I had letters of support from all over the world at the time, but the one from Mrs Forbes was a bit special. She wrote:

Dear Mr Bird,
This is from an old lady of eighty-nine. I want to tell you how you bucked me up when I heard you on telly last night and read about you in the *Sheffield Star*. Congratulations and good luck to you wherever you are. I must tell you how refreshing it was to meet what I call a real Englishman. They are few and far between these days. As you will guess I am a true cricket fan. I used to visit Bramall Lane when they played cricket there, and I have seen most of the greats of the game. I just love it, and even at my advanced years I watch cricket on the telly. Thank you for being so loyal to England and to the game. Good luck.
    Yours sincerely,
    Mrs H. Forbes.
    P.S. This is the first fan letter I have ever written.

On another occasion I was standing chatting to a friend back home in Market Street, Barnsley, when suddenly a grey-haired old lady in a blue raincoat gripped me by the arm. 'I just wanted to tell you,' she said, 'that it's nice to know there are still some people about who don't put money before everything else.'

A couple of minutes later a man emerged from a nearby coffee bar, saw me, stuck out his hand and said, 'Shake, sir. It's grand to know there are still men of principle in this country.'

If I had any doubts about the decision I had made, they were quickly dispelled by that kind of reaction, which was typical of cricket lovers everywhere.

Deep down, I always knew I had done the right thing, both for myself and for the game I love. There were those who said that I was a bloody fool for turning all that money down – most of the players thought I was quite barmy – but I have made my living through making decisions which I always stick to, and this was no exception.

When I was a pit lad at Monk Bretton I watched my dad crawling on his stomach in a seam eighteen inches high. It was so tight he had to take his trousers off halfway through and leave them to be collected on the way back. But for cricket I would probably have been doing that myself for five days a week. Instead, I'd had a life of sunshine, travelled all over, brushed shoulders with royalty many times, and made wonderful friends in and out of the game. What more could I want?

It was on the Friday of the Jubilee Test that the offer was first made to me. I was sitting alone in the umpires' room at Lord's when there was a knock at the door. I opened it, and standing there was a man who was a household name in cricket. He asked if I was interested in umpiring the Kerry Packer Supertests in Australia later in the year. The amount of hard cash that he was talking about was quite staggering.

I have never revealed the exact amount offered, or the name

of the agent who made that first approach, and I never will. Suffice it to say that the scale of the money involved made me think longer than I would have anticipated before turning it down. Money isn't everything, but when a big sum like that is mentioned it makes you think twice.

However, how could I not be loyal to a game that had been so good to me? How could I give up the chance to umpire Test matches, which is what would have happened had I accepted the offer? To me that was everything, and to take it away would be like taking life itself. I also knew, in my heart of hearts, that I could not possibly turn my back on the established game with which I had been brought up.

All these thoughts whizzed through my head during that Silver Jubilee Test at Lord's, and immediately it was over I went to see Duncan Mutch, my solicitor and a very close friend to whom I always went for help and advice throughout my career. He was like a father to me, and I knew that he would guide me into making the right decision. We had a long chat in his office in Regent Street, back in Barnsley, and he advised me to ring Donald Carr, the Secretary of the Test and County Cricket Board, and tell him about the offer that had been made. When I spoke to him, Donald did not seem at all surprised, nor did he try to influence my decision. He just asked to be kept informed of developments.

For the next few weeks the Kerry Packer affair preyed on my mind. I lost weight through worrying about it, and I couldn't sleep. The prospect of not having to worry about paying a bill for the rest of my life was a mighty powerful attraction, especially for someone who had been brought up in a home where money was always scarce, but I never really doubted that I would turn Packer down. Cricket had given me so much, that he didn't really stand a chance. I wasn't a hero for making that decision, as some people said. I did what I thought was best for me; and what I thought was right. I have never, ever, regretted my choice. When I was contacted again I told the caller that I had given the offer a great deal of thought, but was going to turn it down. He said, 'Well, it's your decision, and yours alone.'

I rang Donald Carr and told him what I had decided. He simply said, 'Well done, Dickie,' but I am sure he was delighted. I respected Donald very much. If I had any problem I would go and sit with him in his office at Lord's and talk to him. He was always only too pleased to help. We had a lot of respect for each other, not only as man to man, but as players – I had often played against him when he was with Derbyshire. He was a very good cricketer, who more often than not used to catch me out at slip. Many a scorebook entry read, 'H.D. Bird, caught Carr, bowled Jackson'. And for not many runs, either!

Shortly afterwards an International Cricket Council meeting at Lord's decided to ban all the players who had signed up for Packer. More than fifty of the greatest players in the world at that time, including the entire West Indian side, and most of the Australians, were to be outlawed from Test cricket. Had I accepted the offer, that fate would have been mine, too.

Most of the players who took part in the Jubilee Test signed up with Packer, and, with the West Indians, Pakistanis and Indians joining him as well, all the cream of Test cricket was suddenly taken away. The game as I knew and loved it was under threat. It was a very worrying time.

Test cricket survived, however. In fact, it grew and flourished as young players, who might not otherwise have been given a chance, came through and blossomed. One of them was Ian Botham. The Packer exodus was certainly a blessing in disguise for him. He was thrust into the international arena and went on to become one of the great all-rounders.

Looking at the way England have struggled in recent times

makes me think that it might not be too bad if another Packer came along and lured away some of the current crop of other international players so that we could start afresh again.

The day after the ICC meeting to ban the players, I was at Trent Bridge for the England v Australia Test. Needless to say, the Aussies could not resist having a go at me. 'Jeez, Dickie,' one of them said, 'you must be absolutely loaded to turn down an offer like that.'

Alan Knott, who was playing in that match, was one of the 'Packer Men' and he signed off with a magnificent century. As he galloped towards my end he raised his bat in celebration, and the crowd cheered the little wicketkeeper to the echo for what must have been five minutes.

'Knotty, lad,' I said to him, 'you're going to miss all this when you join the circus.'

He looked at me and I could see he had a lump in his throat. 'You could be right, Dickie,' he replied. 'You could be right.'

The irony of it all is that I went to Australia myself that summer, and it caused quite a stir amongst the media men. It was during the tea interval on the Monday of that Trent Bridge Test that the attendant came into the umpires' room with a message to ring a number in Sydney, Australia. I thought it was someone taking the mickey, but the attendant insisted that it was genuine.

'Doesn't this fellow in Sydney, whoever he is, realise that I am in the middle of umpiring a Test match?' I said to him.

However, I thought it best to find out what it was all about, so at the end of the day's play I sought out Rodney Marsh, the Australian wicketkeeper, and asked him what was the best time to make the call.

'Nine o'clock in the evening,' he told me.

That night I was in the Trent Bridge Inn, just outside the ground – the landlord Norman Mee is a friend of mine and I often used to pop in for a steak there during the evening of a Test match – and I asked if I could use the phone. Norman was a bit put out when I told him I was ringing Australia, but the colour returned to his cheeks when I added that it would be a reverse charge call.

The number rang for a long time, and I was just about to put the phone down when a sleepy voice muttered, 'Hello, who the devil is that? Do you realise you've just woken me up?'

Full of apologies I replied, 'So sorry to trouble you, but what time exactly is it out there, then?'

'Six o'clock in the morning,' he fumed.

Obviously Marshy had slipped up somewhere along the telephone line. Either that or he had done it deliberately – and I wouldn't put that past him.

I apologised once again, but the chap forgot all about the irritations of his unexpected early-morning call when I told him who I was. He explained that he was Bill Currie, the managing director of Currie Advertising, and his company wanted me to do an advert on Australian television. He said, 'Is it possible for you to come out here straightaway?'

I replied, 'Well, not immediately. You see, England still need another 189 to win this Test match.'

'What about when the Test match is over? Could you squeeze in a visit before your next appointment?'

As it happened, I did have a free week coming up, and Bill Currie was willing to pay me a good fee, as well as all my expenses, so I told him that I would go. I would have to clear it with Lord's, but that should present no problem.

Bill nearly fell out of bed at that. 'Great,' he said. 'That's settled, then. And don't forget the white cap. They go barmy over here for your white cap.'

It turned out that Bill and his company had been looking for someone associated with cricket for the ad, but they felt that all the players had been somewhat over-exposed already, in view of all the publicity generated by the Packer affair, so they started casting around for personalities, who it seemed, were few and far between Down Under just at that time. It was then the thought struck them – why not an umpire? And I was the one who immediately sprang to mind.

'Sure,' they said. 'That's it. Perfect. Dickie gets on well with the players. Indeed, he's got a tie presented to him by the Australian 1975 team which he says he would not sell for £3,000. He's become a father figure to guys like Marsh and Lillee. This bloke lives and breathes cricket. Couldn't be better. He's the man for the job.'

Donald Carr gave me permission to go, providing that I was back in time for the Gillette Cup semi-final, which was my next scheduled match.

It just so happened that the England versus Australia Test was due to start at Headingley, and all the newspapers thought that I was flying out to Australia because I had changed my mind about joining Packer's Circus. To add to the rumour and intrigue, Bill Currie's representative in London had told me to say 'no comment' to the newsmen at the airport because they did not want the rival channels to know about the adver-tisement I was doing. That, needless to say, increased the speculation that Packer was involved.

After an exhausting flight I was taken by a chauffeur-driven car for a quick wash and brush-up before going on to the television studio. I dressed in my regulation gear, read the script, filmed the ad, and it was put out the next night. Incredible.

Next day I was invited to sit with Dennis Lillee, one of the banned Australian players, who was in the television studio commenting on the Headingley Test, which was being beamed live. I was dog tired, but I soon forget about that in the excitement of watching my old pal Boycott playing in a Test match on my home ground of Headingley thousands of miles away, while in the company of the bowler who could have made such a difference to that series.

I asked Dennis if he was already missing Test cricket, and he said, 'Deep down, yes,' but he added, 'I also think, Dickie, that the Packer series will be a big success,' and he was right.

Also in the studio was former Australian opening batsman Keith Stackpole, who proved a very amusing companion, with a host of stories to tell. One of the classics was the tale of a Test match confrontation in the West Indies.

There was a fast bowler called Uton Dowe, from Jamaica, and Stacky was giving him some fearful stick on his home ground at Sabina Park. Dowe was quick, but terribly erratic, and he kept dropping the ball short. Being a tremendous hooker, Stacky relished this, and proceeded to hit the poor man all over the park. After six overs had conceded 63 runs – a remarkable number off a Test match bowler in his opening spell – West Indian captain Rohan Kanhai took him off to spare him further punishment.

Later in the day, with Stackpole at the crease, Kanhai decided to risk giving Uton another try, but, as he was marking out his run, a voice in the crowd shouted, 'Kanhai, haven't you heard the eleventh commandment? Dowe shalt not bowl!'

It was a hectic, but thoroughly enjoyable trip, and Bill Currie gave me a huge koala bear to take home as a souvenir.

On the plane home, I sat next to a woman who told me, 'I recognise you. You're Dickie Bird, aren't you? Do you know, I am so glad that you turned Packer down. All cricket lovers in Australia feel the same way. Please take this as an appreciation.'

She handed me an Australian version of the Queen's Silver Jubilee coin. I still have it, and 'George', the koala bear, still sits in his favourite armchair in my lounge. Memories . . .

On the way home there was a hold-up at Bombay, which had me whittling about whether or not I would get back in time to do the Gillette Cup semi-final at Lord's. However, I landed at Heathrow with hours to spare, and as it turned out I need not have worried anyway. The game was abandoned for the day because of the weather.

Relaxing at home afterwards I thought to myself, you must be mad, Birdy. All that way to Australia and back to advertise VW cars – and on Kerry Packer's Channel Nine station at that! I should have insisted on a Rover ad, really: British is best.

Four years later I was approached again, this time to umpire matches in South Africa, a country which at that time was banned from international cricket because of the apartheid problem. Several players, including Geoff Miller, Mike Hendricks, Peter Willey and Derek Randall, had already been approached with a handsome pay-out for providing Test-strength opposition for the outlawed South Africans. Others who later agreed to go included the G-force trio who were all being talked of as leaders of English cricket – Mike Gatting, David Graveney and Graham Gooch – along with Geoff Boycott and John Emburey.

Again it was an offer which would have set me up for life, but my answer was the same as before. I turned it down because of my loyalty to the Test and County Cricket Board, who paid my wages, and to the game itself, which had given me so much. If the authorities were against us going out to South Africa, then that was good enough for me. It would, of course, have been nice to have gone back there, having spent ten very happy winters coaching schoolboys for the Transvaal Cricket Union prior to the Gleneagles Agreement, but I was not going to go against establishment wishes.

I have since been able to return on South Africa's reinstatement to international sport and I am delighted that they are back in the fold. As I said earlier, a lot of credit must go to President Mandela, who is fully committed to uniting the blacks and whites in his troubled country. It would seem they are sorting their problems out, and I sincerely hope everything works out for them.

All the English players who took part in that 'rebel' tour were later welcomed back after serving a ban, and because I did not go out there it does not mean that I was critical of those who did. It was up to the players what they did. Every man has to choose his own path. They chose theirs and I chose mine.

I did not want to get involved with apartheid, or anything like that, because colour of skin means nothing to me. I have always looked upon everybody who plays cricket, from whatever country, and whatever colour, in the same way. For me, however, the issue was once again loyalty.

Anyway, I thought, what is the good of money in the bank when the sun is shining in June and you have nowhere to go?

10

CENTENARY TEST

WHAT should have been one of the proudest occasions in my career provided me, instead, with the worst day of my life as an umpire. The date is engraved on my mind – Saturday, 30 August 1980, the third day of the Centenary Test between England and Australia at Lord's.

The match had been arranged to celebrate a hundred years of competition between the two great cricketing nations, and I regarded it as a tremendous honour to be appointed to stand as one of the umpires, my colleague being David Constant. But that Saturday turned into a nightmare for both of us.

The problems resulted from the fact that on the Friday we had torrential rain. Although we played for most of that day, later on the ground was awash as the heavens opened. To give you some idea of how bad it really was, spectators were actually diving in and swimming at the Tavern end of the ground. That is how deep the water was. It was just like a lake. Frank Bough, speaking on television that night, expressed the opinion of most reasonable people that any prospects of play on the Saturday were extremely remote.

Credit to the groundstaff for doing a marvellous job with the means at their disposal, working through the night under floodlights to try to get the water off, but they were always

137

fighting a losing battle. It might have been different if they had listened to Conny and me. We pleaded with them to get extra cover for the lower part of the square, but they did not do so. As a result, the areas which turned out to be crucial to the events of that notorious day eventually resembled a mudbath.

It was still chucking it down when we arrived early on the Saturday morning, but it finally stopped at about nine thirty. The clouds began to part to reveal lovely blue sky, and it was a glorious day from then on. However, it was impossible to resume play before lunch because the lower end of the square down to the Tavern was absolutely saturated. The problem was that they had been unable to protect that part of the ground because they did not have sufficient covering, and they had declined to try to obtain some from another source as Conny and I had suggested. The area was not only wet, but muddy as well, which made it extremely dangerous, and if somebody had been badly injured because we had played on it, everyone would have blamed the umpires.

One way we could have made an earlier start was to put matting on the problem area, and Conny and I suggested this to the two captains, Ian Botham and Greg Chappell.

Greg said, 'If it will help you two lads to get the game started then I will go along with that,' but Both disagreed, believing his players might receive a serious injury if their spikes got caught in the matting. So the idea was scotched, delaying us further. There was nothing for it but to keep making inspections and hoping that conditions would improve quickly.

Meanwhile, the crowd was becoming more and more restless, and hurled abuse at us, which was very unsettling and slightly unnerving. We bit our tongues, took everything that was thrown at us, and did all in our power to get the game going as soon as we possibly could, because that was what we wanted as much as anybody. However, the onus was on us to make sure that there was no danger to the players through the very wet underfoot conditions. We tried to be fair to all parties, but we were in a no-win situation.

Eventually we said to the two captains, 'Come on, lads, we can't keep going on like this, we've got to make a start. Let's give it a go in another fifteen minutes.' Billy Griffith, who was then President of the MCC and a great man for cricket, had been in and out of the dressing room consulting with us all day, and he agreed that we should give it a try.

We had just arrived at that decision when the trouble started. It was three thirty and I thought we had done well to be able to resume play fifteen minutes after that, considering the amount of water that had been on the ground.

I was still out in the middle with the groundsman, Jim Fairbrother, directing him in putting sawdust on the wet areas to dry it up, when I noticed that there appeared to be a bit of a rumpus around the members' enclosure, although at the time I was not sure what was going on. I walked back into the pavilion a few minutes later with the crowd still shouting abuse at me, but I was never physically assaulted.

I was deeply shocked when I reached the dressing room and saw the state of David Constant. He was very dishevelled, his tie was askew, and he was in a state of distress. He told me that he had been grabbed by the tie and pushed and jostled in a very ugly scene that was more reminiscent of a football terrace than the members' enclosure at Lord's. He was clearly very dispirited and depressed, and when I heard his story I felt the same. It hurt me that so much abuse had been directed at me, but even that was nothing compared to what Conny had suffered. We both sat there with tears in our eyes. I have never experienced anything like that anywhere in the world, not even at Headingley!

I became angrier still when I read the newspapers the following morning. A typical report claimed, 'In the Long Room at

Lord's, the temple of cricket, Ian Botham and Dickie Bird were both struck on the head in angry scuffles as frustrated spectators waited for play to begin in the rain-battered Centenary Test.'

That is absolute rubbish. I was never struck. I was never manhandled. I was still out in the middle when the incident took place. Nobody came to check the facts with me, and that is bad reporting. Some of the Press lads, especially those on the news side, are a law unto themselves. 'Don't let the facts get in the way of a good story' appears to be their motto. They are the ones who are not really interested in the game, but are just looking for a scandal, or a sensational headline.

Those who follow us round covering cricket regularly are generally pretty fair, but even the majority of them were way out of order on this occasion. One notable exception was Ian Wooldridge, who got it right when he reported in the *Daily Mail* that Constant was assaulted, but not myself.

Denis Compton, for example, wrote that, 'Umpires Dickie Bird and David Constant had to be rescued by the two captains, Ian Botham and Greg Chappell, from angry MCC members in unprecedented scenes. Constant was manhandled and assaulted by two members and Bird was reportedly groggy and staggering after being hit.'

Wrong! I did not have to be rescued. Wrong! I was not hit.

Compton also wrote that the outfield was still soggy from the early-morning rain, but the square was entirely covered and risks to the players would have been minimal. He was right about the outfield, but that was not the problem. We were concerned about an area which, despite what Compton suggested, had been left uncovered, on the right-hand side as you leave the pavilion and down towards the Tavern. We are talking about an area of twenty yards and more which had not been protected from the weather.

Writing in the *Sunday Times*, Robin Marlar was also very critical, and very wrong, alleging, 'It is my opinion that the fussiness of the two umpires, Bird and Constant, was wholly responsible for the ugly mood which developed. There was no justification for their concern with the bowlers' run-up at the Pavilion End, nor for the area twenty yards towards the Tavern.'

Mr Marlar does not know what he is talking about in this instance. Just take note of what the two captains had to say about it all, and they were in the best position to pass judgement – apart, of course, from the two umpires.

First of all, Greg Chappell: 'When we arrived early in the morning for practice, the covers were down on the best part, but elsewhere on the square it was uncovered and very wet. If you had walked on those old pitches you would have been bogged down ankle deep. It certainly was not fit for play then. We saw it again, with the umpires, at about three thirty, and at that stage it was fairly playable.'

He added, 'The umpires suggested putting a mat over the problem area, but Ian [Botham] rejected this. The umpires suggested sawdust, and this was, in fact, done. There was not much disagreement between the captains. Ian was understandably a little more reluctant as he felt the fielding side was at a disadvantage. The umpires were keen to start. I felt we were let down by the groundsmen for not covering the square in advance and not doing enough to dry it out. If there had been more sawdust and more work we could probably have started two hours earlier.'

Botham said, 'When we first saw it, it was a mudbath, and obviously unplayable for quite some time. At three thirty the outfield was quite a lot better, but the square was still unfit. It was muddy. Even when we started, a cricket boot still made a heavy impression through the sawdust and mud. You cannot blame the umpires. It was a cock-up and people are trying to make them the scapegoats.'

I rest my case.

It was also reported that at one time it looked so bad that fellow umpires John Langridge and Lloyd Budd had been asked to stand by to take over. What utter nonsense! Where do they get these stories from?

We had the full backing of the TCCB and the MCC, whose secretary, Jack Bailey, apologised to us as well as the two captains for the conduct of some members, which, he said, had been 'inexcusable'. He roundly condemned the disgraceful behaviour and ugly scenes. I felt a lot of sympathy for Bailey. After all, to blame the MCC for the inappropriate behaviour of one or two members would be like condemning football clubs in the eighties and early nineties for the behaviour of a minority of hooligans who gave the sport a bad name.

It was Chappell who reported the incident in the members' enclosure to Mr Bailey and pointed out two alleged culprits. However, after taking them into his office, Jack Bailey said he was satisfied that they were either the wrong people, or that nothing serious had taken place.

'I am convinced,' Jack Bailey said, 'that these two people did not assault anybody. At the time members were getting slightly heated and frustrated with waiting. I can only suppose that a lot of them were around and pushing forward.'

Clearly an assault of some kind had taken place on David Constant, however, and it was also alleged that Botham had been struck on the back of the head.

That was not quite the end of the trouble. David was still very shaken when play resumed in front of a capacity crowd, many of whom had been waiting outside unaware of what was happening in the ground itself, and I tried my best to gee him up. Unfortunately, he was then involved in a controversial decision which hardly helped his morale.

Groundsman Jim Fairbrother had moved the pitch slightly

before the Test started because he said he was worried that there was a little bit of a ridge, which he wanted to avoid. As a result, the new pitch markings were mixed up with the ones on the old pitch, and Conny gave Bruce Laird not out as he tried to make his ground following a run. The television replay showed that Laird should have been given out.

What had happened was that Conny had mistaken one of the old marking lines for the new one. As you can imagine, this got on top of him all the more. It was not his fault, though, and no one could blame him for an error like that. The markings were the problem.

The Press, bless 'em, also had a go at my old mate, Geoff Boycott. Australia had made 386 in their opening knock, England replying with 205, and the Aussies then declared their second innings at 180 for 4, leaving England with 360 to win. When England finished up on 244 for 4, people looked at all those wickets in hand and claimed that England could have won it had Boycott not been too slow. They said he should have got a move on and gone for the runs. The Press slated him, and he got some almighty stick.

I felt that Boycott saved that Test for England, however. He made a magnificent unbeaten 120 after the first three wickets had fallen quite cheaply, and it is my opinion that Australia would have won if they had got him out. Dennis Lillee obviously agreed with me. Bowling from the Pavilion End, where I was standing in that second innings, after he had whipped out the first three English batsmen he said to me, 'If I get your mate Boycott out, Dickie, you'll be back up that motorway to Yorkshire in next to no time, because then we will go on to win the game comfortably.' Yet the crowd booed Boycott and the Press crucified him.

His was one of three magnificent centuries in that match, which, after all the trouble, developed into a very good Test.

Kim Hughes made 117 and Graham Wood 112 for the Aussies. There was also some fine bowling from Lillee (4 for 43 in the first innings) and Len Pascoe (5 for 59), and England's Chris Old (3 for 91 and 3 for 47).

Incidentally, I always thought that Old was an underrated bowler. He swung the ball, and swung it late, and he was not bad with the bat, either, and today he would be classed as a good all-rounder. However, one of his problems was that he was injury prone. He was also a bit of a hypochondriac, as witness one game at Headingley when he was playing against his old club for Warwickshire.

Bowling from my end he produced one of the best spells I had seen from him, taking six wickets, and as he walked back past me I looked at him and queried, 'Chris, are you all right?'

He stopped in his tracks. 'What makes you say that, Dickie?'

'All these wickets,' I said. 'I thought they might be affecting you. You don't look too well, you know.'

He replied, 'Funny you should say that, Dickie. I've not been feeling too well all day. Will you excuse me, I'm going off.' And he walked off, never to return in that innings.

As far as that Centenary Test goes, if we could turn the clock back, knowing what we know now, Conny and I might well say, this is a very special occasion, so we're going to play, and that's it. If a player gets injured, he gets injured. That's the risk, and we have to take the responsibility.

At the time, however, we were simply abiding by the law, playing it by the book, and the over-riding factor was that the pitch was not fit for play.

It was a very sad day all round, and it included the blackest hour of my career. A marvellous occasion was ruined by that one day. I have always said that you can tamper with the laws of the game, you can tamper with the playing conditions, you can alter this and alter that, but all you really need is for the sun to shine. Pitch the stumps, go out there, put the bails on, and, if the sun shines, you will not have any real problems. I pray every morning for no bad light or rain, so that day I must have done something really bad to upset my Lord so much that he sent down all that rain on my parade.

The worst thing is that everybody recalls the downside of that Test, all the controversy and aggro, and they fail to remember the many good things: top-class batting, bowling and fielding, and a game played in the right spirit by two great sides. It was a tremendous occasion because all the outstanding cricketers who had played in Tests between the two countries, right back into history, were brought to Lord's. Everybody who was anybody was there, and I regarded it as a great honour to be asked to umpire the game.

There was one touching moment after the match when Dennis Lillee came up to me with a parcel. He said, 'This is for you, Dickie, but I don't want you to open it until you get home.' I nursed it carefully all the way back to Barnsley and as soon as I got inside my cottage I tore off the wrapping. Inside I found Lillee's official touring tie with a message which read, 'Going back to Australia with an open-neck shirt. You can have my tie because you are a great guy and we all think you are a fair umpire.' It was signed 'Dennis Lillee'. Of all my mementoes, that tie and that message are something I treasure as much as anything. It meant so much to me – coming from an Aussie!

For the record, the two teams on that landmark occasion were as follows:

England: Graham Gooch (Essex), Geoffrey Boycott (Yorkshire), Bill Athey (Yorkshire), David Gower (Leicestershire), Mike Gatting (Middlesex), Ian Botham (Somerset), Peter Willey (Northamptonshire), David Bairstow (Yorkshire), John Emburey (Middlesex), Chris Old (Yorkshire), Mike Hendricks (Derbyshire).

145

Australia: Bruce Laird (Western Australia), Graham Wood (Western Australia), Greg Chappell (Queensland), Kim Hughes (Western Australia), Graham Yallop (Victoria), Allan Border (New South Wales), Rodney Marsh (Western Australia), Dennis Lillee (Western Australia), Ashley Mallett (South Australia), Ray Bright (Victoria), Len Pascoe (New South Wales).

Another Test match which was troubled by rain was between England and the West Indies at Headingley in 1991. The day before it was due to start there was a torrential downpour and no one gave us a chance of getting the game underway on time. However, Keith Boyce and his groundstaff did a wonderful job, working right the way through the night and bringing waterhogs up the motorways from Trent Bridge, Old Trafford and Edgbaston to help suck up all the water. They carried on working under grey skies on the Thursday morning and we managed to start only an hour late, which I considered a remarkable achievement.

Curtley Ambrose opened the bowling from the Football Ground End, where I was on duty, and I thought, great, here we go, then. My home ground, a full house, a great Test in prospect – I'm really going to enjoy this.

Graham Gooch played the first four balls back to Ambrose. I shot my cuffs, hunched my shoulders, twitched, then stood motionless as Curtley prepared for the fifth delivery. It never came. I stood there waiting and wondering where on earth he was.

Then I heard him shout, from about halfway down his run-up, 'Oh, Mr Dickie, we've got big problems here, man.'

I said, 'There can't be any problems. Come on, Amby, get on with it.'

He gestured to me, saying, 'Come and have a look here, man.'

I walked to where he was standing and I could not believe what I saw. Water was oozing up over his boots, and he was paddling

Michael Procter, second only to Sobers as the greatest all-rounder, and batsman Barry Richards, his South African colleague, who were both a great loss to international cricket when their country was banned because of the apartheid issue.

Former Prime Minister and Yorkshireman Harold Wilson, with Geoff Boycott and me.

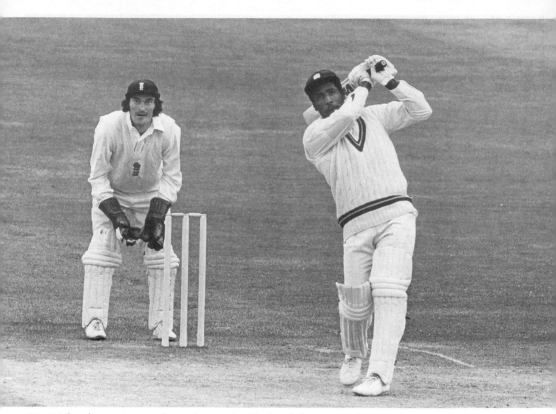

Viv Richards putting on the style, watched behind the stumps by an admiring Alan Knott.

Three of the all-time great fast bowlers, Freddie Trueman, Ray Lindwall and Dennis Lillee, enjoy a drink and a chat.

Allan Border, who did such a good job as Australian captain, adds a few more runs while I look on from square leg.

Receiving my World Cup final medal from Prince Philip after the late-night finish in 1975.

Stepping out to officiate at a one-day international in Sharjah with Indian umpire Swarup Kishen.

Ian Botham and Mike Brearley.
They had mutual admiration
and respect.

'Sorry, but that's out', had to
be my verdict despite Gordon
Greenidge's dash for the line
in the World Cup game
between England and the West
Indies at Lord's in 1983.

Why does it always have to happen to me? The bomb scare at Lord's in 1973 when it seemed to me that the safest place was sitting on the covers out in the middle.

Happy to receive treatment from the England women's team after injuring my elbow when I slipped in the showers after umpiring the Women's World Cup in New Zealand in 1982.

How's that? Pretty painful, I can tell you as Graham Gooch's boundary-bound shot raps me on the ankle during an England v Australia Test at Old Trafford.

'Whispering Death' Michael Holding in delivery stride.

Dennis Lillee, whom I rated the greatest fast bowler of them all, appeals for another wicket.

Malcom Marshall, another of the fearsome battery of West Indian fast bowlers, and a great thinker about the game.

Appealing to the better nature of that wonderful Australian character Merv Hughes, who called me 'a legend' – among other things!

Kapil Dev, the current holder of the record number of Test wickets – over 400.

Sir Richard Hadlee, whose record Kapil Dev broke. Note that lovely action.

about in it. I just stared down in amazement, giving my famous Victor Meldrew impression. 'I don't believe it,' I gasped.

'You'd better believe it, man,' he said.

I glanced up at Curtley's six-foot eight-inch frame, and then back down at my boots, which were gradually sinking like his beneath the waterline.

I shouted across to my colleague, David Shepherd, who was standing at square leg. 'We've got a problem here, Shep,' I said. 'There's gallons of water oozing up.'

'Throw some sawdust down, then,' he suggested.

'Sawdust,' I replied. 'We'll need at least four lorryloads of the stuff, and even then it might not be enough, mate. Better come and have a look for yourself.'

Shep ambled over, and almost immediately up came the water over his boots. 'See what you mean, Dickie,' he said. 'We've got to take them off.'

'What, and paddle about in bare feet?' I chuckled.

'Not the boots, you fool,' he said. 'The players, of course.'

I looked at him thunderstruck. 'What?' I shuddered. 'Take them off at Headingley? In a Test match? After only four balls? Do you realise what you are saying? The crowd will crucify me.'

But Shep insisted, 'We've got to get this water away before we can carry on.'

I realised that, of course, but I still did not fancy facing the crowd as we trooped off, and sure enough, they started having a go at me. 'You're here again, Bird. Every time you come to Headingley you bring them off. What can it be this time?'

I shouted back, 'There's nothing I can do about it. It's the drains. There's water oozing up all over the place. It's not my fault, is it? It's the drains. They couldn't take all that rain. You don't need an umpire out there, you need a plumber.'

We had to stay off until the groundstaff managed to get the

water away. Thankfully, it was just that one section of the ground, and it was not too long before play resumed. It was still very wet out there, but we slapped a lot of sawdust down and got the Test going again. It had been unbelievable while it lasted, though and, not for the first time, I wondered why it always had to happen to me.

Then there was the one-day international between England and Australia at The Oval in 1977 during which we were forced off the field for an hour because of torrential rain. There seemed little chance of finishing the game that day, but we knew we had to do so if humanly possible because of all the Silver Jubilee celebrations going off in London the following day. So both captains, Mike Brearley and Greg Chappell, agreed to play to a finish, come hell or high water. If it was not exactly the first, it was certainly very nearly the latter.

Conditions for the last twenty minutes or so were absolutely horrendous. I have never umpired a cricket match anywhere in the world in weather like that. It rained cats and dogs, then turned to sleet, and finally we were bombarded with hailstones. We were cold and wet, and pools of water began to form on the field, making it hazardous for the players, who were slipping and sliding all over the place. I could feel the water running into my boots and it was extremely uncomfortable, but we soldiered on. In the end the Aussies, beaten in the first two internationals, aquaplaned their way to a two-wicket victory with just two balls remaining.

It was eight twenty and almost pitch black when man-of-the-match Greg Chappell drove Chris Old for the winning runs, taking his own score to 125 not out, and I well remember watching myself on the television news that night, peering through the gloom from behind the stumps, with the rain and the sleet beating down.

Me, stop play for rain or bad light? Don't you believe it.

11

BOWLING THE MAIDENS OVER

My father warned me about cigarettes, drink and women, and I've taken his advice on all three.

I've never smoked, drunk only in moderation, and I've never married. Not that I don't care for the ladies. I do. I've had lots of proposals of marriage, including quite a few since I announced my retirement. However, my sister, Marjorie, has warned me that it is too late now. 'Dennis', she says – she is the only one who calls me Dennis these days – 'it just wouldn't work. You're too set in your ways.'

She's right, of course, as she has been in most things. What I would have done without her all these years I don't know. If I have any problems I can always ring her and she's there to help. She also cleans my seventeenth-century cottage and does all my washing. In fact, she's one in a million. The only things left for me to do are make my own bed and wash the pots up, and I hate doing both.

The fact is I'm married to cricket. To all intents and purposes, cricket is my wife. I've given my whole life to the game, and in return it has repaid me many times over. It has given me the chance to see the world, meet wonderful people, and enjoy a life of relative comfort.

I have lived out of a suitcase since I was a nineteen-year-old signing on for Yorkshire, and, although I had girlfriends when I was younger, relationships never lasted more than a few months. I could never settle down. I did not think, even then, that marriage was for me. It simply would not be fair on a girl to have to traipse around the country with me, living in hotel rooms, or patiently waiting alone and bored back home while I was away for days, weeks and possibly months on end.

There was, however, one time when I gave the question of marriage serious thought, while I was out coaching in Johannesburg in the 1960s. There was this girl and I thought she was the one for me. She was beautiful – blonde, tall, and very well educated. She was studying Afrikaans and psychology at Wits University. She had everything. Most importantly, she liked cricket. We spent many evenings together and felt very much at ease in each other's company.

When I had to return to England for the summer cricket season, she had to remain in South Africa. I realised then it would never work. There were too many obstacles. She said she would travel with me when she had finished her studies, but I could not be sure. It would not, in any case, have been fair on her. If I was being honest about it, looking back, deep down all I could see in front of me was cricket, cricket, cricket. A wife would have to play second fiddle, and that was a recipe for disaster.

So we sadly said our goodbyes in 1964, and that was it. I never saw her again. She understood. I have seen so many many divorces in sport, couples ripped apart because one or other has been living and working away from home, and I didn't want it to happen to me. I believe there has to be total commitment in a marriage, and I could not offer that.

However, the one regret of my life is that I have not had a family. I would have loved to have had a son who played cricket, if only at local league level. It would have given me a lot of pleasure, and I do feel sad about missing out on that.

Mind you, it could have been a cricket-playing daughter. There are some good female cricketers, as I came to discover when I was asked to stand at the Women's World Cup finals in New Zealand during January and February in 1982.

Women's sport is often regarded as something of a joke by men whose opinions are based on the differences in sheer power and physique which make it impossible for the two sexes to compete on anything like equal terms. I always say that, even in sport, one sex is no better than the other, just different, and I can say, with some authority from first-hand knowledge, that the fairer sex play a pretty mean game of cricket. While they lack the strength of their male counterparts and cannot achieve the same pace with their bowling or power with their batting, those at the top have tremendous ability.

I first came into contact with women's cricket when I umpired a three-a-side indoor competition featuring girls from the Lady Mabel College of Physical Education at Wentworth, near Barnsley. They subsequently made me their official coach and I soon came to appreciate that they were serious about improving their cricketing standards.

The most significant meeting I have had with women's cricket came while I was opening the innings for the Barnsley youth team. One day we played a Wakefield youth team and were a little surprised to discover that the driving force behind it was a woman. Her name was Mary Britto, and she really impressed me, not only with her tremendous enthusiasm, but also her knowledge of, and feel for, the game of cricket.

We went our separate ways, although I often wondered what happened to her. My answer came one cold and frosty morning in 1981 when I received a letter from her. It turned out that she had emigrated and was now chairman of the

151

New Zealand Women's Cricket Council. She wanted me to umpire the Women's World Cup which her organisation was promoting. Not one to miss a chance of escaping the chill of an English winter for sunnier climes, I wrote straight back saying I would be delighted to accept the invitation.

It was not a new venture. The first Women's World Cup was staged in England in 1973, when a businessman named Jack Hayward provided the financial backing and seven teams took part: England, Australia, Jamaica, New Zealand, Trinidad and Tobago, Young England and an International Eleven. England beat Australia by 92 runs in the final.

Only four countries took part in 1978: England, Australia, India and New Zealand kept the flag flying, and the Aussies reversed the result of the first final to take the trophy. Determined to give the competition a higher profile when their turn came to stage it, New Zealand formed a World Cup committee and, with Mary at the helm, it was far better organised.

Unfortunately, the West Indies and Holland withdrew after initially accepting invitations to compete, so an International Eleven was recruited to join England, Australia, India and the host country.

I umpired several of the matches, including the final, which gives me the unique record of officiating at both the men's and women's World Cup finals. New Zealander Fred Goodall also stood during the competition, along with a number of women umpires, and I was impressed by the whole operation, which went very smoothly and efficiently.

Australia retained the trophy, beating England by three wickets with an over to spare in the final, and I have to say that the standard of cricket was pretty high. There was some excellent strokeplay and the girls certainly gave very little away in the field. In fact, many of them looked good enough to hold down a place in a reasonable league team in England.

Sharon Tredrea, the Australian captain from Victoria, was the quickest bowler on view, and I can think of one or two male batsmen who would have been wary of her on a pacy pitch. She was a strongly built girl with a good action and I once told Paul Allott, the former Lancashire and England bowler who is now doing television commentary work, that she was as quick as him. He was not impressed.

I travelled with the England team to New Plymouth, but we were all a bit taken aback when we saw the aircraft which was to transport us there. It was very much on the ancient side, with four propellers, so when it was announced that there was to be a delay we feared the worst. We were told that the captain could not get it started and were amazed when he came and asked us if we would give him a push. It did the trick, though, and I bet a lot of photographers regret not having been around that day to grab a wonderful shot of Birdy and the England women's cricket team putting their shoulders to the rear end of an aeroplane to get it kickstarted.

Jan Brittin stood out amongst the English girls. The Surrey all-rounder was a superb athlete who had represented English schools at athletics. She scored 391 runs in the competition and had the highest aggregate, displaying a wide range of quality strokes. She is still playing for England to this day.

Another good cricketer was Jan Southgate, of Sussex. She did not play in the early matches, but I watched her in the nets and believed that the selectors ought to have second thoughts. I had a quiet word on her behalf, and they must have taken notice, because she was selected for the next match and did well. She went on to become one of the most successful English batsmen. That, by the way, is not a slip. The girls themselves refer to batsmen rather than batswomen because it sounds more natural.

All the teams and the umpires were invited to a big reception given by the Prime Minister, the Right Honourable Sir Robert Muldoon, at Parliament House in Wellington, and when I returned to New Zealand early in 1997 I met quite a few of the girls who played in that competition. I was also delighted to renew my acquaintance with Mary Britto, who is now vice president of the New Zealand Women's Cricket Association.

She asked if I could take two bats autographed by the England and New Zealand Test teams and deliver them to Hoffman's pie shop in Wakefield. Sadly, it was not possible, because of all my baggage, but I would have loved to have obliged because, along with Charlesworth's in Barnsley, Hoffman's sell some of the best pork pies in the world. Whenever I travel by train from Wakefield to London I pop in for a couple and eat them with a cup of tea on the way down. I still wonder where those bats are, and if ever they found their way to Wakefield.

Mary lives in Wellington, which is known as the Windy City, and when I was there for the Women's World Cup it lived up to its name with a vengeance. Even the weighted bails would not stay put. When England's Sue Goatman and Barbara Bevege of New Zealand tossed up, the coin was blown almost to the boundary, and the players could hardly stand up as the wind whistled straight down the pitch. From one end the bowlers were driven along so much that they found it difficult to stop to deliver the ball at the appropriate moment, while at the other end they could hardly fight their way to the stumps as their run-up was reduced to a crawl. It is to their credit that they all battled away with great spirit, and I did not hear one complaint.

Competing so seriously, women obviously need the same sort of body protection as the men – plus a little bit more besides! I umpired a game between England and Australia, who had Denise Alderman in their side, the sister of Western Australia's Terry, a great fast bowler in Test cricket, who spent a season in England with Kent. While Denise was batting, the England bowler, wicket-keeper and close fielders all appealed for a catch behind. I heard some contact, but was not certain that the ball had touched the bat. It did not have the right sound for that, so I gave not out.

When Denise got down to my end a little while later she looked at me and grinned. 'That was a neat decision, Dickie,' she said. 'The ball hit my metal chest protector.'

I must say I enjoyed being with the ladies, and I discovered another advantage. When I showered I always used to put on floppy sandals to prevent myself from slipping. Once, in New Zealand, I forgot, and, sure enough, down I went, landing quite heavily and bruising my right elbow. Suddenly I found the place full of budding Florence Nightingales, and I could not help but make a speedy recovery.

Some years later I had a similar experience at Old Trafford. I was standing at square leg when the batsman whacked a leg-side long hop straight at me. It whistled through the air like a tracer bullet, bounced on a patch of artificial turf covering the trench where the ground-cover balloon is housed, then flew up and hit me fair and square in the privates.

Down I went in agony. My eyes watered for a different reason on that occasion. Now, it just so happened that the Lancashire physio was a young lady called Sheena Storah. She was summoned on to the field, but decided that this particular injury should be treated in the privacy of the medical room, far away from the prying, all-seeing eye of the television cameras and the millions watching at home.

I was helped off, told to lie down and drop my pants – what a sight greeted me. I'm telling you I was black and blue and a size you would not believe possible. I had never seen anything like it; nor, judging by her expression, had Sheena. I said to her, through clenched teeth, 'Do you think you could do

something about the pain and the bruising while still retaining
the size?'

In Auckland I was honoured by an invitation from the mayor
and council of Birkenhead to visit their city, and I took along
a booklet about Barnsley to give to them, always eager and
willing to promote the cause of my home town. I wonder if
they still have it?

New Zealand Airways sponsored my trip, and their wonderful hospitality led to another of my most embarrassing
moments on the flight home. The captain turned out to be
a cricket fanatic – as was often the case – so he invited me on
the flight deck, where I spent a fascinating few hours learning
how everything operated, as well as talking at length about the
game. When I returned to my seat he asked the stewardess
to give me a couple of bottles of their best wine. I put these
carefully in my bag, but as we changed planes in Los Angeles,
I dropped the bag on the floor and the bottles smashed to
smithereens. There was wine all over the place. Everything
in my bag was soaked through, and to this day the souvenir
World Cup final programme I brought home remains crinkled
and blotchy, although it still retains a very pleasant aroma.

While I've been umpiring I've seen my share of streakers
– and very enjoyable it's been, too. In July 1986 I was flabbergasted when a buxom blonde, Joanna Duchesne, brought a
Test match to a halt when she ran on to the pitch, grabbed the
bails and put them down her panties. Edgbaston was aghast;
batsmen Phil Edmonds and John Emburey were bewildered;
and my colleague Barrie Meyer and I were just a little more
flustered than usual.

The problem was, how to get the bails back without being
accused of indecent assault? Eventually, policewoman Lorraine
Arscott saved the day, and our blushes, by retrieving them.

Then there was the young lady down at Hastings during a

Sunday League match between Sussex and Kent. Although she was fully dressed, she had obviously had a drink or two and would take no notice of the stewards who were trying desperately to persuade her to go back over the boundary ropes.

Finally, Kent captain Chris Tavare persuaded Alan Whitehead and myself to go over and ask her if she would mind leaving the field. So we marched over and popped the question.

'I won't go until Dickie Bird gives me a kiss,' she said. So, naturally, I obliged and very nice it was, although I rather think that Alan was just the tiniest bit jealous that I'd won that particular battle of Hastings.

Alan, incidentally, is mad on fillies of another kind. All he does on the morning before any match is go through the *Sun*'s racing pages picking out what he hopes will be winners. I keep saying to him, 'A mug's game that, mate. Get you nowhere, backing horses. Be a good boy and listen to your Uncle Dickie. Put that money in the bank.'

Although I don't gamble, I have to admit that I have had a racehorse named after me. It won once in its first seven races and that caused some merriment down at Canterbury, where I was umpiring the game between Kent and Worcestershire. The crowd erupted and everybody in the Ladbroke's marquee was on their feet, cheering like mad, when it was announced over the Tannoy that Dickie Bird had won the four thirty race at Glorious Goodwood. Every time I see Whitehead now I tell him to get some money on Dickie Bird.

I saw Willie Carson and Walter Swinburn at the BBC Sports Review of the Year in London later that year, and I said to them, 'Ey up, you two, I want a good jockey to ride Dickie Bird next summer. How about it?' I'm still waiting to hear from them.

I came across some more beautiful birds at the annual Caged Birds Society show at the NEC in Birmingham. It is the equivalent of Crufts in the canine world, and I had been asked along, as a Bird myself, to judge the talking parrots section. I got very friendly with a big Australian cockatoo and was delighted when he hopped up on my shoulder. Then, just like the blackbird in the nursery rhyme, he pecked at my nose, and there was blood all over the place. I had to have a tetanus vaccination there and then.

I went back to the cockatoo afterwards and said to him, 'Look what you've done. You've been a very naughty boy and I want you to be a good boy from now on.'

This bird was a brilliant talker, just like a human being, but I was not quite prepared for his answer. He swore at me. I dare not repeat his actual words here, but there were two of them, and the second was 'off'!

On another occasion when I was judging the talking bird contest, Billy, an Amazon parrot from Aylesbury, tried to bite me. But I was too quick for him that time. I whipped round and warned, 'Here, steady on, don't bite that finger. That's the one I give 'em out with.'

12

AROUND THE WORLD

AROUND the world in eighty days. That always used to be the dream, didn't it. So much so that it inspired a book and a film. But early in 1980 I did it in six weeks. In that period I covered 48,000 miles on a sponsored tour that took me to Bombay, Singapore, Hong Kong, Sydney, Melbourne, Perth, Auckland, Wellington, Christchurch, Tasmania, Barbados, Karachi, and back to Bombay again before returning home. When I arrived in London at the end of the trip I was feeling rather dizzy and wondering not only where I was, but what day it was – and even who I was.

It was an exhausting schedule which included lectures to umpires, radio and television appearances, and a rare outing as a player in a charity match. Unfortunately, with such distinguished colleagues as Richie Benaud, Tony Greig, Bobby Simpson and Bill Lawry, it is hardly surprising that I did not get a bat. I did, however, have the opportunity to cover myself in glory with the catch of the day. Sadly, the ball hit my thumb, bounced away and fell to the floor, much to my extreme embarrassment. I didn't know where to look. Someone kindly asked, 'How's that, Dickie?'

'Bloody painful,' I answered, and went off for treatment from the English team physiotherapist, Bernard Thomas.

I had a warm welcome wherever I went during my trip, and was delighted to be invited into the Australian, England and Indian dressing rooms for a chat and a drink with the players.

At one stage of the tour I went down with a slight touch of sunstroke in Sydney, where my mind was beginning to reel with all the time changes in the different countries I was visiting. The doctor who was called into the hotel to have a look at me came, by coincidence, from Leeds, so we had a good old-fashioned chinwag about all manner of topics from the changing face of the city to the state of Yorkshire cricket. After prescribing some tablets he said, with typical Yorkshire bluntness, 'Whoever arranged your itinerary is either a genius or a madman.'

While in Australia I was a guest at the third Test between England and Australia at Melbourne, during which I did an interview with David Colley, of Australian television. Filmed highlights were later shown back home in England.

I also managed to see Harold Larwood, who lived near the Oval Cricket Ground in Sydney, and who had settled very contentedly in Australia, despite the wrath that descended on him during that controversial Bodyline series. He proved to be a great character, full of common sense about cricket, and with strong feelings about what is right and wrong. I spent a fascinating few hours with him, learning about his experiences and what it had been like to be a professional at the time we refer to as 'the good old days'. He made it clear to me that, in many ways, they were not as good as we believe, and left me in no doubt that the lives of ordinary cricketers in the 1920s and thirties were very, very hard. They had to know their place and enjoyed none of the perks which have become part and parcel of the modern set-up.

One big difference to which he referred related to the advent of Sunday cricket. Larwood and his contemporaries always used to have Sundays off, which is why he made a habit of having a night out on a Saturday, when he enjoyed a pint or three in the company of his great friend and colleague Bill Voce, who also played for Nottinghamshire and England.

He recalled one night in particular when they emerged from a public house in what might be described as a mellow mood. Voce, stumbling over a wheelbarrow in the backyard of the pub, suggested that Larwood should have a ride down the street in it. Larwood obligingly clambered in and off they set. However, they had not gone very far when they were stopped by a patrolling policeman, who had been alerted by the racket they were making. He did not view their antics in too favourable a light.

'Right, me lads, let's be having your name, then,' he demanded, confronting Voce. He took out his notebook, licking his pencil and preparing to make the obligatory 'I was proceeding along Baker Street at eleven thirty on the night in question' report preceding the caution of two miscreants.

'I'm Bill Voce, the Nottinghamshire and England fast bowler,' came the reply.

'Oh, yes,' said the policeman sarcastically. 'And I suppose you'll be telling me next that's Harold Larwood in the barrow.'

When I flew from Sydney to Bombay I got the VIP treatment on arrival, even at ten thirty in the evening. There seemed to be about 10,000 people crowded into the area round the airport all pushing and shoving, but a number of officials, all looking very important in a variety of impressive uniforms, took pains to assure me that I would be well looked after, saying, 'Do not worry, Mr Dickie, we will give you priority. You will soon be through passport and customs control.'

That comforting message was relayed to me at regular intervals, yet it was not until four thirty in the morning that I finally managed to limp through the last of the formalities. I dread to think how long I would have been kept waiting had I not been given priority treatment.

While in India I watched the Golden Jubilee Test between India and England – and what an occasion that was. It was an event that captured the imagination of the whole nation. There is always a fanatical interest in cricket out there, with Test matches attracting crowds of 85,000 every day, and another 85,000 outside trying to get in.

I discovered that, in accordance with longstanding custom, tickets were generally duplicated and sold twice. Thus, when an Indian appealed for lbw, the 85,000 inside the stadium immediately appealed in support, to be joined seconds later by the 85,000 outside as news of a possible home-team success reached them, either by radio or word of mouth.

England won that Jubilee Test, arranged to mark the fiftieth anniversary of the formation of the Indian Cricket Board of Control, and I proudly watched Graham Stevenson, a former Barnsley player from just down the road at Ackworth, take two wickets and score 27 not out on his international debut in that 10 wicket triumph. Graham was a good cricketer, and in fact I thought he had more natural ability than Ian Botham at that age. Unfortunately it all went to waste.

Another big event during my stay in India was an eclipse of the sun. The Indians are a very superstitous people – they even stopped the Test match for the eclipse – and they all warned me not to look at it or I'd go blind. Some bowlers may have thought I was blind already after having numerous lbw appeals turned down, but I was taking no chances, so I stayed in my hotel until it was all over. I stretched out on my bed and caught up on some much-needed sleep.

When I was about to move on, Geoff Boycott came up to me and pushed a bundle of letters into my hand. 'Will you post these for me when you get back to England?' he asked. Always willing to give Boycs a helping hand I put them in my luggage, and did not notice, until I was about to pop them into the London post box, that he had neglected to put any stamps on them. I am still waiting for the money for those stamps to this day.

The tour was a wonderful experience and I enjoyed every minute of it, but it was very, very tiring. All I seemed to do in those six weeks was fly in aeroplanes, sleep in hotel bedrooms, do radio and television appearances, and talk to umpires. There was very little time for relaxation or sightseeing. I felt I didn't want to see the inside of a jumbo jet again for a long, long time. When I got home and drove my car into Barnsley I still felt as though I was at 20,000 feet.

The previous winter I had one of the most terrifying experiences of my life when I spent a six-week, expenses-paid holiday in the West Indies after agreeing to do a series of commercials using the slogan 'Dickie Bird flies with British Airways'.

I was swimming quite a way out in the warm, clear sea off the coast of Barbados when I suddenly felt the tentacles of a giant jellyfish on my arm. Unfortunately I panicked. I tried to fling the thing off and it landed on my back, giving me more painful stings. I was told afterwards that had I plucked it off I would not have been so badly hurt, but I was terrified at the time.

I got out of the water as quickly as I could and an old Barbadian lady, who had a stall on the beach, took a lime, cut it in half, and spread the juice over my arm and back.

I was then taken to a doctor, who told me that I had been stung by a poisonous Portuguese man-of-war, and that the woman's immediate action had probably saved me from far more serious effects. He also warned, 'Tonight you will get the shakes all over your body, but do not worry, because tomorrow you will start to feel better, and you will soon be well again.'

It is a good job he gave me that warning, because otherwise I would have died of fright. I had a terrible night, sweating and shaking and sometimes delirious, and I often wonder what would have happened had that little old lady not been so kind and resourceful. I could have died – it has been known after receiving particularly severe stings and failing to obtain prompt attention.

During my stay I did a fifteen-minute spot on television, plus two radio interviews, gave talks to umpires, and umpired schoolboy matches, as well as enjoying a holiday break with a sting in the tail. I also met Sir Garfield Sobers and Clyde Walcott, two of the great West Indian cricketers, and I was introduced to the Prime Minister of Barbados. It was amazing how many people knew me wherever I went, simply because they had seen me on television.

The jellyfish incident incident shook me up so much, however, that I decided to return to England a week early, to find the country shivering in the first really cold spell of the winter – another shock to the system after the sultry heat of the Caribbean islands – but, in many ways, it was good to be home.

Another frightening experience came when I spent five weeks in Nigeria, another emerging nation in the cricketing world, during November and December of 1980, having been invited to do some coaching and lecturing on behalf of the West African Cricket Board of Control.

My Nigerian expedition got off on the wrong foot. On the day I was due to fly out to Lagos my tickets had still not arrived, so I contacted Nigerian Airways, who assured me that the tickets would be left at the airport. Only too well aware of such unfulfilled promises, I remained uneasy, so, on arriving in

London, I called first at Lord's to check with TCCB secretary Donald Carr, who brought his influence to bear, and the tickets were duly collected from Heathrow.

I had no further trouble until I landed in Lagos to find no one there to meet me, apart from 30,000 very hungry mosquitoes who obviously enjoyed their unexpected dish of a rare-cooked Bird. As I tried desperately to fend them off I saw the airport staff casually boot my luggage from one end of the reception area to the other. My protests fell on deaf ears, and my unease began to turn into a sense of fear and foreboding. I have rarely been as frightened as I was at that moment.

I looked again at my letter from the West African Board of Control, who were responsible for all the arrangements, and everything checked out. Someone should be there to greet me. Then I noticed that three hotels were mentioned. My prospects of finding them on my own in a strange country in the middle of the day would have been remote; in the dark it was an impossibility.

I managed to persuade a security guard to give me a helping hand. He found me a taxi and gave instructions to the driver. I felt no better when he took me down a series of roads unmarked by signposts, but liberally dotted with potholes that jarred and shook me as we bounced along. To make matters even worse, the first two hotels we tried had never heard of me. That did nothing for my frayed nerves, and I hardly dared ask if they had a reservation for me when we arrived at the last address on the list. Imagine my relief when it turned out to be third time lucky. Yes, they were expecting me. And yes, my room was ready and waiting.

I slumped on my bags in sheer relief, and I could easily have fallen asleep there and then, but I was startled to hear a voice I recognised, 'Birdy, what the heck are you doing stuck out here at this hour when all decent folk are tucked up in their beds?'

165

David Bell, from Hull, loomed up out of the darkness to shake my hand and remind me yet again that the world really is a very small place indeed. He just happened to be working for a firm in Nigeria and knew the ropes well enough to settle me in and raise my spirits. It was not such an out-of-the-way place after all.

Even so, I sat up all night on my bed, finding it impossible to sleep, despite the fact that I was so tired. I wittered away, wondering what tomorrow would bring, and the mosquitoes continued to whizz around to keep me company.

I felt really down next morning when there was still no one to meet me, not even a telephone message. I was lingering over breakfast, not knowing what to do for the best, when another Englishman came up and asked if he could help. 'It looks as though you might have a bit of a problem,' he said.

'Problem? Problem?' I squawked. 'I'll say I've got a problem. In fact, I've got problems on top of problems,' and I poured out the whole sorry story.

'Look,' he said, sympathetically, 'I'm going back to London via Paris this morning. I'll see if I can get you a seat on the same plane if you like.'

Two more Englishmen then joined us, and one of them advised me to stay put. 'Don't do anything hasty,' he said. 'You need a lot of patience in this country. Don't panic, because nothing ever gets done in a hurry.'

However, they took me to the British Consulate, who got in touch with the Nigerian cricket authorities, and mercifully some officials finally appeared, full of excuses and apologies. 'So sorry, Mr Dickie Bird,' they explained. 'You see, we met the wrong flight, and when you did not turn up we assumed that you would be coming later.'

I am happy to say that once things were cleared up and I had fully recovered my composure I had a superb time.

The West African Cricket Board of Control provided me with a car and a driver in order that I could fulfil all my engagements, which was just as well. I could not possibly have managed without the chauffeur because the traffic in Lagos is impossible to describe. The volume is too much for the road, so drivers are allowed to use their cars only on certain days, according to the registration of the vehicle.

I found that Nigeria boasted some decent cricketers, and I spotted several youngsters who gave me the impression that, with the right kind of coaching and tuition, they could go on to become quality players. I imagined that standards would quickly improve as the game caught on, but sadly this has not happened, and all those promising young players fell by the wayside. Cricket, you see, remains very much a minority sport. The Nigerians are too wrapped up in football: they enjoy a quick game, and cricket is too slow for them.

There is a spectacular sports complex in Lagos, with a football stadium that can seat 90,000 people, and I was privileged enough to see the World Cup qualifying tie between Nigeria and Tanzania. I was the only white man in that capacity crowd.

There was just one more slight hiccup before I left: an electricians' strike left me without running water at the hotel. 'What am I supposed to do for a bath?' I asked the manager.

'Open your fridge,' he said. 'You will find bottled water in there.' Just imagine having a good scrub down in a couple of pints of bottled water and you will get a good idea of the impossible task I had. And then I had nothing left to drink.

When the time came for me to leave, Nuna Uzoh, secretary of the Nigerian Cricket Association, handed me a letter to give to the customs office at the airport. It read, 'At a cocktail party arranged in his honour by the Association, several groups presented Mr Bird with an ebony walking stick, a carving of the head of the Oba of Benin, and the yellow traditional dress, with cap to match. This letter is aimed at soliciting your co-operation in ensuring that he takes these gifts home.' It did the trick in Nigeria, although there were one or two raised eyebrows at Heathrow.

Three years later the Kenya Cricket Umpires Association invited me over, and I stayed at the Treetops Hotel, where thirty-one years earlier the Queen had learned of the death of her father, King George VI.

It was a tremendous trip, and a fantastic experience to see all the wild animals come down to the water for a drink at the game reserve. The management there employ a guard, because you have to walk about two hundred yards from the car park to the hotel, and the animals that freely roam about are always on the look-out for a tasty morsel, whatever the time of day or night. I discovered that the guard at that time was originally from Lancashire, so we were able to reminisce about all the old Roses rivalry.

Treetops had been destroyed by fire in 1955 and completely rebuilt; elephants had tried to demolish it by headbutting and charging it so that the entire building shook, and baboons regularly took tea on the veranda as they stole bread and cakes from visitors. There was never a dull moment there, and of all my travels throughout the world, visits to famous game reserves such as this, and the one in Kruger Park, South Africa, have provided me with some of my most memorable and enjoyable experiences, because I just love animals.

There is now a lot of interest in cricket in the region around Dubai and Sharjah in the United Arab Emirates, and my first trip out there was a hectic one to say the least. I had been invited to umpire the Asia Cup in 1984. The competition took place in March and April, during which I travelled 13,632 miles by air in the space of fourteen days in order to umpire three matches

– including a return trip to England to attend an important umpires' meeting at Lord's.

When I originally agreed to go I did not know the date of the umpires' meeting, so it was quite a blow when I received the letter asking me to attend. It was the one meeting in the year that we could not miss, and it seemed I would have to call off the Sharjah trip.

However, when I rang the organisers in Sharjah to tell them, they wouldn't hear of me pulling out. They said they were all looking forward to my visit so much that expense was no object. They offered to fly me home for the meeting, then fly me back to Sharjah the following day. It was quite unbelievable. If you read of such a thing in *Roy of the Rovers* you would say it could never happen in real life. They were obviously going for it in a big way, and they were not going to let a little thing like an umpires' meeting at Lord's thousands of miles away upset their plans.

I was the only neutral umpire in the competition, and also the only white man, the Cup being competed for by the black cricketing nations of the world, with the exception of the West Indies, who were still involved in a Test series with Australia. I stood with officials from the three competing countries of Pakistan, India and Sri Lanka.

There was so much interest in the competition that we had to have a police escort to and from the ground every day because of the massive crowds milling around. The series was won by India, who thus added the Asia Cup to the World Cup they had won in England the previous year. They beat Sri Lanka by 10 wickets and Pakistan by 54 runs. In the other match Sri Lanka, just beginning to make their presence felt on the world stage, surprisingly beat Pakistan.

I thoroughly enjoyed the experience, but it was so hot out there in the middle. It was 115 degrees in the sun and 96 in the shade, so you can imagine what it was like standing out there for eight hours, with just the usual breaks for lunch and tea.

The chap behind the emergence of cricket in the United Arab Emirates was Abdul Rehman Bukhatir, a forty-year-old Arab, schooled in Pakistan, who owned thirty businesses in Sharjah, including the city hotels. Such was his love of cricket – he idolised such players as Hanif Mohammad when he was a youngster – that he spent £3 million building the magnificent stadium right in the middle of the desert sands.

I could not believe what I saw when I first laid eyes on it. As well as the stadium itself, enclosing an all-grass cricket field that was well up to Test match standards, there were fantastic practice facilities, and the accommodation was out of this world.

Once the tournament was over I sat in that empty stadium, watching the sun setting, with the sultry breezes wafting across the ground, and I still found it difficult to believe that I had actually taken part in a cricket competition in the middle of the desert.

Camel racing and football had been the two main sports of the country, but now cricket was arriving with an almighty bang, and it continues to thrive to this day, with the Asia Cup an annual event. Tickets for that first series cost £30 each, yet every game in the 35,000 all-seater stadium was a sell-out, and thousands more were locked outside. The interest was quite amazing.

Abdul Rehman Bukhatir always insisted he was no Kerry Packer. 'He makes money out of cricket,' he said. 'I give money to it.'

I returned the following year for a competition which this time featured England and Australia, as well as India and Pakistan, and I was asked if I would take some stumps out with me. I ordered a set from Duncan Fearnley and carried them all the way from Barnsley to the United Arab Emirates, along with all my luggage. When I arrived my arms and my back were killing me. After all, it's a long way to Sharjah – as the Bird flies. India eventually beat Australia in the final, which I umpired.

The England team included Martyn Moxon, a Barnsley lad who went on to captain Yorkshire. Unfortunately he was too nice to be a captain, and players took advantage of him. He was always, however, a very fine opening batsman and deserved to play for England many more times than he did.

There were one or two other players who I always thought were very unlucky not to receive more international recognition. Tim Robinson of Nottinghamshire was one. I rated him very highly. You have only to look at his figures to see his consistency: 1,600 runs every season and averaging in the 50s. Then there was Kim Barnett of Derbyshire, one of the best county captains, and again a consistently high-scoring batsman with a 50-plus average season after season.

Along with Jack Russell, Glamorgan wicketkeeper Colin Metson is another who has suffered in recent times as a result of the policy of not playing a specialist wicketkeeper. Metson is capable of turning a match by his performances behind the stumps, yet he has not even managed to make the England A or B teams, and I simply cannot understand that.

When you stand out there seven days a week umpiring you see these kind of players and you have to wonder why they are continually overlooked by the England selectors.

During that tournament in the United Arab Emirates, I was approached by Tony Lewis on behalf of the BBC to do an interview for Radio Four. I agreed, but was not quite prepared for what followed. Tony went off to find a taxi, and in we got. The driver appeared to have little idea of where he was going. We bumped and shuddered over rough tracks and I began to fear the worst. I could see the headlines: 'Dickie Bird Lost In Desert'.

However, after what seemed like the duration of a Boycott century, we finally came to a juddering halt outside a tin hut, from the roof of which protruded a radio mast. We sat down and miraculously contacted London with the aid of a man who sat up on the roof holding some wires. In a temperature of around 115 degrees, the cat on the hot tin roof had nothing on him! To my great surprise the conversation was relayed to listeners back home with no trouble at all, and we were told that the reception had been excellent.

When I visited Dubai again with a party from the *Cricketer* magazine, I really got myself into the most terrible muddle – as usual. I had carefully arranged to leave myself with several hours to spare before my evening flight, so, arriving in London mid-afternoon, I called into a café for a cup of tea. I decided, before going on my way, to double check that I had everything I needed for the trip. A sudden surge of panic gripped me when I realised that I did not have my passport. I could picture it on my study desk, where I had left it so that I would not forget to pack it.

Instead of being able to make my way to Heathrow untroubled and at a leisurely pace I was now faced with a desperate race against time. Frantic with worry I dashed across London at Linford Christie speed, breathlessly to pour out my sorry story to an official at the British Airways offices.

'Sorry, sir, that's it, then,' he said. 'Top and bottom of it is that you can't go. Nothing I can do.' Then, seeing the startled look of consternation in my eyes, he added, 'Course, you could try the Passport Office. They may be able to help.'

Sweat poured off me as I rushed round to the Passport Office, more in hope than expectation, and I was in despair when I saw the length of the queue. Now, I do not like using my name to seek favours, but this was an emergency. I had to do something, and quick. I knew that in a few minutes they would be shutting up shop and it would be curtains for me, so I pushed through to the front of the queue and informed a startled young lady, 'I'm Dickie Bird, the Test umpire, and I must see the manager immediately.'

Although taken aback, she reacted at once, and the manager quickly appeared. Thankfully he happened to be a keen cricket fan, so pulled out all the stops to help me. 'If you can get a quick photograph of yourself we will process a passport straightaway,' he said.

So off I ran again, still with all my luggage in tow – which by this time was beginning to weigh a ton – to find the nearest photo booth, which happened to be in a Tube station. I can't remember what the picture was like, but it can't have been very complimentary. I must have looked a nervous wreck.

Back at the Passport Office we got through all the details, and, clutching the vital document as if my life depended on it, I completed the journey to Heathrow with seconds to go before booking in for my flight.

When standing at the Sharjah Cup final in 1988 I had to be carried off the field by two of the West Indian players, Roger Harper and Courtney Walsh, after keeling over in the cruel heat. It was my sixth game in eight days, standing in temperatures well over 100 degrees, and I was suffering from dehydration. Obviously I had not drunk enough to counteract the loss of fluid through sweating. You could wring the water out of our shirts. I had felt it coming on in the morning and had a bit of a do during the first session, when I went dizzy. Then, in the afternoon, I simply passed out. Next thing I knew I was in the umpires' room. My blood pressure was sky high, and people were trying to pour drinks down me.

David Shepherd stood at both ends for the remainder of the

game, which the West Indies won by 11 runs in front of a crowd of nearly 50,000.

Despite all the marvellous facilities at Sharjah, it being in the middle of a desert, sand was bound to be a problem at times, as former Yorkshire and England cricketer Richard Hutton will testify. Richard, a very good player who lived in the shadow of his father, the great Sir Leonard Hutton, and is now editor of the *Cricketer* monthly magazine, was captain of a group of English professionals playing a Select XI on a matting wicket.

The English team was fielding when all of a sudden a terrific sandstorm blew up out of nowhere. One minute everything was going along quite nicely, the next we couldn't see a thing. I had never experienced a sandstorm before, and neither had Richard.

I heard him shout, 'Gentlemen, I can hear you, but I can't see any of you. Dickie, are you still there?'

'Don't worry, Richard,' I answered. 'I've not gone anywhere. What do you want me to do?'

'Well,' he said, 'I don't know about you, but I think we ought to call a halt to this match right now.'

I agreed. There was nothing else for it. I had brought players off the field for bad light and rain, but this was the first time that a sandstorm had stopped play.

Amsterdam is not exactly a noted centre of cricket, but the game is growing in popularity in Holland and I was invited there to talk to Dutch umpires. The standard of cricket in Holland has, incidentally, come on in leaps and bounds since my visit.

During my stay I was taken to the restaurant L'Auberge Maître Pierre in the Annex Hotel, and there on the walls were pictures of such celebrities as Shirley Bassey, Liz Taylor, Richard Burton and others from the world of entertainment, as well as one of the greatest footballers of all time, Dutch international Johan Cruyff.

No sooner had we sat down than the owner appeared. He came over to me. 'May I say how honoured I am to have Mr Dickie Bird, the great umpire, in my restaurant.'

'Surely I can't be that famous in your country when you play so little cricket,' I said.

He threw up his arms as though appealing for a catch behind the wicket. 'Everyone knows you. Please give me an autographed picture and I will put it in a place of honour on the wall.'

'You've already got that great footballer Johan Cruyff in the place of honour,' I chuckled.

'Give me your picture and I will remove him from my wall and put Mr Dickie Bird in his place,' he exclaimed. He refused to accept any payment for the meal, and offered me a bottle of cool gin as a present. I still have that bottle in my showcase. I never touched a drop. It is a memento of a wonderful occasion.

I promised to send him the autographed picture, but whether I replaced Cruyff or not I have never found out.

Incidents like that please me a lot, not through any sense of personal glory, but because they reflect the significance of cricket. That occasion brought home the message to me yet again that those of us who are readily recognised, in any sport, and are so much in the public eye, have a big responsibility for furthering that sport and ensuring that it is presented in a good image wherever we travel in the world.

In 1996 I paid a one-day visit to India just to make an ad. The invitation came from Pepsi, who wanted the ad to be shown on Asian television in the build-up to the World Cup. When I arrived I found the hospitality at my Bombay hotel excellent, as usual, and I was given VIP treatment.

The ad was to be filmed at a cricket venue in the centre of town. While travelling there in the morning was not too bad, the return trip was horrendous. It was just like being back in Lagos. It seemed to take us hours to crawl through the traffic, and I thought we were never going to get back to the hotel in one piece. Was I glad that we managed to get all the filming done and dusted in one day. It would have driven me mad to have had to go through all that again.

When I arrived there in the morning, they donned me up as a judge, with a gown and wig and a big hammer. I didn't have any lines, and all I had to do was bring the hammer down to smash a block of ice, but I went through an action replay of that more times than Geoff Boycott has run out his batting partners. Right there in the middle of a cricket field in Bombay in hundred-degree temperatures, the sweat rolled off me underneath my gown and wig, trickling down into my shoes. Needless to say, the ice kept melting, and they had to keep fetching more and more blocks from the refrigerated storage in the pavilion, yelling, 'New ice, more ice, plenty ice.'

The ad was built around Sachin Tendulkar, who filmed his part on a different day. How they put it together I'll never know. The idea was that I was passing judgement, and when I brought my hammer down on the ice out shot a can of Pepsi cola, to be caught by the Indian batsman.

I flew home the following day, and I never did see the finished ad.

A visit to New Zealand for the Women's World Cup in 1981 gave me a chance to umpire the Shell Shield final – the equivalent of our Benson & Hedges – between Wellington and Canterbury at Lancaster Park, which also stages both cricket and rugby Test matches. The ground has an area behind the bowler's arm at one end which is similar to the Hill at Sydney, although on a smaller scale. When the fans there have had a few beers it tends to get rather lively.

In this particular final the crowd threw cans on to the field and reflected the sun into the batsman's eyes, a little trick they enjoyed performing whatever the state of the game. Eventually one of the batsmen got rather fed up with this and asked me to do something about it.

I marched off towards the offending group, intent on giving them a talking-to, but, as I did so, I noticed all the fielders laughing amongst themselves.

'All right, gentlemen,' I said. 'What's up and what's to do, then? Let's have it. What do you find so funny?'

'You'll find out if you tangle with that lot,' they said, pointing to the noisy mob, sprawled out in the afternoon sun. 'They don't need an umpire to talk to them. What they need is a lion-tamer.'

Undaunted, I went over to the boundary, and fixed them with my beady eye. The shouting and jeering grew as I approached. I held up my hands, as if in surrender.

'Excuse me,' I said, 'but do you mind if we continue this match without these constant interruptions? It really isn't necessary, you know, and it's certainly not fair. That's all I have to say, gentlemen. Thank you very much.'

Whether it was the fact that I had addressed them as gentlemen that tickled them I do not know, but they roared with laughter. 'That's more like it,' I said. 'I'll come over and have another chat if I get chance later on, but I don't want any more funny business. Understand?'

It would seem that they did, because they cheered me all the way back to the middle and behaved themselves impeccably for the rest of the game, much to the astonishment of the players. How to make friends and influence people . . .

I have umpired Test matches in New Zealand and I returned again early in 1997, accompanying a group on a tour organised by All-Ways Pacific Travel, in conjunction with the *Daily Telegraph*. I had also been asked to speak to the international panel of umpires who were taking charge of the Test series and one-day internationals between New Zealand and England.

There was typical Bird-like chaos at the start of the trip. It could only happen to me. I put my luggage on the shuttle from Manchester to Heathrow and was told there would be no problem. It would be transferred straight to my Auckland flight and I would be able to pick it up on arrival in New Zealand.

Once we had landed, I went to collect my luggage from the carousel. Bags kept coming round and round the conveyor belt, and I was convinced that mine was not there. The carousel kept going. Sure enough, the last bag was taken off and still no sign of mine. I reported the fact to the lost baggage department, who were very good. They said it was not their fault but they would look into the matter. Computer checks revealed that my bags were still at Heathrow.

So there I was in New Zealand, rather dishevelled and sweaty after a twenty-nine hour flight, with only the clothes I stood up in. Ian Botham offered to lend me some of his, but they were miles too big, so I made do with what I had, although I did have to go out and buy a new toothbrush, some toothpaste and shaving gear. I got the bags next day, so it was not too bad, but I could still have done without all the hassle.

I was already confused with the time lapse. After a flight of that length you find yourself having set off on Monday and landing on Wednesday, and wondering where on earth Tuesday has gone. They say you catch up the time on the trip back, but it baffles me.

In between the Test matches I had time to do a bit of sightseeing and it reminded me what an extraordinarily beautiful country New Zealand is. All the lakes, the rivers, the greenery. It is much like England in many respects, but so clean and spotless.

Amazingly, all the cricket grounds over there are really rugby stadiums, except for the one at Wellington. The All-Blacks play international rugby straight across the ground in the winter and they then get the squares ready for cricket in the summer. They prepare some magnificent pitches, and I just do not know how they do it.

One of the most memorable parts of my visit was talking to some of the great Australian players of the past. I always enjoy chatting to older players because they usually know what they are talking about. They have been there, seen it, done it. It was a tremendous thrill to meet the likes of Keith Miller, Neil Harvey, Alan Davidson, Ian Johnson, Bill Brown – all great Australian cricketers – who had been members of the team that had toured New Zealand fifty years earlier.

Miller and Davidson told me that Ray Lindwall, the legendary Australian fast bowler, had clean bowled more than 100 of his first 200 wickets in first-class cricket, a truly remarkable ratio.

The great England batsman, Len Hutton, had told me years before that the bowler he feared most was not Lindwall, but Miller himself: 'Miller would come in from six paces, then off a long run, then he'd try a few leg spinners. You just did not know what to expect next.'

Dear old Len. He used to come into my dressing room, sit with me, and have a natter about the game in general. He always used to finish by asking, 'Can this lot play, Dickie? Can they really play?'

And I used to tell him, 'Oh, aye, Len. They can play. But not as good as thee.'

I was going to stay out there for the one-day internationals, but a request from a certain lady had me cutting my visit short and hurrying home. Her Majesty The Queen had invited me to Buckingham Palace for a reception for sports personalities arranged by the Central Council for Physical Recreation. How could I refuse, even if it meant a gruelling twenty-nine hour flight over thousands and thousands of miles?

There were hundreds of people there, but only ten of us were invited to meet her in the White Room, where she, Prince Philip and the Duke of York came to talk with us and enjoy a buffet. It was just like greeting an old friend, because it was the twenty-seventh time that we had met.

The Queen said to me, 'You've done very well to come all the way from New Zealand to be here.'

I replied, 'Well, Ma'am, I was actually outside the palace gates four hours ago. I didn't want to be late, you see.'

Another of those introduced to Her Majesty was BBC's *Match of the Day* presenter Desmond Lynam, who was questioned by a chap from the CCPR before being allowed into the White Room.

'Are you Press?'

'I'm Des Lynam,' came the reply.

'Oh, and who do you work for?'

Des turned to me and quipped, 'I bet he doesn't watch much television, Dickie.'

I had considered flying back to finish my New Zealand itinerary, but the doctor advised against it. The risk of dehydration would have been far too great, and could have seriously affected my health. So I took his advice and instead of flying back Down Under I took the train back to the north of England,

I arrived home a very tired man, but it had all been worth it. It had been a lovely evening and I had enjoyed it so much. I wouldn't have missed it for the world.

13

THIS IS YOUR LIFE

P EOPLE often ask me what stands out most in my career – three World Cup finals; the Centenary Test between England and Australia at Lord's; the Bicentennial Test; trips all over the world; and much, much more. But what thrilled and delighted me more than anything else was to be awarded the MBE in the Queen's Birthday Honours List in June 1986. That was undoubtedly the highlight, the pinnacle of my career. That MBE means more to me than life.

It even earned me a standing ovation at Old Trafford. Imagine that! Immediately after the award had been announced I was on duty for the county championship match between Lancashire and Worcestershire and as I walked out with John Jameson at the start of the morning's play the crowd all stood up and cheered me to the middle. There was I, a Yorkshireman, at Lancashire's cricket headquarters, receiving a standing ovation. Needless to say, the hankie was out again.

That was the game of cricket acknowledging the award, which I regarded as an honour for the sport in general. It was also an honour for my home town of Barnsley, the county of Yorkshire, and, of course, for all umpires throughout the world, who do a very important job and, on the whole, do it very well.

I was, naturally, even more nervous than usual when I went down to Buckingham Palace to receive the MBE. I had to be there at twenty past eleven in the morning, so I arrived at half past seven. There was hardly a soul around, which is not really surprising. However, after a while the crowds began to gather, and there I was, outside the Palace gates in my top hat and tails, feeling a little bit like Fred Astaire and fully aware that everyone was staring at me. Thankfully I had my sister Marjorie and my niece Rachel for company. We chatted to the sightseers and tourists until the time finally came for me to go inside.

There were tears in my eyes when the Queen handed me my medal. I was very emotional but she has this happy knack of putting everyone at their ease and soon we were chatting away like old friends. She said to me, 'I'm coming to the Test match on Friday, so I'll see you there. You will give me time to sit down and have my cup of tea won't you?'

'Yes, of course, Ma'am,' I said.

Then she added, 'Oh, by the way, I don't want you bringing them off for bad light.' We both had a chuckle about that.

That little tête-à-tête illustrates what a wonderful, caring, down-to-earth person the Queen is. I hope she reigns until she is 100. I am a royalist through and through and not ashamed to admit it. I think that the Royal Family, and particularly the Queen, does a wonderful job promoting this country and all it stands for. Of course, there are problems. It cannot be easy for Her Majesty to go through all those countless functions with heads of state and the like, and I honestly feel that she really enjoys meeting and talking to the man and woman in the street, ordinary people like me.

Remarkably, I have met the Queen twenty-seven times, one of those occasions being a lunch at Buckingham Palace in November 1990. I was sitting at home one day when the phone rang in my study. When I picked it up a voice at the other end of the line said, 'This is the Master of the Household ringing from Buckingham Palace. I have been commanded by Her Majesty The Queen to see if you are available, Mr Bird, to have lunch with her on Tuesday, November the twentieth.'

I thought at first it was somebody taking the mickey. Well, wouldn't you? But I told him, 'If I really have been invited to have lunch with the Queen at Buckingham Palace I will walk from Barnsley to be there.'

'That's all I wanted to know,' he said. 'The invitation will follow.' And it did.

Like the award of the MBE that invitation meant so much to me. It was not as if there was to be a big crowd of people, just the Queen, her lady-in-waiting, Prince Edward and one or two other specially invited guests.

Needless to say, I was up with that other bird, the lark, and arrived at King's Cross station at twenty past eight in the morning. Even taking it steady I was outside the Palace at twenty past nine for a one o'clock appointment. Recognising me a policeman enquired, 'Are you down here sightseeing, Dickie? I can't see you umpiring a match in the middle of November.'

'No officer,' I replied. 'I've been invited to lunch with the Queen.' And I showed him my invitation.

'Hmm,' he said, 'well, you've got quite a while to wait, I'm afraid. We've got the Changing of the Guard first. Can't stop that. Not even for Dickie Bird.'

So I toddled off to yet another coffee shop, for nearly four hours.

However, it was another great day. To sit in the lounge of Buckingham Palace after a magnificent lunch and talk to the Queen over a few drinks was something very, very special for me.

There was a story put round at the time that I had sent a bunch of grapes rolling all over the Palace floor, but, as is so often the case with newspaper stories, there was only a grain of truth in it. What happened was that I was offered some grapes to finish off the meal. The Queen said, 'Would you like some fruit, Dickie?' pointing at the grapes. 'There are some scissors there to cut the stalks.'

'No thank you, Ma'am,' I said. 'I've had such a wonderful lunch that I couldn't possible eat anything more.' Actually they looked delicious and I wouldn't have minded one or two, but I dare not touch them. I had this vision of trying to cut one or two off and sending them cascading on to the floor for the corgis to pounce on.

When I hailed a cab outside the Palace to take me to the railway station for the trip home, the cabbie said to me, 'Now then Dickie mate, what are you doing down here in the middle of winter? A spot of sightseeing?'

'No,' I replied. 'I've just had one of the best days of my life. I've just had lunch with the Queen.' To this day I'm not sure that he believed me.

There was another royal occasion on Monday, 20 June 1977 during the England v Australia Test at Lord's in the Queen's Silver Jubilee year. Both the teams and the two umpires – David Constant and myself – were invited to Clarence House to meet Queen Elizabeth, the Queen Mother.

When I was introduced to Her Royal Highness she said to me, 'Dickie, I've been watching the game on television and I noticed that you were not wearing your white cap today. Why was that?'

'Well, Ma'am,' I said, 'it was rather overcast today. I didn't really need it.'

'Well, I think you ought to wear it all the time,' she answered. 'I always know it's you with your white cap, as well as by your little mannerisms – pulling up your arms, your twitches, tugging at your umpire's jacket.'

It was marvellous to know that she had noticed these things, and again it all added up to a wonderful evening.

I had another pleasant surprise in 1991, when I received an invitation from the then Prime Minister, the Rt Honourable John Major MP, to attend a buffet luncheon at Chequers. I stayed overnight at a small hotel not far away and was on his doorstep at nine o'clock the next morning for the 12.30 luncheon. When I say 'doorstep' I mean I was sitting in my car in one of the country lanes around Chequers wondering if I dare risk knocking on his door a bit early.

Eventually, at about 11 o'clock, I plucked up the courage to pull up at the top of his driveway, where all the security men and police were stationed, and told them about my luncheon invitation. They said, 'Bit early, aren't you? Just a minute, we'll see what the Prime Minister says.'

They buzzed down to the house and said, 'Excuse us, Prime Minister, but we've got a right early Bird here, what shall we do with him?' And the Prime Minister told them, 'If that's Dickie send him down.' So I made my way down the driveway, parked the car just outside the entrance to Chequers and sat with John and Norma – that's what they insisted on me calling them – for an hour and a half, drinking coffee and talking cricket until the other guests arrived.

Norma, by the way, showed a great interest in the game. She is a lovely lady and does a tremendous amount of work for charity.

There were big names from all walks of life there. I don't know why I was invited. But it was the second invitation I had received from a Prime Minister. The first had been from Lady Thatcher in November 1981. It seems like only yesterday that I walked down Downing Street for a reception attended mainly by show business people including Eric Morecambe, Ernie Wise, Terry Wogan and Ronnie Barker. The former trade union leader Joe Gormley was also there.

I have met Mr Major many times. He used to pop in to see me in the umpires' room at Test matches, either during the lunch or tea interval. The attendant would stick his head round the door and say, 'Your friend's here to see you again, Dickie.' And in would walk the Prime Minister.

The first time I was introduced to Mr Major was in Paul Getty's private box at Lord's. By that time Mr Getty and I had become firm friends. He is a very kind-hearted man who gives a lot of money to charity. The friendship started when I received a letter from Sally Munton, who organises his Cricket XI, asking if I would go and umpire one of his Sunday matches. He has his own cricket ground, a magnificent affair, at Wormsley in Buckinghamshire, near High Wycombe. He got Harry Brind, the inspector of pitches for the Test and County Cricket Board, to lay the pitch for him and a very good one it is too.

Mr Getty gets everybody to play there – celebrities from television, films and the stage, politicians, and touring cricket teams. After that first visit, whenever I had a blank Sunday during the season I would umpire a match for him. Whenever I go he invites me to stay overnight in his magnificent mansion overlooking the ground, and I have dinner with him and his lovely wife, Victoria. In fact, he did say that when I retired completely he would like me to be his resident umpire. Maybe that is how I will be spending most of my summer Sundays in future. It really is a wonderful day out. There is supposed to be an hour for lunch in the marquee which is specially erected for the occasion, but the lunch is so good that very often the interval spreads to an hour and a half. The food and wine are excellent.

I once presented Mr Getty with one of my National Grid umpire's jackets and he keeps saying that one day he's going to wear it while umpiring a match with me. That is one of his ambitions.

It was a great honour to be the subject of *This is Your Life* on television. People often wonder if the celebrities really are as surprised as they look when they are confronted with the famous red book. Well, I don't know about the others, but as far as I was concerned I did not have the slightest inkling of what was going to happen.

I had a telephone call from Don Mosey, the well-known cricket commentator, asking me if I would go on a Yorkshire Television programme to relate some of my funny cricketing stories. We arranged to record it during a break in my trip up to Durham for a county championship match, and I emphasised that it shouldn't take too long because I wanted to get to the north east in good time for an overnight stay before the match began.

When I arrived at the studios in Leeds I was told that they were not quite ready for me, and I said, 'Well, just remember, I'm in a big hurry. I've got to get up to Durham. I can't hang about all day.' Eventually they got the set all ready and the show began to roll. I sat and chatted to Don in front of a television audience, but what I did not realise was that it was made up of television workers and backroom staff enlisted to make me believe that the show was for real.

Everything went swimmingly until he asked me, 'Tell me, what's the most awkward situation you have encountered in your career?' Now, I wasn't expecting that. It was one question I had not been given notice of, and I felt a rising sense of panic as I cast around in my mind for something to say.

'Well?' probed Don.

'Er, awkward moments eh? Well, let me see now. The most awkward moment. Er, well, ee, Don, that's a bit er . . .'

It was then that Michael Aspel walked on. 'Hello, Michael,' I said. 'What are you doing here? Are you on the show as well?' He produced the famous red book and replied, 'No, you are on the show with me. Dickie Bird, this is your life.' Don Mosey's question was finally answered. Here was the most awkward situation of my career.

I could not believe it. They had to take me into a dressing room to calm me down – and it took a glass or three of champagne to do that! Then I was led into a bigger studio where there were so many people I knew. Sir Garfield Sobers had even flown from the other side of the world to be there. There were filmed tributes from Dennis Lillee in Australia, Ian Botham, Vivian Richards, Graham Gooch, Allan Border, David Gower, Imran Khan, Michael Parkinson, Brian Johnston – and even John Major. When they got in touch with him he said that normally he would not do such a thing, but for Dickie Bird, yes.

All the Yorkshire team was there to support me, along with former players Geoffrey Boycott, Raymond Illingworth, Brian Close and Freddie Trueman, with John Hampshire representing the umpires. Alf Broadhead, the man who took me under his wing at Shaw Lane when they turned me away as a youngster, was brought on in a wheelchair, and that was a very emotional moment for me. When 'Chunky' Charlton, my old pit manager at Monk Bretton Colliery, walked on, I blurted out, 'Mr Charlton . . . I thought you were dead.'

As well as my family, other guests included Stan Richards, who plays Seth in Emmerdale; Ashley Jackson the painter; Kathy Mutch, the widow of my old friend and solicitor, Duncan Mutch; *Barnsley Chronicle* sports editor Keith Lodge, who had been a big help to me during my career; my chemist, Brian

Ellison; Jack Sokell, Lord and Lady Mason, and John and Pat Perry.

Brian Ellison has always been invaluable whenever I have had to travel abroad. He is the one who advises me on vaccinations and tablets, and what to avoid. I used to go into his shop on Huddersfield Road in Barnsley and stock up before I left. Then I would pop across the road to the doctor's surgery where the nurse, Avril, would give me all the necessary vaccinations for such things as cholera, malaria and hepatitis. I did not like the malaria tablets. They upset my stomach and made me feel quite ill, but they had to be taken. The manager at the chemist's shop, Dean Chester, tells me that he does not know of anyone who takes his obligations so seriously. I used to cover absolutely everything to make sure I stayed healthy and able to do my job properly.

Jack Sokell, another of the guests on *This is Your Life*, is secretary of Wombwell Cricket Lovers' Society and a member of the Yorkshire County Cricket Club committee. I have known him for many years. Whenever I have wanted any advice he is one of the people I have turned to, because he is very knowledgeable about cricket and his heart and soul is in the game.

He has done a lot for youngsters in the Barnsley area, giving them a chance to be seen by Yorkshire, whereas in the past they may have been overlooked. When I was with Yorkshire it was always a fight to get recognition, coming from my part of the county. The club always looked to the Bradford and Huddersfield Leagues for up-and-coming youngsters, or so it seemed to us. Jack made it so that South Yorkshire lads were given a much fairer crack of the whip, and now the current committee really do scour right the way through the county for talent.

Jack can take pride from the fact that he has helped bring to the attention of the county club such outstanding players as Martyn Moxon, Graham Stevenson, Arnie Sidebottom and England youth internationals Alex and Zac Morris. Players who have gone to other counties include Tim Boon (Leicestershire), John Walters (Derbyshire) and Peter Hepworth (Leicestershire). All these are products of the coaching classes at Wombwell Cricket Lovers' Society which Jack was instrumental in setting up.

I have umpired all over the world, and wherever I have been a card from Jack has found its way to me, wishing me all the best. For every little thing I have achieved there has been a note of congratulations from him. Mind you, he bombards everyone with letters. Anybody who is anybody in cricket has spoken to Wombwell Cricket Lovers' Society simply because Jack refuses to accept no for an answer. He just keeps writing and writing until they finally agree to go, if only to stop the flood of mail postmarked Barnsley. He has worked wonders getting so many famous people to speak at a place they had probably never heard of before.

I am honoured to be a patron of Wombwell Cricket Lovers' Society alongside Keith Miller MBE, Sir Colin Cowdrey, E.W. Swanton CBE, Lord Rix CBE, Fred Trueman CBE, Geoffrey Boycott OBE, Michael Parkinson and Don Wilson. There is a tremendously hard-working committee – always has been – but if we are all honest about it, we will admit that had it not been for Jack, the Society could well have fallen by the wayside. There are Cricket Lovers' Societies throughout the world, but I believe that Wombwell stands out as the best of them all, and that is down to Jack.

Jack told me that he once heard of a Barnsley Cricket Club member who asked, 'What do they know about cricket in Wombwell? Nothing ever lasts there.' Well, the Society has lasted. Jack has always maintained that it was that remark which gave him the incentive to succeed.

He is also an outspoken member of the Yorkshire CCC committee, never afraid to speak his mind. He feels that maybe the game of cricket is losing its way, but hopes against hope that he is wrong. His main worry is the attitude of some Yorkshire supporters, who are the first in line when the freebies are handed out, but all too anxious to criticise the very players who are giving them. Jack told me that one particular member had it in for Martyn Moxon when he was captain, making it rough for him at a time when he needed support most of all.

Jack and I have the same feeling for the game, believing that it is foremost in the world for comradeship, meeting people, building friendships. It is completely different from football, for example, where they all go their own ways as soon as the game is over. In cricket you linger, mingle and chat with the opposition, forging friendships which may last a lifetime. I have friends all over the world through cricket. I admire Jack Sokell. He is a 'one-off'.

John and Pat Perry, from the Livermead Cliff Hotel in Torquay, are a wonderful couple who have been extremely kind to me. I could never possibly repay them for all they have done. They invite me down to their hotel at the end of the English season, and again in the New Year, and I have been going for thirty years and more, ever since I was in Devon coaching. It is a lovely part of the country to go and relax, and relax I do.

John knows I like fish and there are always kippers and haddock on the menu. He makes sure that he is well stocked up before I arrive. He is also a cricket fanatic, and a member of the MCC. He was a very close friend of the late Peter May, the former Surrey and England captain. They were at school together and Peter was John's best man at his wedding, and vice versa. The Mays used to go down to his hotel to relax as well. If ever I need my batteries recharging or somewhere to think things over, I head for the Livermead Cliff Hotel and the Perrys. Indeed, it was there that I finally made my decision to retire from international cricket.

From all this you will gather how much I feel I owe to the game of cricket. The beauty of it is not only to be found on the playing field itself, but also in the comradeship and fellowship you find. It is a game which knows no boundaries. I have met so many people, from royalty, Prime Ministers and millionaires to ordinary people from many walks of life, and I can mix just as comfortably with them all through the common bond of cricket.

I can sit and have a lovely meal at Brooklands; snatch a tasty sandwich in The Crickets up Regent Street in Barnsley; sample the stew and dumplings in Madge's Cafe; or dine with the richest people in the world. From a bacon sarnie in Barnsley to a sumptuous banquet at Buckingham Palace, that is the road I travel. That is what cricket has done for me. It has been my life and it has been a marvellous one.

14

NINETY-NINE
NOT OUT

WHEN I flew out to officiate at the World Cup in India
and Pakistan in 1987 I was hopeful that I would achieve
two additional honours. If everything went according to plan I
would reach the momentous milestone of one hundred international appearances, and there was also the exciting prospect
of standing at a fourth successive final. The England team
denied me both, however.

Because I missed two of my scheduled internationals due to
fever, I was left dangling on 99 not out in my bid for that magic
century, and the success of the England lads meant that I was
also robbed of the distinction of becoming the only umpire to
stand at all four finals.

It was very, very disappointing to miss out on that, particularly as the World Cup organising committee had told me that I
would definitely be standing at the final. Before the semi-finals
were played I was called in to a meeting in the Taj Palace Hotel
and told that I would be one of the umpires for the final.

I said to them, 'Well, that's very kind of you, gentlemen, but
we haven't even played the semi-finals yet. We don't know who
is going to play in the final. What if England get through?' Times

had changed. In 1979 I had been allowed to stand at a final involving England, but now neutral umpires were all the rage, and I was resigned to the fact that if Mike Gatting and the boys did get through it would scupper my dream of another final.

It was obvious to me, from the way they were talking, that the organisers were convinced there was going to be an India v Pakistan final, so all their best-laid plans went very much awry when England and Australia won the semi-final encounters instead. I was hardly surprised when they called me to another meeting, this time to tell me, 'So sorry, Mr Dickie Bird, but as England have reached the final, that rules you out as an umpire.'

The two captains, Mike Gatting and Allan Border, both appealed on my behalf, saying they would still like me to stand, along with Tony Crafter, the Australian umpire. Border pleaded, 'I would like Dickie Bird to do the final, and I speak for all the players and the Australian Cricket Board of Control. We know England are in the final, but we want Dickie Bird.'

The World Cup committee declined to go against their principles of completely neutral umpires, which was only to be expected and quite fair, but at the same time it was a tremendous personal compliment that the teams wanted me to be in charge.

Crafter, incidentally, had been involved in one of the two major incidents in the competition. At a crucial stage of the match against India, Martin Crowe of New Zealand was given out stumped when the wicket-keeper, More, had apparently failed to gather the ball, and in England's game against Pakistan at Rawalpindi, Crafter had the temerity to give Javed Miandad out leg before wicket.

The fact that the ball was straight, would have missed off and leg stumps but could hardly have avoided middle, and hit Miandad just below the knee-roll of his pad, makes no difference. Miandad had enjoyed something like diplomatic immunity in such matters. You just didn't do what Crafter did, at least not if you were a Pakistani umpire. Hence Miandad's astonishment.

Crafter wondered whether he was going to be lynched by the crowd.

'I could feel them watching me,' he told me, 'and it went so deathly quiet.'

Miandad had a go at Mike Gatting, who claimed he said nothing more inflammatory than, 'Come on mate, you're out,' although the television replay suggested otherwise, and Crafter reflected, 'That could have been nasty.'

Crafter had been involved in another run-in with Miandad in Perth, when, in a notorious incident, Dennis Lillee aimed a kick at the Pakistani, who reacted by charging Lillee, bat raised, intent on braining him.

My disappointment at missing out was mixed with pride in England's achievement. It was lovely to see them go all the way to the final, and I would dearly have loved to have seen them win it. They played extremely well throughout the competition, and their professional approach was the key to their success.

The pressure of carrying the hopes of all their home supporters led to the downfall of both India and Pakistan at the penultimate stage, and when England beat India I went into the England dressing room and told them they had robbed me of a fourth final.

'Never mind, Dickie,' they said, 'we'll go out and win.'

Unfortunately they didn't, which made it doubly disappointing. I was particularly sorry for skipper Mike Gatting, who had taken a lot of stick because of a reverse sweep which resulted in his dismissal at a crucial stage of the game. Had it come off he would have been a big hero, and such is the thin dividing line between success and failure. However, I did not regard it as a failure by England. It had been a magnificent achievement by them to reach the final.

I stood in five matches during the competition, four of them involving India – against New Zealand in Bangalore, Australia in Madras, New Zealand in Nagpur, and Zimbabwe in Ahmedabad.

The fifth game was the semi-final between Pakistan and Australia at Lahore, which was my only trip into Pakistan. A crowd of 120,000 turned out for that match, the biggest I had ever umpired in front of, and even the smallest crowd for my matches numbered 85,000 for the India v Australia clash in Madras. The organisers considered that a poor gate, yet the previous biggest crowd at any match of mine had been 42,000 for a full house at Lord's.

I managed to avoid the dreaded 'Delhi belly' by sticking to my usual diet, but a fever confined me to my bed for three days and caused me to miss two games, Pakistan Test umpire Khalid Azhaz deputising. I felt very, very ill, and the England lads were obviously rather worried because they kept popping in to pay me a visit and try to cheer me up, which possibly made me feel even worse.

The crunch came when Allan Lamb visited me in my room. 'Now then, Lamby,' I said weakly, 'have you brought me some flowers, or better still, some chocolate?'

He said, 'I've brought you nothing, but there is one thing.'

'What's that, then, Lamby?'

'This,' he remarked, dramatically opening the door wide.

The corridor of the hotel was full of army guards, with rifles, all on security duties. Lamby brought six or seven of them into the room, lined them up at the foot of the bed, and barked, 'Right. Put the poor bugger out of his misery. Ready! Aim! Fire!'

It was not the first time, nor the last, that I had been caught out by one of Lamby's practical jokes, and on two occasions he really did have me hot under the collar.

Once was when I was having a morning coffee and a quick read of the paper prior to a match between Northamptonshire and Gloucestershire at the County Ground. The next thing I knew the paper was ablaze. Everybody was in a panic – not least me. I jumped about all over the place in a bit of a flap, threw the paper on the floor and stamped on it to try to put it out, burning the carpet in the process.

Lamby again. He had crept up to set fire to my paper, thus providing the hottest news of the day.

Then there was a game between Lancashire and Northants at Old Trafford when I was sitting in the umpires' room with my colleague, Raymond Julien, waiting for the bell which signalled resumption of play after lunch. When it rang we got up to go, only to find we could not get out. The door was locked. Then, to our consternation, we saw smoke billowing underneath the door. Thankfully, Ron Spriggs, the Lancashire attendant who looked after the umpires and players, and was the best in the world at his job, found a fire extinguisher and put the fire out, and unlocked the door. We went out into the middle, coughing out mouthfuls of smoke, to be greeted by the two Lancashire batsmen and a giggling Northamptonshire team, led by Lamby. He had somehow obtained a key to lock the door, put a load of waste paper at the bottom of it – and set fire to it!

As we were walking off at the end of the game, Lamby came up to me, all apologetic. 'I'm so sorry about that little prank, Dickie,' he said. 'No hard feelings, I hope.'

Always game for a laugh, I answered, 'Of course not, Allan. You know I don't mind a little joke now and again. Providing,' I added, 'that it does not get out of hand.'

'That's very good of you, Dickie,' said Lamby. 'See you later in the season, then.'

I went to the dressing room, had a shower and changed, packed my bags, and went to the car park to drive home. I could not believe what I saw. There were no wheels on my car. Lamby had taken all four of them off, left the car still jacked up, with the wheels all stacked up neatly at the side of the car-park railings.

There, on the windscreen, was the message, 'All the best, Dickie. Have a good journey home.'

That was one of the times when I wished Geoff Grundy had been with me. He owns the garage just round the corner from where I live and he has been a great help to me through the years whenever I've had trouble with the car. But here I was, landed with a car with no wheels and Geoff a couple of hundred miles away back in Barnsley.

I soon recovered from my Indian fever, and from Lamby's firing-squad prank, and felt well enough shortly afterwards to attend an official dinner which turned out to be something rather special in that I was mentioned in a cleverly arranged menu in my honour which included a main course of 'Dickie Bird (grilled chicken with pimento coulis)'.

I am not sure what some of the courses were, or what they tasted like, but I can tell you it was one occasion when I deserted my usual safe diet of boiled eggs and really spread my wings.

All sorts of problems invariably beset me on my travels, and on this occasion some of them turned out to be of the liquorice variety. The Sheffield-based firm of Bassett's, famous for this type of sweet, had read about my fears of foreign food, and, just as I was about to get into my taxi, back home at the start of my trip, a big van rolled up loaded with Liquorice Allsorts.

'We've been sent with a month's supply, Dickie,' said the driver. 'We don't want you wasting away,' and he handed me a giant-sized box. Mind you, it wasn't bad publicity for them, seeing as how the Yorkshire Television cameras had turned up to film my departure.

The taxi driver was not best pleased, though. The minutes were ticking away and he was becoming anxious that he might not get me to the train station in time. It turned into a bit of a pantomime as I kept checking and rechecking I had got everything. I thanked the van driver for the Liquorice Allsorts, and humped the box into the taxi alongside me on the back seat, with the rest of my luggage safely stowed away.

I was greatly relieved to catch my train with only a few seconds to spare, and looked forward to a bit of peace and quiet on my trip to the airport in order to recover my composure. I could even, I thought, have a Liquorice Allsort or two.

So there I was, contentedly munching away, when the crown came off one of my teeth. Worse still, I swallowed it. Panic set in, but there was nothing I could do, and I tried to put it to the back of my mind.

I did not feel too bad until I was airborne, when I felt a twinge, which developed into a constant ache. By the time I reached India I was in agony. It did not help that there was some landing problem and we seemed to fly three times round the country before finally touching down in Delhi.

For part of that journey I was joined by the West Indian party, and Malcolm Marshall proved a big help. He could do nothing about the toothache, but he could, and did, help with the potential stomach trouble.

'You listen to me, Dickie,' he said. 'Get yourself a bottle of Angostura Aromatic Bitters and put some in everything you drink. You'll be as right as rain then, man.' He was right. It did the trick, and I still keep a bottle for emergencies in the little cocktail bar in the corner of my cottage.

The first port of call on my arrival in India was the hotel

room of the England team doctor, Tony Hall, who advised me
to go straight back home.

'You must be joking,' I said. 'I've just flown halfway round
the world to umpire in the World Cup. No way am I going
back. I must get it fixed here.'

Needless to say, the England team had little sympathy, and
found it amusing in the extreme. 'One out, all out,' they
chorused, and then fell about laughing when Dr Hall agreed
for me to have the necessary treatment, providing I had an
injection first.

'Get on the bed and drop your trousers,' ordered Dr Hall,
a man who really believed in getting to the bottom of things.
'There,' he said, 'now you can go and find a local dentist.'

The Secretary of the Indian Board of Control, Mr I.S. Bindra,
was a tremendous help to me. He summoned a taxi, and the
driver was instructed to take me to a well-known local dentist.
With my toothache continuing to rage, another part of my
anatomy still rather tender, and the taxi a sticky sweat-box, I
had almost passed out by the time we reached our destination,
and I had another panic attack when I was ushered into a
dilapidated building that was as far removed from the starched
white surgeries in England as you could possibly imagine.
Conditions were basic, to say the least.

The dentist, a charming man, sat me in the chair and set
about the offending area with his drill. Within seconds I had
almost literally hit the roof as he struck a nerve, and my
pained reaction sent both dentist and drill hurtling halfway
across the room.

The dentist crawled about on his hands and knees to retrieve
the drill, which he then proceeded to wipe on his sleeve, appearing totally nonplussed. 'Mmm,' he observed with supreme
understatement, 'it does seem a little bit sensitive. But never
mind, Indian dentists are the very best in the world, much

better than in England, as you will see. I will sort you out pretty quick.'

With that he began poking about again before suddenly asking, almost as an afterthought to the whole situation, 'Have you still got the crown?'

'Well, I don't really know,' I answered.

'How do you mean, you don't know? You either have or you have not. Simple.'

'It's not really as simple as you might think,' I explained. 'You see, I swallowed it.'

'Even so, surely you looked for it,' he insisted.

Eventually, and no doubt flushing a little, I managed to convince him that the crown had gone for good, and he agreed to fit me with a new one if I came back the following day.

Unfortunately, when I returned, the crown did not fit to his satisfaction, but he said not to worry, he would soon fix that. He turned to a small boy sitting in the corner of the room. 'You get on bicycle and hurry pretty damn quick,' he told him, adding some instructions that sounded complete gibberish to me but were obviously well understood by the lad, who ran off, mounted his bicycle, pedalled away furiously, and returned barely half an hour later with the crown adjusted to perfection by some Indian dental mechanic.

I can happily report that the tooth has not given me one moment's further trouble from that day to this, and I was particularly pleased to find that I never had to pay a penny. Either the Indian Cricket Board footed the bill, or the dentist let me have the treatment free because of my celebrity status in his country.

Before long I had forgotten all about my ordeal and was eating quite normally again, until I bumped into Geoff Boycott, who was now writing for the *Daily Mail*, having retired the previous season as Yorkshire's opening batsman.

'Just the man I was looking for,' he said. 'Come with me, Dickie lad, and I'll treat you to something to eat. I know how careful you have to be with your stomach, but you'll enjoy this.'

I was looking forward to a gourmet meal, so I was more than a little surprised when he led me, not into the restaurant of the hotel, but down a corridor to the little shop where he bought two bars of fruit and nut chocolate. One for him and one for me.

'I know how expensive chocolate is out here,' he said, 'but don't you worry about the cost. This is my treat. It will do you more good than anything, so eat it all up.'

Unfortunately, one of the nuts must have somehow slipped into the bar with its shell still intact, because I just couldn't chew it. No wonder. It wasn't a piece of nut, but a filling which had come out.

The next day I found myself back with my old friend the dentist, who spent a couple of minutes replacing the filling and a couple of hours talking about cricket, telling me how India were going to win the World Cup again. He was wrong about India, but did another excellent job with the filling which, like the crown, is still in place.

Food and dental care apart, it was very hard work out there. We had to stand in temperatures up to 110 degrees with dust swirling around all the time. There was tremendous pressure on us, and constant noise from the crowds, with fireworks exploding throughout the matches. It was particularly difficult, in all that din, to pick it up if someone got a slight nick.

The thousands and thousands of miles we had to cover on internal flights, merely to get from one match to another, was also very tiring, although the hotel accommodation was first class. Driving from the hotels to the grounds came as a shock to the system. It was quite unbelievable to see the poverty and squalor all around, with people living – and dying – in the streets.

The schedule was very demanding, as you will see from my itinerary. On 1 October I flew from Delhi to Madras, which took about two and a half hours, and then had the luxury of spending a whole day in one place. After that, however, I began to feel like a Bird of the feathered variety as I winged my way from place to place. Things became really hectic and my programme read: 11 October, Madras to Bangalore; 15 October, Bangalore to Bombay; 19 October, Bombay to Delhi; 23 October, Delhi to Ahmedabad; 27 October, Ahmedabad to Bombay; 28 October, Bombay to Nagpur.

Without any shadow of a doubt life was very much harder for the organisers in India and Pakistan than when the World Cup took place in England, where the grounds are relatively close together with motorway links between them, and travel is quick and easy, despite the traffic jams and roadworks which pose minor problems from time to time.

In India and Pakistan flying is essential, and there is, of course, so much more scope for things to go wrong, as they invariably did for me. For example, my flight from Bombay to Delhi was due to take off at eight forty in the morning, so I got up at four thirty, had a bath, packed my things, booked a taxi, and arrived at the airport by six o'clock.

I waited in vain for my flight to be called, and expected that at any minute someone would arrive to tell me what was happening, but no one came. I made some enquiries of my own, and discovered that the departure time had been changed to late afternoon. Nobody had bothered to tell me.

There was nothing for it but to return to the hotel, but by that time my room had been cleared ready for the arrival of another guest. I had to sit in the lounge, trying desperately to get some much-needed sleep. I closed my eyes, but could not drop off, and by the time I was eventually airborne some hours later, I was exhausted.

Worse was to come. A hold-up developed at Delhi, and I had still not cleared the airport at midnight. All the airport staff were very kind and understanding. In fact, throughout my visit I was struck by the warmth and affection of the Indian people towards me. They treated me like a king, although that did not help when I was constantly told, 'No problem, Mr Dickie, we are looking after you,' only to find that there was, indeed, a problem, and apparently nothing anyone could do to get me to my destination any quicker.

I was almost past caring when I finally arrived at my Delhi hotel, only to be told that they were full up.

'Well,' I informed the manager, 'if you do not find me a room there will be no cricket match here tomorrow. You will be having a funeral instead. Mine!'

Thankfully a bed was found. I collapsed into it and was asleep as soon as my head touched the pillow.

I very often find great difficulty in getting off to sleep. Umpires have to endure long sessions in the field, seven hours a day, seven days a week, for six months of a cricket season, making us overtired. I sometimes have nightmares, too, shouting out in my sleep things like 'Catch it' and 'How's that'. I find I need real peace and quiet. When at Lord's, for example, I make arrangements with the hotel just across the road from the ground to book me in the quietest room they have. That night in Delhi, however, a herd of elephants could have rampaged through the bedroom and they would not have disturbed me. I could have slept on a clothes line in the middle of Picadilly Circus, I was so tired. And to think that the next day I was due to umpire an important World Cup match.

I had another very unfortunate experience in Madras when the other English umpire, David Shepherd, accompanied me for the group match between Australia and India. Shep and I were very well looked after, and given a car and driver for our use. However, on our arrival, we felt more like taking a gentle walk to get some air into our lungs after all that tiring flying, thinking it would do us a world of good and help relax us.

Instead of driving around drenched in sweat in a hot and sticky car, therefore, we headed for the nearest beach to cool off. It was not very far away, and soon we were walking contentedly along the water's edge.

'By, Shep,' I said, 'but this is the life. Sea, sand, sun and all this wonderful scenery. I feel better already.'

Suddenly Shep pulled me up short. 'Here, just look at your feet,' he gasped. I looked, and was alarmed to see some distinctly unpleasant stuff covering them. We had not been warned that this part of the beach was used for the sewage disposal system for the area.

It was awful – all over my training shoes and my legs. It needed a quick trip into the sea to wash it off. So there I was, in my T-shirt, shorts and trainers, paddling along like an overgrown schoolboy.

Thankfully, the dip did the trick, and we hurried back to the hotel to take all our things off, have a bath, splash it all over, and come up smelling rather more like roses.

Having thus learned a lesson the hard way, we never took a chance with another walk by the seashore. It was cars and taxis from then on, sweaty and sticky or not.

Incidentally, my Pakistani umpiring friend Shakoor Rana turned up during that World Cup, causing me a moment of alarm when he had the gall to telephone me in the middle of the night. Still half asleep, I was almost too scared to answer it because I simply could not imagine why on earth someone should be ringing me in a hotel on the other side of the world in the middle of the night unless it was really bad news.

'Hello,' I said. 'What is it?'

'This is your good friend Shakoor Rana. I am wanting you to get me a ticket for the World Cup game and you should be able to do this for me.'

So it was that he came to my hotel next day and I handed him two tickets.

He was delighted: 'You must come and meet my family,' he said. 'They will be thrilled to meet you.'

I said, 'Sorry, but I have such a tight schedule that I am afraid it will be impossible.'

I did not want to get involved in any kind of social activity. All I wanted to do was rest up as much as I could. In fact, the England boys promised to buy me a microwave bed to help me get a few hours of shut-eye in only ten minutes!

'Never mind, Dickie,' said Shakoor. 'I understand. You can come and meet my family next time you visit Pakistan. But, meanwhile, perhaps you could give me one or two of your white caps. They are worth more than money in my country.'

He took a couple out of my bag before I could reply, said his goodbyes, and I haven't seen him since. However, our paths did cross indirectly not too long afterwards, as I will explain later.

It was all a great adventure for me, but all too soon it had to come to an end. Australia won the World Cup, with England finishing gallant runners-up in an exciting final watched by millions of people all over the world on television.

Shep and I travelled home on the same plane as Geoff Boycott, who received a lot of attention. We all enjoyed a laugh as we recalled the events of those exciting few weeks, and then the pilot invited me on the flight deck, where he and I talked about cricket while Boycs slept.

'You do know that Geoff Boycott is sitting back there,' I told him, 'one of the greatest batsmen the world has known.'

He shrugged his shoulders. 'I preferred to attack the ball myself,' he said, suggesting that Boycs was possibly not quite so cavalier in his approach to runmaking, and then he emphasised the point with some dashing imaginary strokes.

'Here, steady on,' I said. 'I'd much rather you kept your hands on the steering wheel.'

He roared with laughter at that. 'Don't you worry, Mr Dickie Bird. You are very safe with me. Much safer than the bowlers, I can tell you.' It occurred to me that he must be one of the very few batsmen who thought they were better than Boycott.

Looking back, all the cricket in that World Cup was of very good quality, but the fielding was probably the outstanding feature of the competition. Gone were the days when the more ponderous members of a side could hide in the field, or when key batsmen were allowed the luxury of strolling about. I have always said that the one thing that has been improved almost beyond recognition in the modern game has been the fielding, which is now generally excellent. Some of the catches that are taken these days are quite unbelievable, and the ground fielding is brilliant.

I almost ended up back in Pakistan later that winter. I was looking forward to a quiet evening of relaxation at home when the phone rang. It was an official of the Test and County Cricket Board.

'Dickie,' he told me, 'I want you to be prepared to catch the earliest flight to Pakistan. You will be aware of the umpiring problems they are having out there and we have been asked to put you on stand-by for the third and final Test between Pakistan and England.' Apparently both teams had agreed that, if possible, I should be brought in to umpire the game, along with David Shepherd. There were problems to overcome, so nothing was cut and dried, but I was told to pack my bags just in case.

That night I did not sleep a wink, for worrying and wondering. For instance, I didn't know what to do about my cholera and yellow fever vaccinations, which no longer covered the period I would be there, and there were all sorts of domestic arrangements to make. Then there was the flight to consider: a fourteen-hour journey, not allowing for any delays, at the end of which I would be virtually stepping off the plane and on to the pitch to umpire an important Test match in very controversial and tense circumstances.

I was therefore pretty relieved to receive a further call at six thirty the next morning saying that the TCCB had found it impossible to obtain visas in time, and that other plans had been put into operation for two neutral Indians to stand at the game.

I would have gone, if necessary, but it would have been difficult. You have to be mentally prepared for any Test match, let alone one with the eyes of the world focused on you after problems involving umpires in the previous two Tests. If I had been given a week to go out there and prepare, there would have been no problem, but it was really asking too much in the time available.

The Pakistan Cricket Board had not helped matters by originally nominating Shakeel Khan and Khizar Hayat for the game. The former was dubbed 'the assassin in the white coat' after his series of controversial decisions cost England eight wickets, including that of the reluctant Chris Broad in the first Test, while the latter had strongly supported my old mate Shakoor Rana in his volatile finger-pointing confrontation with Mike Gatting in the second.

An immediate objection from England tour manager Peter Lush resulted in an about turn by the Pakistanis, who then indicated that they would be happy to have neutral umpires, or even two from England. The initial reaction was to send for me, but it was not as simple as that. The Pakistanis had not left enough time for the move to be practical, and in the end there were two Pakistani umpires for the match after all – Mahboob Shah, the official England had asked for all along, and Khizar Hayat.

I eventually completed my hundredth international the following May, when rain and bad light, the twin scourges of my cricketing life, threatened to ruin what should have been a memorable occasion. That one-day game between England and the West Indies at Lord's saw four stoppages for rain and bad light, which cut out four hours and ten minutes of the third match in the series, and there were slow handclaps and jeers from a capacity twenty-five-thousand crowd. When I eventually led the players off the field at the scheduled seven fifteen close of play, we had the best sunshine of the day, and the spectators showed their annoyance by throwing seat cushions on to the pitch.

The rain certainly did its best to spoil the occasion for me. Only one ball had been bowled at the start of play before the heavens opened, then, when we finally got some bright sunshine at the end of the day, we had to come off. I can well understand the frustration of the spectators, but, believe me, it is just as bad for players and umpires in such circumstances. Unfortunately the law stated that play had to stop at seven fifteen if there was no possibility of a finish on that day, and that was the situation.

I was very upset at the time, but after the day's play I was invited to dinner at the House of Lords by Lord and Lady Mason of Barnsley, which made up for all the aggravation that had gone before. It was a marvellous gesture by Lord Mason, which I really appreciated. He had been at the match and took the opportunity to congratulate me personally on my one hundredth international.

The game reached its conclusion on the Tuesday – the West Indies referred to it as my 101st international – when England completed the clean sweep in the Texaco Cup series by recording a seven-wicket win.

Looking back over the two days there is no doubt that the bad weather created problems, but it was still a wonderful occasion for me. It was something special to reach the century milestone after such a long time waiting for it, and I was delighted to receive silver salvers from the Australian and West Indian Cricket Boards of Control to mark the occasion.

I also received another memento which has pride of place in my home. Jim Bailey, a well-known master blacksmith from Ivybridge, in South Devon, had always been a very keen fan of mine, and in recognition of my contribution to the game of cricket over those one hundred internationals, he fashioned a wrought-iron weathervane in the style of the famous Father Time figure that reigns over Lord's. Jim is a great character and a true cricket lover, and when I travelled to his forge to receive the weathervane I was very moved. It is a magnificent piece of craftmanship and something I have always treasured.

15

THE ONE-DAY GAME

BEING of the old school and very much a traditionalist at heart, I have to admit that, to me, the one-day game, enjoyable and exciting though it may be, simply isn't cricket. But there is no doubt that it is here to stay, because it is the type of cricket that most people want to watch. Travelling home after a game having seen a result is an appealing notion and, of course, popularity brings instant financial rewards as the thousands click through the turnstiles.

This was brought home in startling fashion in New Zealand in 1997. Test matches and one-day internationals are played in two of the big rugby stadiums which can seat up to 60,000 people. For the Test matches against England both those grounds looked virtually deserted, with spectators scattered around the vast arenas. Yet for the one-day internationals the same two grounds were almost packed out.

It is not quite the same in Australia, the West Indies, Pakistan or, to a lesser extent, England, where Test matches are still the big attraction, but even in those countries the one-days are sell-outs. It is a trend that worries me. I do not think it can possibly be for the good of cricket as a whole. If too much emphasis is placed on the one-day game, Test match players will be unable to develop the different skills and techniques that are required for a five-day encounter. They will get into bad habits, playing shots that they would never get away with in Test matches. It is happening already and it will get worse.

People may argue that it has not affected standards in Australia, for example. It does not seem to have affected Pakistan. Both still have very powerful Test teams. But they do not play as much one-day cricket as we do in England. If I was in a position to decide, I would certainly be looking at abandoning one of the one-day competitions, probably the Sunday League. Test cricket must always be the ultimate. I am tempted to ask, is it because New Zealand are putting so much store by the one-day game, that they are so weak at Test level?

I must confess that when one-day cricket was first introduced in 1963 I had my doubts that it would take off, but it did and there seems to be no stopping it now. We have, therefore, to try somehow to combine the requirements of the one-day game with the greater demands of Test cricket. It will be difficult, and I certainly do not pretend to have the answer, but it must be done because financially the one-day game is where the big rewards are. In this country more people turn up for one-day games than for county championship matches.

Having said that, however, I do feel that we have got the formula right in the county championship with four-day matches. There is a good argument, though, for introducing two divisions to provide a greater element of competition, particularly at the end of the season, when, apart from one or two teams contesting the championship, interest declines.

Returning from the heat of the West Indies in 1993 where I had been on Test match duty, it was not just the cold but the outfit waiting for me at home that left me with a touch of the blues. The light blue coat, dark tie and purple trousers came as a bit of a culture shock, and the Panama hat with multi-coloured band that was to replace my famous white cap in the Sunday League pyjama game made matters even worse. I never thought that I would live to see the day when we were kitted out like that. The spectators thought we were milkmen!

I am a big believer in cricket, of whatever variety, being played in whites, with a red ball and a white sightscreen. In New Zealand last winter they even played each player's favourite record as he went out to bat in the one-day internationals, and there was pop music between the overs. What are we coming to? To me that's not cricket, yet it seems to appeal to people and it pulls in the crowds, so who am I to criticise?

As a player I took part in the first-ever one-day match at Old Trafford on 1 May 1963, when Lancashire played Leicestershire, but it developed into a two-day affair because rain brought about a delayed start. Both teams were struggling near the bottom of the championship table but, when our skipper, Maurice Hallam, put the home team in to bat, Lancashire produced one of their best displays of the season to rattle up 304 for 9 off their 60 overs. Peter Marner hit 121 to qualify for the first man-of-the-match award. Marner was a powerful striker of the ball and a bit unlucky not to play for England. His temperament was against him. He was far too impetuous, getting himself out by hitting across the line. It often worked in one-day cricket, but it would not have worked at Test level.

We were up against it when we replied, and were eventually bowled out for 203. H.D. Bird was clean bowled by Brian Statham for 7. I wish we had a bowler like Statham in the England team today. We would win a few Test matches then, I can tell you. He and Freddie Trueman made a formidable combination. Statham, 'George' to his colleagues, had everyone in trouble except Hallam, who made 106. His 12 overs cost only 28 runs and he took five wickets into the bargain. He always bowled at the stumps, just like the great West Indian, Michael Holding. If you missed, he hit – as I proved. He was a great bowler, both in the one-dayers and at Test level. There have not been many better.

I could never hit him off the square. Occasionally I would edge him through the slips and I'd be so embarrassed I would apologise to him.

'Don't worry about it, Dickie,' he would say, 'that's another four runs for you.' Typical that; he was a kind man. Edge Fred through the slips and the air would be as blue as my Sunday League jacket.

Mind you, I did not think Statham was all that kind when he and his colleagues bowled us all out for 37 – Leicestershire's lowest total since the Second World War – in a game in 1960. It was a flier of a pitch and a ball from Statham hit me on the knuckle. I was in agony. I retired hurt after scoring just one and did not go out for the second innings.

To be honest, I was not a very good one-day player. Some people may claim I was not all that hot over three or four days, but that was certainly more to my liking.

When I umpired the semi-final of the Gillette Cup between Lancashire and Gloucestershire at Old Trafford in 1972, we ended up playing by the light of the silvery moon. Lancashire were desperately chasing the runs and falling further and further behind the required rate. It got to the stage where the light was so bad that Arthur Jepson and I were duty bound to offer it to the batsmen. But Lancashire skipper Jack Bond, who was at the crease, replied, 'There is no point going off. We can't possibly win, so we might as well see it through to a finish tonight.'

He was right. There was a full house, with people spilling over on to the grass. The gates had been locked since half past nine that morning. We could not – we dare not – go off now.

But then Gloucestershire captain Tony Brown, who is now the administration manager for the English Cricket Board, put on spinner John Mortimore to bowl, and David Hughes hit him for 28 in one over to win the match for Lancashire in almost pitch blackness and against all the odds. To this day I cannot understand why Tony did not recall one of his fastest bowlers, Mike Procter, who still had six overs left. Bond had already said he was going to play through to a finish, so he would not have appealed.

At one stage, as we were discussing the worsening light with the players, Arthur Jepson reflected, 'I don't know what you're all worrying about. The moon's shining brightly. Let's get on with it.'

My first Gillette Cup final also involved Lancashire, their opponents in that 1973 clash being Middlesex. It was a slow pitch and it needed a man of power to get on top of it. Lancashire had that man in Clive Lloyd, who produced a magnificent knock of 73 not out to win it for them.

Middlesex, batting first, made 180 for 8, with Larry Gomes, the West Indian Test player, top-scoring with 44. Peter Lever (2 for 47), Peter Lee (3 for 38) and Bob Ratcliffe (3 for 25) were the Lancashire wicket-takers.

Although the light was again not too good – they would probably have gone off in a Test match – it was generally thought that Lancashire would knock off the runs to clinch a fourth Gillette Cup triumph, but they struggled to get the ball away, and after 38 overs they were only 73 for 2.

It was then that Lloyd ambled to the crease, peering through the gathering gloom from behind thick-rimmed glasses.

'I can hardly see the ball, Dickie,' he said as he took guard. For someone who could hardly see it, he did not do a bad job, clouting it to all parts of the ground. Although he was fortunate to be dropped by Mike Smith at mid-on, he went on to win the trophy for his side and was rightly named man of the match by Tony Greig. He was very well supported by a young lefthander called Andrew Kennedy, who made 51. Kennedy later received the cricket writers' Young Cricketer of the Year award but, sadly, he was yet another highly promising player who fell by the wayside.

Lancashire were there again when I stood at the 1976 final, but Northamptonshire, who had never reached that stage of the competition before, sprang a surprise by beating David Lloyd's side by four wickets with 11 balls left. It was the first trophy success in their ninety-eight year history.

The only thing that went right for Lancashire that day was the winning of the toss, but even that rebounded on them. Lloyd decided to take first knock, only to see his opening batsman, Farokh Engineer, bowled round his legs for a duck by John Dye in the first over. Poor Farokh was distraught. He came up to me afterwards and said, 'Dickie, I must have made a big mistake. I must have asked you for the wrong guard.'

'What guard did you want?' I asked.

'Leg stump,' he replied.

'Well, that's what I gave you,' I told him.

He was mainly a leg-side player, and in his anxiety to get the ball away through to the mid-wicket area, he had gone too far across, leaving his left peg open to a ball which pitched on leg and carried on fairly straight to take leg stump.

Lancashire were eventually restricted to 195 for 7 and Peter Willey, now a first-class umpire, led Northants to victory with a man-of-the-match knock of 65, he and Roy Virgin putting on 103 for the first wicket.

My first Benson & Hedges final came in 1974 and was memorable for a hat-trick by Ken Higgs, the former Lancashire and England bowler, who was now playing for Leicestershire. He finished with 4 for 10 in seven overs. Yet he did not get the man-of-the-match award. That went to Surrey's John Edrich, as much for his brilliant captaincy as his batting which produced 40 runs as he led his side to their first success in limited-overs cricket.

I went on to stand at twenty-one domestic finals in the Gillette, NatWest and Benson & Hedges competitions. My first earned me £60, my last £800. My first Test match brought a cheque for £25. When I retired the fee had risen to more than £2,000. I am still trying to work out whether that was merely keeping pace with inflation.

I chalked up my half century of internationals after only ten seasons on the first-class umpires list when I officiated at the Prudential Trophy one-day match between England and Australia at Lord's in June 1981. Thankfully there were no problems on the day, which was made all the more memorable by an England win engineered by my old mate Geoff Boycott.

However, more rule changes, this time involving experimental regulations restricting fielding positions in Benson & Hedges Cup ties, brought a good deal of controversy in a tie between Yorkshire and Derbyshire at Derby in May 1981.

The regulations, based on those used in Kerry Packer's World Series Cricket, called for four fielders, in addition to the wicket-keeper, to be positioned within a thirty-yard radius of each set of stumps. If there were less than four fielders inside the circle the square leg umpire had to call a no-ball.

Barrie Wood was bowling to Chris Old from my end, and Chris had noticed that there were only three fielders inside the circle, which was marked with white discs, so he had an almighty heave, confident in the knowledge that even if it failed to come off he could not be given out. But he was. The ball skied high in the air, he was well caught, and Chris stood there waiting for the no-ball call which never came. There was pandemonium out there in the middle.

'But there are only three players in the circle,' Chris protested. 'Look – one, two, three.'

Arthur Jepson, a great character and a lovable man, countered, 'Well, I don't know, I'm tryin' ter watch bowler for throwin'; I'm lookin' all around t' field ter see where ivverbody is; I've got ter watch for run-outs and stumpin's; 'ow the 'ell do they expect me to see if the's three inside t' circle or four, on top of ivverything else? Do they think I've eyes in me backside?'

So there they all were, arguing on a lump. There was nothing I could do. I couldn't give the decision. The law said it had to be the square leg umpire. I was powerless. So I suggested we rang Lord's for clarification of the ruling. We all trooped off the field and there was a fifteen-minute delay while we sorted things out. The decision was that we should re-instate Chris Old. So he went back out to resume his innings and we carried on.

It just goes to show the problems that can arise when you have different playing conditions for different competitions – Sunday League, Benson & Hedges, Gillette Trophy, NatWest, county championship, one-day internationals, Test matches . . .

All the tinkering with the laws meant that we had so much on our plates, as Arthur had pointed out in his own blunt way. It seemed ridiculous that all the responsibility should be put on one man's shoulders like that. The new law was a good one, and beneficial to the competition if it was operated successfully but, like all new regulations, there were teething problems.

I also pressed for solid lines rather than discs to mark the circle; there are times when the disc is almost hidden by the grass, especially early in the season, and sunlight glare sometimes makes it difficult to see the discs clearly. No one took up my suggestion but I still think it would be a big help.

Incidentally, the Benson & Hedges game ended happily for Yorkshire, thanks to a remarkable 103 from wicketkeeper David Bairstow, who shared a last-wicket stand of 80 with Mark Johnson.

There was embarrassment for me in 1984 when Yorkshire were drawn to play a Benson & Hedges zonal tie against Scotland in Perth. Yorkshire had hired a coach for the long trek north, and John Holder and I decided to travel with the team. Holder had also been standing with me at the county championship match between Yorkshire and Nottinghamshire at Headingley.

Unfortunately, the championship match dragged on late into Friday evening, Yorkshire winning by six runs with just two balls remaining, so we boarded the coach immediately after the game rather later than planned. As it had been an exciting and, as far as Yorkshire were concerned, triumphant finale to the day's play, everyone was in good spirits at the outset. That did not last long.

The coach coughed and spluttered along at a snail's pace, but every time someone yelled, 'For goodness sake put thy foot down driver,' he mumbled something about his tachograph, whatever that might be. It must, I suppose, be some kind of ailment that prevents a driver putting his foot down on the accelerator.

Now everyone knows I like to get to bed pretty early, and it was long past my usual retirement time before we had even crossed the Yorkshire border, with many miles still to go. Some of the lads settled down for a kip but I found it impossible to nod off. I kept looking hopefully at my watch, and there were times when I was sure that the hands were going in an anti-clockwise direction.

It was nearly two o'clock in the morning by the time we reached the outskirts of Perth, and one Yorkshire journalist shouted over to me, 'There now, Dickie, it's only five miles to Perth. Not long now, then you'll be able to get to bed.'

'Not long? Not long?' I spluttered. 'It might not be long for you lot, but I've another eighty miles to go. I'm staying in Inverness.'

As it turned out, I had to abandon those plans. The friend who had arranged to meet me had long since given it up as a bad job and gone home. I still did not get much sleep that night, and was understandably bleary-eyed and a little tetchy the next morning. What happened next, as they ask in *Question of Sport* circles, hardly helped to improve my mood.

Scotland were making a pretty good attempt at chasing Yorkshire's 231 for 7 when, after the completion of the twenty-fifth over, John Holder and I called for tea in the usual manner. The players seemed rather bewildered by the decision, which puzzled us somewhat. The mystery may have remained unsolved had not Robin Prentice, a Scottish Cricket Union official, had a quiet word with us.

He told us that the laws had been changed. The TCCB had decided to move the tea interval in the Benson & Hedges competition from 25 overs to 35 overs in the second innings to ensure that the breaks for lunch and tea came at a comparable point during each side's knock. It was the first John or I had heard about it. Why, we wanted to know, had nobody taken the trouble to inform the two umpires of this momentous decision? We were flabbergasted.

As the ground at Perth is in the middle of a park, with the nearest phone some distance away at the rear of a sports centre, there was a problem in getting immediate instructions from Lord's about the matter. So what should we do? As I sat down pondering my next move, a very elderly gentleman, wrapped in a heavy overcoat, his neck protected against the elements by a thick woollen scarf – off a Scottish sheep I have no doubt – came up to me, pushed his face into mine and gasped, 'I am 92 years old and I've been an umpire in the leagues for more than fifty years. I have always wanted to meet you, Mr Bird. You are the best umpire in the world.'

'That's as maybe,' I said. 'But what do you think I should do about tea?'

What we eventually did was take the teams off the field again ten overs later for a second tea interval at the right time, upon which the flummoxed Scottish PA announcer broadcast, 'Aye, they sure like their tea these English lads.'

The Scots argue to this day that the double interruption to their progress cost them the game, and it is true that they spluttered to a grinding halt after a good start. But they were still 45 runs short of the total at the end of their overs, with only two wickets left, so it was not exactly a close-run thing.

Holder and I took some stick in the Sunday papers, and the debate was still raging on the return coach journey when Phil Carrick came round with a can collecting for the coach driver. He came up to me and said, 'Boycs is asleep, Dickie, can you put a quid in for him?' I was not exactly in the best of spirits, so I am afraid I snapped, 'What? For Boycott? You must be joking. I'd never get it back.'

You can guess what I found waiting for me on the doormat when I arrived home in Barnsley. Yes, there it was, a letter from the TCCB telling me about the changes in playing conditions for the Benson & Hedges tea interval. I was not a happy chappie.

That was also the year when I was presented with the first man-of-the-match award of my career when Middlesex beat Kent in a thrilling NatWest Trophy final at Lord's. The only trouble was that it belonged to Middlesex batsman Clive

Radley. I was sitting there admiring this beautiful gold medal after the presentations when 'Radders' and Clive Lloyd, the match adjudicator, came rushing in. It turned out that there had been a mix-up when the awards were presented, and I had been given the man-of-the-match medal by mistake. I didn't mind, but 'Radders' had been given my umpire's medal and he was rather more keen to do a swap.

That was the first, and I suspect only, time that an umpire had been given the man-of-the-match award.

The game itself was a marvellous affair, with Middlesex hitting a four off the last ball to win by four wickets, and it certainly rates high on my list of top one-dayers. There was only one winner that day – not me, not Clive Radley, not Middlesex, but the game of cricket itself.

Most people will have heard the story of Allan Lamb and the mobile phone, which is related elsewhere, but a similar incident occurred at the start of play in the final one-day international between England and Pakistan in 1987.

This time it was Ian Botham who walked up to me and commanded, 'Look after this for me, Dickie.' It was not the great man's cap, not his sweater, not his sunglasses, not even his chewing gum. It was his mobile phone.

'What do you expect me to do with that?' I asked him, without thinking that 'Beefy' might possibly tell me in no uncertain terms. However, for once he restrained himself quite admirably.

'Just put it in your pocket,' he said, 'and if it rings, answer it.' Well, it did ring – not once, not twice, but three times. First it was his business manager, then his wife and finally an acquaintance trying to finalise details of an angling trip. Mind you, I did think there was something fishy about it at the time.

Sadly, that game was marred by some of the worst crowd

scenes I have ever witnessed at a cricket ground in this country. Hundreds of banner-waving Pakistanis held up play every time an England batsman was dismissed. They raced on to the pitch and the police could not hold them back. It was very frightening and such a great shame, because it was a marvellous game of cricket. There were unpleasant incidents at the close, when I had Ian Botham's sweater snatched from my grasp; and colleague Ken Palmer was bundled to the ground. Worst of all, one fan was taken to hospital with a gaping wound after being hit by a missile. I felt very, very sad. I never thought I would see a day like that in cricket. I just could not believe it when I saw blood on the seats afterwards. Apparently some spectators had used the poles from the banners as spears.

One very interesting statistic emerged from the World Cup competition in India and Pakistan in 1987: nineteen of the twenty-seven games were won by the side batting first. Until then, it had been widely felt that chasing, rather than setting, a target offered the greater advantage. The World Cup suggested otherwise and English county captains duly took note. A tactical awareness developed in the limited-overs competitions, with more and more teams electing to bat on winning the toss.

I suppose W.G. Grace gave the best advice when asked what he would do on calling right.

'If it is a good pitch,' he said, 'I bat. If it looks as though there might be something in it for the bowlers, I think about it for a bit, and then I bat. If it looks as though there might be a lot of help for the bowlers, I think about it for a little longer – and then I bat.'

I also recall a famous bowler expressing his disgust when asked by his captain about the possibility of putting the opposition in.

'Well, if tha does,' he said, 'I 'ope tha bowls 'em out, 'cos I shan't.'

223

It also brings to mind the Benson & Hedges match between Yorkshire and Scotland at Headingley in May 1986, when Scotland put the home team in after winning the toss. Yorkshire amassed a formidable 317 for 5 in their 55 overs.

'At least we know how many we have to get to win,' observed one Scottish official, seeking to restore morale.

'Oh, aye,' observed another, 'a damn sight too many.'

There is a lot in that. You have to have really good reasons for putting the opposition in. I would always bat first.

While I have eventually been persuaded, after initial doubts, that the electronic eye is a great help, at least as far as line decisions are concerned, it did bring another moment of acute embarrassment during the one-day international series between England and the West Indies in 1995. I declined to make use of the third umpire for his second opinion of a run-out based on the video replay, and was shown to have been in error in ruling that Neil Fairbrother was out. I held up my hands. I had made a mistake and I admitted it.

However, once bitten, twice shy. I wasn't going to be caught out again, and at Headingley in a later game I caused a certain amount of merriment when I mischievously called for the camera evidence to 'confirm' that Brian Lara had made his ground by miles.

It was during that tour that the West Indians decided to call me 'Uncle Dickie'. That was nice, but I wonder what they would have called me had I given Lara out?

If I am not umpiring I like to go to watch the one-day finals as a spectator. It makes a pleasant change, with all the pressure off. I was particularly looking forward to one NatWest Trophy final at Lord's because I had been invited into a private box by millionaire Paul Getty, with whom I had struck up a great friendship.

True to form, I arrived at Wakefield railway station in plenty of time for the train, so took the opportunity to pop into the cafeteria for an early morning cuppa. It was only as I was about to step on board the train that I realised I had left the pass needed to get into Mr Getty's box in my car.

I asked the guard if I could fetch it, but he said, 'Sorry, Dickie, we can't hold the train up, we've got to go.' The driver noticed what was going on and I had a word with him.

'The guard's right, Dickie. We can't possibly hold the train up.' However, on seeing how flustered and upset I was he relented.

'Oh, very well then,' he said. 'Seeing as it's thee. But be sharp about it.' As I ran back to the car park he shouted after me, 'Mind you, we wouldn't have 'eld train up for thy mate Boycott.'

On another occasion, while waiting at Wakefield station for a train to London, a guard asked the friend I was travelling with, 'Who's that with you?'

'Dickie Bird, the Test umpire,' said my friend.

'I thought I knew the face,' said the guard. 'I wouldn't mind a job like his, but I couldn't stand all that travelling up and down the country.'

It certainly is tiring clocking up all those miles between engagements, and there was one season when I had hardly had a break and was feeling particularly shattered. After a four-day match between Surrey and Kent at The Oval I was faced with a drive down to Bristol for my next fixture – a one-day game between Gloucestershire and the touring West Indies.

I packed my bags, took them to my car and set off for the south west. Calling in for some petrol on the way I decided, for some reason, to check my boot. It was then that I noticed that something rather important was missing. I had not loaded my gear into the car after all. It was still standing in splendid isolation in The Oval car park.

Thankfully a phone call to the ground resulted in an express delivery – faster than anything even the West Indies themselves could offer – to the Gloucestershire venue next morning in time for the start of play, and I was able to turn out fully equipped and attired after a sleepless night worrying about what I was going to do if my bag didn't turn up.

In the event I was all shipshape and Bristol fashion, you might say.

16

STANDING THE TESTS OF TIME

I N June 1976, for the second time in three years, I was called upon by Lord's to answer an SOS to take charge of a potentially explosive Test between England and the West Indies.

The first time had been as a replacement for Dusty Rhodes, who pulled out with an eye infection. Now Arthur Fagg had developed a back injury, and TCCB secretary Donald Carr contacted me while I was on duty at a John Player League game between Sussex and Kent at Brighton, asking me to report for the first Test of the series at Trent Bridge.

I was shattered by the call, as it meant that I would be standing at three of the five Tests. It was truly remarkable to do so many in one series. Once again, of course, the pressure was on me because of all the publicity surrounding the West Indies' pace attack and the threat of a bumper war.

Sure enough, I was again to discover the truth of the old saying, 'It's tough at the top.' The knives, it seemed, were well and truly out. I was accused of 'hogging the spotlight', with even Jim Laker, who was usually very kind to me, having a bit of a dig. He wrote in the *Daily Express*:

> At Trent Bridge the man to leave the biggest mark on the first Test
> was umpire Harold Bird. Now I believe Bird is a first-class umpire
> – he and Frank Chester are two of the finest I have ever seen – but
> the best umpires, like the best soccer referees, are seldom noticed.
> This, sadly, could not be said of Bird, and I cannot believe that it
> was purely coincidental that every incident in this match seemed
> to involve him. In my days, umpires took charge, gave decisions
> firmly, and everybody got on with the game.

I was upset by this accusation. Everyone knows I have always
been a bit of a flamboyant character, but I have never allowed
that to detract either from fairness or firmness in giving
decisions, and I do not believe I did so in this game.

I watched a new young New Zealand umpire, a chap called
Bowden, last winter, and it struck me that he was very flamboyant, with some unusual quirks. I did not mind that, and
people have often said the same about me. The key question
was, though, did he make the right decisions? I have never met
the fellow, but if he makes good decisions and therefore earns
the respect of the players, his antics are irrelevant. However,
he cannot afford to draw attention to himself in that way if
he does not make good decisions, as it would only highlight
his mistakes. Maybe Bowden is highly strung and nervous, like
myself. His chattering and gesticulating might be his way of
releasing his nervous tension. I have always found it a help to
chat and have a joke with players, while being very careful not
to let things go too far, but I have never allowed it to interfere
with my decision-making.

Nothing went right during that Trent Bridge Test, and I was
even given the bird for my inability to shoo away persistent
pigeons who insisted on repeatedly taking up close-catching
positions, thus causing numerous interruptions.

It was just one thing after another, what with disputes over
bad light, pigeons, a swarm of invading bees, the repeated

moving of the sightscreens, a misunderstanding over a West Indian runner, problems with Wayne Daniel running on to the wicket, bad light – inevitably – and a seven-ball over.

That latter incident involved the dismissal of David Steele in England's first innings when he was caught for 106 off what was reckoned to be the seventh ball of Daniel's over. What happened was that there had been a wide earlier in the over, but, because I was so concerned about warning Daniel for persistently following through on to the pitch, I failed to signal the fact to the scorers. The players themselves knew, and there was no problem out there in the middle.

However, the alarmist reaction of the Press was typical of that game. Every little incident was blown up out of all proportion, which made it one of the hardest matches I have ever had to umpire.

As everyone knows, Geoff Boycott is not the ideal partner when it comes to running between the wickets – as I know to my cost – but his worst moment of all came during the England versus Australia Test at Trent Bridge in the Silver Jubilee Year of 1977.

Boycott was joined at the wicket by Nottinghamshire batsman Derek Randall, who was so keen to do well in front of his home crowd, who loved him. Derek was very popular wherever he went. He had achieved worldwide fame after his 174 in the Centenary Test in Melbourne earlier in the year, but it had not changed him one iota. He was a very charming man. Derek was, however, a natural fidget, and he was a mass of nerves when he strode out to a deafening reception.

Trying to be friendly, as always, but also trying to calm himself down, he said to the Australian wicketkeeper, Rodney Marsh, 'Hello, Marshy, nice day for it.'

Marsh was not in the mood for small talk. 'Just get on with it. This isn't a tea party, you know.'

So Randall did get on with it, asking me for two legs as he took guard. English players usually take leg or two legs, whereas the bulk of the Australians prefer centre. He had made only 12 when Boycott ran him out.

I was at the bowler's end, and as soon as Boycott played the ball back down the pitch, just to the right of Jeff Thomson, I could see there was no run in it, but Boycott shouted, 'Run, run,' and charged down the pitch. He would never have got back had Randall said, 'No.' At first it seemed that the little man might do just that, but, after a moment's hesitation, he set off.

The Aussies shouted to Randall, 'Stand your ground, man, stand your ground.' They wanted Boycott to be the man run out. Boycott, however, was almost past Randall before the latter made his move. Derek is a fast runner, but he had no chance of beating Thomson's accurate throw to Marsh, who knocked all three stumps out of the ground.

Boycott was now at my end. He stood beside me, completely shellshocked, then threw his bat and gloves down, and held his head in his hands. 'It was my fault,' he moaned. 'I've run him out in front of his own supporters.' There were boos for Boycott among the sympathetic cheers as Randall walked dejectedly back to the pavilion.

It was quite extraordinary that Boycott should have wanted to run. He did not hit the ball very hard, and even if Thomson had missed it, I doubt that it would have gone twenty yards. It would seem that the pressure on him was so intense in his first Test back after years of isolation, when he had said that he was not available for Test cricket, that he acted quite out of character. Boycott's critics claimed that it was another example of his selfishness, but he protested at a Press conference afterwards that he had not run out many batsmen in the previous three years, after setting out to cure a fault he had acknowledged. He claimed that during that period he had been run out more times than he had run out his partners, although I was not entirely convinced about that.

As if trying to make amends for his aberration, Boycott went on to score a century, but the Nottinghamshire public never forgave him.

The turning point in the match came when Rick McCosker spilled a simple catch at first slip off Thomson when Boycott was on 20. England went on to win, and, with Dennis Lillee missing the latter part of the tour because of his involvement with Kerry Packer's World Series Cricket, they eventually clinched the series 3–0, thus regaining the Ashes.

One of the most exciting Tests I have ever stood at came at Edgbaston in August 1981, when England played Australia.

What people may have forgotten is that Ian Botham was captain at the start of that series. The Aussies won the first Test, and Botham's form was very poor. He could not get a wicket or a run to save his life. After the Lord's Test he lost the captaincy, England bringing in Michael Brearley to lead the team at Old Trafford.

Brearley had a word with Botham before the Test and said he was thinking about leaving him out. 'Both' pleaded, 'No way. I want to play in this match.'

After a lot of thought, Brearley decided to stick with Beefy, who went out in that Old Trafford Test to score a magnificent century, as well as getting amongst the wickets. He never looked back during that series. With the burdens and shackles of captaincy taken away from him he was a different player, and it turned out to be a golden year for him.

In the Headingley Test he scored another glorious century at a time when England looked to be down and out, and a tremendous spell of bowling by Bob Willis then clinched victory against all the odds in a remarkable game of cricket.

So convinced were they that it was all over, that on the Saturday night England had booked out of their hotel. Botham decided to hold a barbecue and invited a few of the Aussies round. They certainly got their fingers burned as 'Both' tore in to them with the bat the following day. He also took a few wickets in that match for good measure.

Then it was on to Edgbaston, and again it looked like curtains for England as the Aussies reached 89 for 3 in their second innings, needing only 139 to win. Everyone thought it was just a matter of time before they knocked off the runs.

Brearley came up to me at square leg for a natter. We often had chats out there on the field, and he always had something significant to say, but on this occasion he did not seem to know quite what to do. 'What do you think, Dickie?' he asked.

'Captain,' I replied, 'I reckon you've had it.'

'Oh dear,' he said. 'Do you really think so?'

'Just look at that scoreboard,' I said. 'They're eighty-nine for three. They only need another fifty runs and they've seven wickets left.'

Brearley persisted, 'Well, what would you do if you were in my shoes?'

'What would I do? If I were you, Captain, I'd put myself on to bowl, chuck them up, let them get the runs as quickly as possible, and then we can all shoot off home.'

'Good thinking,' he said, and strolled off. Then he stopped, turned, came back to me and said, 'Dickie, thanks for your suggestion, but I've decided to try something different.'

'You need a miracle, man,' I told him. 'What can you possibly do?'

Brearley replied, 'I'm going to bring on the Gorilla at the City End.'

Now Botham had a lot of respect for Brearley – he would do anything for him – and, likewise, Brearley respected Botham.

So the captain went up to 'Both' and told him, 'I want you to take your sweaters off and bowl from the City End.'

'Both' looked at him. 'Fair enough, Captain, but I can't keep on working miracles. We've really not got much chance.'

Brearley insisted, 'You can do it. Just fire them in as hard and as fast as you can. Give it all you've got.'

So Botham peeled off his sweaters and went on to take five wickets for one run to win the Test match. It was a remarkable performance. Only one man could have pulled it off, and that man was Ian Botham. The win also clinched the series, the last Test at The Oval ending in a draw.

In the build-up to that sixth Cornhill match, Geoff Boycott had been going through an unusually difficult time. The week before the game he telephoned Yorkshire County Cricket Club committee member Sidney Fielden, who was also a personal friend, and asked if he could arrange for him to have some batting practice. It just so happened that on the intervening Sunday a charity match was being played at the Pilkington's Ground near Doncaster and Sidney arranged for Boycs to play.

The great man was invited to open the innings, but he was caught at short leg for a duck off the fifth ball of the first over. Naturally the big crowd was very disappointed, and some of them called for the head of the short-leg fielder who, they said, 'should have dropped the bloody thing'! There was only one thing for it. Sidney spoke to the two captains and it was agreed that Geoff should bat for the other side, and he scored 120 in quick time. He was exhilarated. He told Sid, 'I'll get another hundred tomorrow now.'

Yorkshire were playing Derbyshire in a County Championship match at Chesterfield and Sid took the day off to watch him. Boycs made 122 not out.

The Test match started on Thursday of that week and Sid went down to watch, staying with Robin Marlar in Guildford.

On the Saturday, when England were due to bat, he told Robin what had happened the previous weekend at Doncaster and at Chesterfield, adding, 'He'll get another ton today, you mark my words.' Geoff made 137. I was there to see it, too, because I was one of the umpires.

It was, of course, typical of Boycott that he should have sought that extra practice. He would never pass up an opportunity to have a knock, whatever the circumstances.

Sid Fielden also loves to tell the story of his wedding to Maureen at St Mark's Methodist Church in Goldthorpe on 16 June 1980. After the ceremony they all went off to the reception at The Old Bells at Campsall. Someone remarked that it was a lovely sunny day, just the sort of day for cricket. Another – misguidedly as it turned out – added that he had a bat and ball in the boot of his car. Boycott's eyes lit up.

'Well, what are we waiting for then?' he asked. And, leaving the ladies and the other guests, half a dozen or so enthusiasts, including the groom, adjourned to the car park, which was, appropriately enough, the size of a cricket field. Boycs got hold of the bat and for over an hour batted with his back to the wall, as if his Test match career depended on it.

Sid and his friends took turns to bowl and they ran about fielding, perspiration dripping from them. But not one of them ever laid so much as a finger on the bat. Boycs refused to give it up and they couldn't get him out. When, after more than an hour, they all returned to meet the wrath of the ladies, the bowlers and fielders at least were somewhat spent, although Boycs seemed fresh enough.

Like Boycott, Ian Botham was a magnificent matchwinner – but he could do it as a bowler and fielder as well as a batsman. He was, quite simply, one of the greatest all-round cricketers I have ever had the privilege of umpiring. He was also a genuine bloke who always had a smile on his face. Whatever he is supposed to have done off the field – and stories about him were legion – on it he was a superb ambassador for the game.

He also did a tremendous amount of charity work for leukaemia, and some of those walks of his were incredible. The stamina and guts he showed was unbelievable. I actually walked with him just a little way during his John o' Groat's to Land's End trek. I met his party off the ferry from Dartmouth, intending to walk with them from Kingswear to Torquay.

However, with my advancing years, I was unable to keep up. I got so far behind at one stage in the country areas around the coast on the way from Brixham to Paignton that a bus driver took pity on me. He pulled up in his service bus and said, 'You're well behind, Dickie. Hop on, and I'll give you a lift.'

Nobody was looking, so I got on that Brixham to Paignton bus and we caught up the rest of the walkers. I jumped off, thanked the driver, got into step alongside the startled Botham, and urged, 'Come on, Both, you're slacking.' What he called me I dare not repeat!

We eventually arrived in front of the Civic Hall at Paignton, where thousands and thousands of Botham's admirers lined the streets. It was amazing. We met the Press, had a few drinks, and then set off on the next stage to Torquay, with people cheering us every step of the way.

Botham was staying at the Grand Hotel in Torquay, and he invited me up to his room for a drink with him and his wife, Kathy, who was a tremendous help to him, and in fact, walked with him some of the way.

'Both' had his shower, came into the bedroom and lay down on the bed, with his towel wrapped round him, while David Roberts, the former Worcestershire and England physio, gave him the once-over, as he did at every checkpoint. I could hardly believe what I saw. His knees were so full of fluid that they were as big as footballs, and the blisters on his feet like golf balls. Roberts burst the blisters, got the fluid on the knee down by using ice packs, and next day Beefy was off again. It was like that every night, but he never gave a thought to packing it in before he had finished what he had set out to achieve. Typical Botham.

Next morning I said cheerio to him as he went on his way and I returned to continue my relaxing holiday at the Livermead Cliff Hotel in Torquay.

I thought I was going to have to take it on the chin, not to mention shin, and miss the second Test between England and India at Old Trafford in June the following year, having been struck by a full-blooded sweep from Essex batsman Ken McEwan during a county championship match between Derbyshire and Essex.

I always stand closer in when spinners are on, in order to get a better view of the wicket-keeper, and I never saw the ball coming. It arrived so quickly that I had no chance of getting out of the way. It was really painful, and my leg swelled up like a balloon. Thankfully the ball did not hit me on the bone, otherwise the leg would have been broken, which would certainly have put me out of the Test match. Dallas Muir, the 6 feet 6 inches slow left-arm bowler, picked me up, cradled me in his arms like a baby, and carried me off.

It was the second time that season that I had been hit, having been knocked unconscious the previous month when a drive from Allan Lamb deflected off the non-striker into my face. The ball hit me on the chin and the lights went out. The next thing I knew two doctors and all the players were peering down anxiously at me as I lay on the ground.

After those two experiences I could say with some feeling that batsmen were striking the ball a lot harder than they used to do.

On the last day of that Old Trafford Test, the Indian tour

manager, Rajsingh Dungapur, captain Sunil Gavaskar, and vice-captain Vishwanath, all said they were looking forward to seeing me at The Oval.

I told them, 'Sorry, gentlemen, but I am not doing that Test match.'

They replied, 'Oh, yes, you are. We spoke with Lord's, and they are agreeable. We want you there.' I felt very honoured that those Indian players should have so much respect for me.

It was a split tour that summer, with Pakistan following on from India, and I stood at the second of the three matches against Pakistan along with David Constant, who had been controversially withdrawn from the first Test involving India following a protest from the tourists.

As far as I am aware, India had come across him only in the Yorkshire fixture at Bradford, where, to the best of my knowledge, there had been no doubtful decisions or arguments. David said he could think of no reason why there should have been any objection to his standing at the Test, and all the first-class umpires gave him a massive vote of confidence.

There were further problems in the game involving the Pakistanis. He had to put up with an unnecessary show of petulance from Abdul Qadir, who proved far too insistent when Ian Botham, missing a sweep, was struck on the pad. Constant immediately said not out, but the leg-spinner continued to jump up and down with his hands raised aloft. David came over to me and said, 'Look here, Dickie, we're going to have to stop play if they don't accept my ruling.'

'Hold on a minute, Conny,' I said, 'let's not be hasty. The best thing to do is have a word with Imran.' So that is what we did and, thankfully, the Pakistan captain, Imran Khan, helped us to sort things out.

In September of that same year came an even more remarkable request. Pakistan took the unprecented step of asking if

I would be prepared to go out there and stand at a total of nine Tests during the winter – three against the Australians and six against India. This bold and controversial move did not come off because of the rules of the World International Cricket Council, which stated, at that time, that each country should appoint its own panel of umpires. However, it showed the way the Pakistanis were beginning to think, led by Imran Khan. They were very much in favour of neutral umpires for Test matches, and they continued, ultimately successfully, to fight to change the system.

I took it as a very big compliment from the Pakistan management, and I would have jumped at the chance of umpiring those matches. I had always maintained that English umpires were the best in the world, and this went a long way towards proving it.

An incident in the Trent Bridge Test of the 1983 series between England and New Zealand had me hopping about with indignation.

As we were taking the field, I said to Ian Botham, 'Which end are you opening from with the new ball?'

'We're opening at the Pavilion End, then I'm coming on from the Radcliffe Road End,' he replied.

I was at square leg for the first over, and then strolled in to take up my position behind the stumps at the Radcliffe Road End, where Botham was preparing to bowl. With every step I took there was a loud explosion which had me jumping about like a cat on a hot tin roof. 'Both' had sprinkled some Chinese crackers all over the place, and there was I, putting my foot in it as usual. That's Botham for you.

Not many people know this, but I was presented with my West Indian cap at the end of the 1984 series. Or, to be rather more precise, I was presented with Joel Garner's West Indian cap. I received the 'award' on the Tuesday morning after the

West Indies had completed an innings victory over England to establish an historic 4–0 lead in the series. Clive Lloyd called me into the dressing room, congratulated me on my handling of the game, and then handed over the cap as a mark of appreciation from all the team.

That Test match also provided me with one of the most embarrassing experiences of my career, as I had to bring a halt to the proceedings right in the middle of a session. The players wondered what on earth was happening when I called over England captain David Gower and West Indian batsman Gordon Greenidge to explain to them, 'Gentlemen, I am afraid I shall have to suspend this Test match. Nature calls,' and off I toddled to the loo.

There was a bizarre moment of cricketing history on the second day of the England v New Zealand Test at Lord's in 1986 when Bob Taylor, who had last played for England in Pakistan two years earlier, was summoned from his lunch table to keep wicket in place of Bruce French. Taylor, who had celebrated his forty-fifth birthday the previous week, did so as immaculately as ever.

French collapsed after being struck by a ball from Richard Hadlee while batting. Fortunately his injury proved to be nothing more serious than a cut on the back of the head which required three stitches, but he was too dazed to continue, and when New Zealand batted, Bill Athey wore the gloves for a couple of overs while a search went on for a more orthodox replacement.

England captain Mike Gatting remembered that Taylor, who had retired from first-class cricket at the end of the 1984 season, was in the ground in his new capacity as a liaison assistant, employed by the sponsors, and was entertaining guests at lunch.

New Zealand's captain, Jeremy Coney, raised no objections

and Taylor, in a mixture of his own and borrowed kit, was soon displaying all his old agility with some good takes down the leg side as the England bowlers strayed off line.

It was a special thrill for me to stand at the MCC's Bicentennial match at Lord's in 1987 because all the great players were there, and there was a wonderful atmosphere. It was also an excellent game, with so many top-class knocks, some good bowling, and magnificent fielding. It was also good to see that, when wickets fell, players did not hug and kiss each other and give the high-fives. It was a game played in a very competitive spirit, which you are bound to get with great players who have a pride in their performances, but it remained friendly and sporting at the same time.

It was just a shame that we did not get the exciting finish that was promised on the last day. It was all set up, with the Rest of the World side committed to going for the runs, and it really would have been the icing on the cake, but unfortunately, rain washed out play completely.

The outstanding memory of that occasion, however, was off the field, not on it. The presentations were made in the Long Room, and we all received magnificent glass goblets, inscribed with the Bicentennial emblem. You could almost feel the presence of all those famous players of the past who had walked through that very room on their way to a memorable innings or a matchwinning bowling performance. It really was a most moving experience.

I made history of another kind that summer. I became the first umpire in Test match cricket to be substituted because of injury. I was left hopping about even more than usual when a sharp return from Salim Malik hit me just below the knee in the first Test between England and Pakistan at Old Trafford. I didn't want to go off, but physio Lawrie Brown said I had to have the wound cleaned. It came up like an egg. Mind you, it would have gone for four overthrows if I hadn't got in the way, so the Pakistanis should be grateful to me. I was back after half-an-hour's treatment, Jack Birkenshaw having deputised meantime.

Unfortunately, the Asian ill-feeling towards David Constant reared its ugly head again when Pakistan this time made a formal request that he should be stood down from the fifth Cornhill Test at The Oval. Hasib Ahsan, the Pakistan manager, said, 'All I can say is that the team do not have confidence in Mr Constant. But we think four of your umpires, Dickie Bird, Barrie Meyer, David Shepherd and Alan Whitehead are very good and very firm. There are no better umpires anywhere in the world.'

Three years later Conny was at the centre of controversy yet again when he decided to stand down from the Cornhill Tests against New Zealand, and that brought another Lord's SOS for me to take an extra spell of international duty. Constant withdrew because he felt unhappy about an incident involving Kiwi batsman Mark Greatbatch during the second Texaco international. Greatbatch had an angry exchange of words with the umpire after complaining that the England bowlers were delivering too many illegal bouncers. Constant, in turn, reported Greatbatch's behaviour to the TCCB, who passed over the matter to the New Zealand officials.

Greatbatch was subsequently fined about £300, but Constant was still not happy about the situation. It was a great shame for him, because he was a very fine umpire, and it was typical of him that he should ring me to wish me all the best when I stood in for him.

It was during the Trent Bridge Test of that series, when I was standing at square leg at the Radcliffe Road End, that Allan Lamb, coming out to bat at number four after England had lost two quick wickets, started to walk towards me rather than taking up his position at the crease.

I admonished him, 'Nay, Lamby lad, what do you think

you're playing at? Have your eyes gone or summat? The stumps are over there. This is square leg.'

He replied, 'I know that, Dickie, but it's you I want. I've got a big problem.'

I countered, 'Not half as big a problem as you'll have if you don't get over there double quick so that we can get on with the game.'

'But it's my hand phone,' he pleaded. 'I forgot to take it out of my pocket when I came in to bat. I put my thigh pads on, strapped on my pads, picked up my gloves and bat, charged out here, and completely forgot about the phone.'

'Well, what do you expect me to do about it?' I asked.

'I want you to put it in your pocket and keep it safe for me. Oh, and if it rings, answer it.'

I stuttered, 'You must be joking. We're in the middle of a Test match, man. You'll get me shot. I'm not putting it in my pocket, and that's that.'

But he argued, 'You must, Dickie. Please. I can't carry it about while I'm batting, can I? Just stuff it in your pocket and hope it doesn't ring, there's a good chap.'

So I did, and off he went to take guard from my colleague John Hampshire, and the Test match rolled on.

Lamby had been out there for about ten minutes, pottering about and getting nowhere fast, when the phone rang in my pocket.

I thought, oh no, now I'm for it. Whatever will Lord's think? I shouted across, 'Lamby, t' phone's ringing.'

'Well, answer it, then,' came the reply. 'I'm expecting some messages.' I pulled the darn thing out of my pocket, ever so gingerly, and whispered, 'Hello, this is Dickie Bird speaking on Allan Lamb's phone. Who's there?' A voice answered, 'This is Ian Botham ringing from the dressing room. Tell that fellow Lamb either to play a few shots, or get out.'

With my sister Marjorie, without whose help and support I would never
have been able to cope.

This is Your Life with Michael Aspel, who really did catch me totally by surprise.

Putting the world to rights with John Major, when he was Prime Minister, during a break in play at Lord's.

Alf Broadhead, without whose intervention I might have been lost to cricket. I owe him so much.

I couldn't believe it when they brought my former Monk Bretton Colliery manager 'Chunky' Charlton on to the *This is Your Life* set. I thought he was dead!

Hamming it up with my former Barnsley batting colleague Michael Parkinson, the best chat show host I've seen and a brilliant sports columnist. A dinner at Ardsley House brought us back together in home-town Barnsley.

In the grounds of Buckingham Palace after the proudest moment of my life – receiving the MBE from Her Majesty The Queen.

A silver salver awarded to me by the National Grid for breaking Frank Chester's world record with my forty-ninth Test, Zimbabwe v New Zealand, in November 1992.

Another Royal occasion, meeting the Queen at Trent Bridge in her Silver Jubilee year. England captain Mike Brearley is making the introductions and further down the line are Derek Randall, Bob Woolmer, Bob Willis, Graham Roope, Ian Botham, Alan Knott, Mike Hendrick and Geoff Miller.

Shaking with a sheikh after umpiring an international tournament in Sharjah.

Shoulder to shoulder with Paul Getty, whose big ambition, he says, is to umpire one of his matches at Wormsley with me.

A Bird-like caricature drawn by John Ireland.

I wave a white handkerchief in surrender during an international tournament in Sharjah – Viv Richards had sent several shots rocketing past my ears like tracer bullets.

This Australian cockatoo was totally unimpressed by my 'that's out' decision. It pecked me on the nose!

Surrounded by the ladies at a farewell dinner at Brooklands Restaurant in Barnsley. *Left to right:*
Lady Mason, Lady Howell, Mrs Gratton, Pat Perry, Lady Byford, sister Marjorie and niece Rachel.

A trio of Lords – Howell, Mason and Byford – at the farewell dinner at Brooklands.

With my lifelong friend Keith Lodge, who has been a marvellous help in writing this book, and has faithfully plotted my career in the pages of the *Barnsley Chronicle*, where he is Sports Editor.

On the balcony at Lord's, holding aloft the plaque presented to me by Cornhill Insurance after my final Test.

The first-class umpires who were on the list in 1995.

Whenever I see someone with a mobile phone now that incident always rings a bell with me.

The 1991 Headingley Test was another memorable occasion, when England beat the West Indies by 115 runs in the opening game of the series. It was a truly marvellous match. You simply did not know what was going to happen next, and the game could have gone either way, right down to the last day. England bowled well, there was some brilliant fielding, particularly by the two new boys, Mark Ramprakash and Graeme Hick, and Graham Gooch played a great innings which, in the end, proved the vital difference between the teams. I also stood at the Test in which he scored his record-breaking 333, but I would rate this as an even finer knock in the context of the game. The uneven bounce and constant interruptions for rain and bad light made it very difficult for the batsmen, which is why Gooch's innings was so remarkable. I reckon that if the West Indies had been able to get him out they would have won easily.

As it was, I saw England beat the West Indies for the first time in eighteen years as a Test umpire. In fact, it was England's first victory over their Caribbean rivals for twenty-two years.

I received the usual barracking from my home crowd during that Headingley Test whenever colleague David Shepherd and I were forced to take the players off the field because of the weather conditions, but we always tried to keep the game going, sometimes in really bad light, and came off only when we had no choice.

Umpiring in those conditions demanded great concentration and one decision in particular required expert positioning and an eagle eye, which was when Robin Smith was run out in the first innings. It was such a close call that no one was sure about it until the television replay backed up my decision. I was therefore delighted that night to hear a glowing tribute from Richie Benaud in his summary of the day's play on the television highlights. 'There were two stars out there today,' he said. 'Robin Smith and Dickie Bird.'

On the day before England were due to play Pakistan in the last Test at The Oval on 6 August 1992, I spoke at a luncheon where I received a Sports Personality of the Year award from the Press, who then proceeded to stitch me up. As far as I was concerned it was a harmless enough speech, consisting mainly of funny stories, and I thought no more about it.

The next morning I was faced with headlines such as 'Bird Says It Will Be War', and there was one photograph of me wearing a tin hat. I had never said anything remotely like that, a fact which was confirmed by the Test and County Cricket Board's Press Officer, who had been present at the luncheon. It was the Press at it again, building something out of nothing just to make a sensational story. The series was tied at 1–1, this last Test would be the decider, and the Press were introducing controversy before the game had even started.

There had been problems in the fourth Test at Headingley, with the Pakistanis claiming there had been quite a few dubious decisions by Ken Palmer and Mervyn Kitchen. I felt it was quite wrong for them to take that attitude. They should have accepted the decisions and got on with the game.

It was bad enough that the umpires had to contend with a difficult pitch, with the ball jagging around off the seam all the time, but there was also a big screen at the ground and all the incidents were being played back, with players stopping and watching every decision. It puts a lot of extra pressure on the umpires and I do not think it is fair. I had every sympathy with Palmer and Kitchen.

Personally, I take no notice of the replays. I never look at them. I have always given my decisions as I see them at the time and then I stand by them. But, if they are given the opportunity, it is only natural that players should want to look to see if they have been treated fairly.

There had also been some trouble at Old Trafford, where Ken Palmer's brother, Roy, had a problem with Aqib Javed, who showed dissent over one decision to such an extent that former Pakistan captain, Imran Khan, admitted that it had been totally unjustified.

He qualified his criticism of his compatriot by claiming that officials should command rather than demand respect, and asked, 'Why is it that Dickie Bird, during his entire career, has never had an ugly incident?' He answered his own question thus, 'He is a great umpire, not because he does not make mistakes, but because of his integrity and his wonderful nature. Bird's greatness is that he recognises that the players are human beings and not robots. So he ignores the little outburst or talks to the bowlers in a soothing manner. An hour or two later the same player tenders his apology and the whole incident is forgotten.'

Pakistan coach Intikhab Alam said he was absolutely delighted that David Shepherd and I had been appointed to the final Test; but I must admit I was really worried when I saw all those press cuttings suggesting it was going to be war out there. 'Oh dear me,' I thought, 'now what's going to happen?' But nothing did. I didn't have a moment's problem with either team as Pakistan won to clinch the series.

In June 1993, I was involved in yet another cricketing first when I stood at the game between England and Australia at Old Trafford. I condemned Graham Gooch to become the first England player – and only the fifth worldwide – to be given out for handling the ball in a Test match.

The England captain, battling from the front to try to prevent the Aussies from going one up in the six-match series, had made a magnificent 133 when, playing a ball from Merv Hughes down into his crease, he appeared to panic as it bounced back towards his stumps, and he knocked it away with his hand. Immediately the Australian players appealed, and I had no option but to give Gooch out, although I felt very sorry for him, losing his wicket in that way at such a crucial stage of the game.

Law 33 clearly states, 'Either batsman, on appeal, shall be out handled ball, if he wilfully touches the ball while in play with the hand not holding the bat, unless he does so with the consent of the opposite side.'

Gooch was obviously in breach of the law, so I asked Australian captain Allan Border if he wanted to uphold the appeal. When he said he did, there was only one decision. 'That's out.'

It was the first time I had given that particular decision in twenty-four years of umpiring first-class cricket. Gooch realised that he would have to go as soon as he knocked the ball away. He could have used any other part of his body. He could have kicked the ball away, nudged it clear with his arm, or even headed it!

He told me afterwards, 'You were quite right, Dickie. You could not have done anything else. It was just an instinctive thing on my part. I knew the law, but just could not stop myself from knocking the ball away with the back of my hand. I could have kicked myself, never mind the ball. We were trying to save the Test when I got out, and I can only blame myself.' Gooch's dismissal, after five hours and ten minutes of defiance, proved to be the turning point. After he had gone the rest of the England batsmen were unable to hold out and the Australians eventually won by 179 runs.

Goochie was again in top form in the first Test between England and New Zealand at Trent Bridge in June 1994, the big crowd who turned up for the third day's play enjoying the spectacle of the opening batsman completing a double hundred as Michael Atherton's team strolled towards an innings victory. They were, however, unaware of a dramatic 'spectacle' of another kind that had taken place off the pitch.

I was horrified, on arriving at the ground by taxi from my hotel, to discover that I had mislaid the special tinted spectacles I had taken to wearing on sunny days. They were an invaluable help to me, and on this particular day, just for a change, the sun was shining quite brilliantly.

A telephone call to the hotel proved in vain, as a search was made of my bedroom, the dining room and the foyer without success. The next SOS was to the taxi firm, who told me, 'Sorry, sir, that particular cabbie had been on the night shift. You were his last fare. He's now gone home to bed.'

By this time I was desperate, so I called the police. I don't know what they thought when I said to them, 'Hello, this is Dickie Bird, the Test umpire here, I've lost my glasses,' but they were great. They went round to the cabbie's house, woke him from his slumbers, and there, in the back of the taxi, were the missing spectacles, which were returned to a profusely perspiring and extremely agitated umpire with just twenty minutes to spare before wickets were pitched. It was such a relief to get those glasses back, but the police told me that the taxi driver had been none too pleased when they woke him up.

The following month I was caught up in the dust storm of the infamous 'ball-tampering' incident during the historic first Test between England and South Africa at Lord's. BBC television pictures showed Michael Atherton, the England captain, apparently take something from his pocket and sprinkle it on one side of the ball, before wiping his hands on his trousers and then vigorously polishing the other side of the ball.

The first my colleague, Steve Randell, and I knew about the incident, or of any controversy, was when we were told, after the close of play, that people had been ringing up to complain about what they had seen on television. The calls had come from all over the world, including South Africa and Pakistan. Steve and I were asked to attend a meeting with match referee Peter Burge and the third umpire, Mervyn Kitchen, along with Atherton and England team manager Keith Fletcher. We watched the video, but were not asked to comment, being there merely as observers.

I can honestly say I could not believe what I saw, nor could I explain it. Atherton is such an intelligent chap, and the last person you would think capable of doing anything underhand.

To captain your country is the greatest honour, and yet it seemed at that moment he was putting his position in jeopardy. It threatened to ruin his career, and he has had to live with the stigma of it ever since. It says a great deal for his character and resilience that he came through it all to continue to lead his country. Indeed, he was still in the job for this summer's Ashes series against Australia, having just become the first captain in five years to win an overseas Test series, leading his side to victory in New Zealand during the winter.

Atherton was fined a total of £2,000 by the Chairman of Selectors, Raymond Illingworth, after admitting that he did not at first tell Burge the whole truth about the ball-tampering speculation. He was fined £1,000 'for using dirt' taken from his pocket, to rub on the ball, and the same amount 'for giving incomplete information to the match referee'.

My Barnsley compatriot, Darren Gough, was also drawn into the controversy, because it was to him that Atherton handed the ball immediately after the incident.

All I can say is that the ball was examined after every over by either myself or Steve Randell, when it was also shown to the players. There was never any evidence to suggest that it had been tampered with.

Only Darren Gough, of the England bowlers, made the ball deviate, and it is my honest opinion that nothing the England captain may or may not have done had any effect on the way the ball behaved.

The fact that Gough did make the ball deviate was down to class bowling and nothing else. His inswinging yorker was magnificent, and he has continued to use it as a vital weapon in his armoury from that day to this. I rate that particular delivery of his even higher than that of Waqar Younis, and I can give no higher praise than that. It therefore annoyed me that we had found a lad who could deliver the goods, yet his achievements were minimised and overshadowed by the ball-tampering allegations.

People forget that De Villiers also swung the ball all over the place for South Africa, yet no one suggested that this was anything other than excellent bowling. It was no different with Goughie.

The ball-tampering controversy rubbed off much of the gloss from what should have been a joyful occasion as South Africa celebrated a historic return to the headquarters of Test cricket after years of banishment by recording a runaway victory by the huge margin of 356 runs.

It was also an emotional game for me, because I had spent so many years coaching in South Africa prior to the Gleneagles Agreement, and I had scored a century against them when they toured here in 1960. I was able to meet up with several players who had featured in that touring side, among them Roy McLean, Peter Pollock, Johnny Waite and Trevor Goddard. Jimmy Cook, whom I had coached as a schoolboy, was also there, disappointed not to be in the squad.

At the end of it all, there was only sadness that a game which had been played in such a good spirit should have been soured by that one incident, while all the good things were forgotten or at least overlooked.

Against the West Indies at Old Trafford the following year there was a remarkable incident involving Dominic Cork. He had made only a few runs when he added another two to his tally by forcing Ian Bishop towards the boundary. As Cork returned to the striker's end I saw him pick up a bail and put it back on top of the stumps, although I had no idea how that bail had ended up on the ground. Bishop was walking past me at the bowler's end, preparing to send down the next delivery, and there was no appeal from anyone.

Just then West Indian captain Richie Richardson strolled over to the square leg umpire, Cyril Michley, and enquired, 'How was that, Cyril?'

'Not out,' said Cyril. 'I saw no contact with the wicket.'

Afterwards Cyril admitted that he should have gone to the third umpire on Richardson's appeal, so, out of curiosity, at the next interval he went and asked the third umpire, Chris Balderstone, what decision he would have given had he called on him for advice.

Balderstone told him, 'My decision would also have been not out, because it was not clear what had happened on the video playback.'

Cyril felt a lot better after that, but a couple of hours later the incident was magnified from another camera angle and it showed that Cork's heel did, in fact, just touch the base of the stumps as he made his shot, which had been enough to dislodge the bail. Cork went on to score forty-odd and England won by four wickets when chasing only just over ninety to win, so it was obviously a crucial moment in the game.

That was an instance when not even the combination of the third umpire and the electronic eye was capable of giving an instant decision that was correct. How much more difficult, then, for the man out there in the middle?

17

MY WORLD SQUAD

URING my years as an umpire I have seen many great players come and go, and I have often been asked who, in that time, have been the best of all. It is not an easy question to answer, and I have had to give it a lot of thought. Eventually I whittled my list of possibles down to a final thirteen, and even now I look at it and think, how could I possibly have left so-and-so out?

Here is my final selection for a Best in the World squad: Barry Richards (South Africa), Sunil Gavaskar (India), Vivian Richards (West Indies), Greg Chappell (Australia), Graeme Pollock (South Africa), Garfield Sobers (West Indies), Alan Knott (England), Richard Hadlee (New Zealand), Michael Holding (West Indies), Dennis Lillee (Australia), Lance Gibbs (West Indies), Andy Roberts (West Indies), and Abdul Qadir (Pakistan).

Two men in that team averaged more than 60 at Test match level – Barry Richards and Graeme Pollock. Only three others managed that: Herbert Sutcliffe (Yorkshire and England) – which is going back an awfully long time – Sir Donald Bradman (Australia) and George Headley, of the West Indies, whom they christened the Black Bradman.

I consider Barry Richards to be the best batsman I have ever seen, and it was very sad that he was lost to international cricket because of apartheid. He played in only five Tests, during which he averaged 75. I know that people will argue that you cannot judge a man on five Tests, but I maintain that he was the best, and there are a lot of very knowledgeable people in the game who agree with me.

Barry Richards was a brilliant opening righthand batsman who could also bowl off-breaks. He hit 1,000 runs in a season in England nine times, going on to 2,000 one year, and he scored three double centuries for Hampshire, the highest being 240 against Warwickshire at Coventry in 1973. However, his most famous innings was 356 for South Australia against Western Australia at Perth in 1970–71, when he made 325 not out on the opening day of the match – a remarkable achievement. In 1970 he appeared in all five matches for the Rest of the World against England.

Sunil Gavaskar is my choice as Richards' opening partner. Like the South African, Gavaskar was a tremendous player off both back and front foot and capable of playing magnificent shots all round the wicket. His Test record is outstanding: he played in ninety matches and scored 7,625 runs at an average of 52.22. A slight, nimble-footed player who was a delight to watch, he made 1,141 runs on his first tour to England in 1971 at an average of 43.88. Three years later he again appeared in all three tests of the Indian tour, hitting his country's only century at Old Trafford. His performances in 1979 improved further, with 1,062 runs at an average of 55.89, including an innings of 221 in The Oval Test. He was an excellent right-hand opening batsman and terrific slip fielder.

It was a very difficult decision to leave out my old Barnsley batting colleague Geoffrey Boycott, and he will certainly not be pleased about it, because he is a big believer in his own ability.

What I will say about Boycs, however, is this. Of all the great players I have seen, if I had to pick a batsman to bat for my life, I would go for Geoffrey. He is probably the best self-made player there has ever been. He might not have the natural ability or flair of a Richards or a Gavaskar, but he would be the man if my life depended on it. His application, dedication, concentration, self-belief and mental toughness set him apart. I do not think there has even been a player quite like him.

Incidentally, Nottinghamshire members will tell you to this day that Boycott used to fancy their bowlers just as much as Fred Trueman used to fancy their batters. Of the 103 centuries he made for Yorkshire, no fewer than thirteen were against Nottinghamshire.

In 1983 he made 214 not out at Worksop and in the return fixture at Park Avenue, Bradford, he followed up with 163 and then 141 not out in the second innings. His good friend, Sidney Fielden, a Yorkshire County Cricket Club committee member, went home with him after that Bradford game and while a meal was being prepared, Boycs said to Sid, 'Come on, I'll beat you at snooker.'

They played two frames and Boycott lost them both. After they had eaten Boycott said, 'You're not going yet, Sid, we've still to finish that snooker match.' So they played a third frame and again Boycs was beaten. The reason, Sid told him, was, 'You can only hit the red balls.'

But the story exemplifies Boycott's attitude to any game. He just hated to be beaten. He always wanted to be the best.

I was shocked when I heard, early in October 1983, that Yorkshire had sacked him. After the committee meeting at which the decision was made, Sid rang his friend and was invited to his home in Woolley.

'But you'll have to come across the fields,' he said. 'Don't try it by road, the Press and television people are everywhere.' He advised Sid to park in a farmyard on the outskirts of the village and trudge across the fields.

When Sid got to Water Lane in Woolley it was just as Boycott had said, so he took his advice and made the final part of his journey across the fields. He tore his suit getting through a barbed wire fence and when he arrived at Pear Tree Farm he looked more like a tramp than a member of the Yorkshire committee. Later, in the early hours of next morning, when all the media had left, the two of them walked round the village. Sleep was impossible.

That story reminds me of the time I paid Geoff a visit. He does not live too far away from me and he once invited me over for lunch – just once, mind you. When I arrived at Fortress Boycott I found that the gates were locked, and Boycs, teasing me on the intercom, would not let me in. There was nothing for it but to clamber over a ten-foot high wall, scramble down a tree on the other side and make my way in that way.

Boycs was waiting for me at the front door, grinning like the Cheshire Cat, only rather more lop-sidedly. He said, 'Better come in now you're here. We'll have lunch in a minute.' I was looking forward to some Yorkshire pudding and roast beef. What I got was a toasted cheese sandwich!

If it was hard to overlook Boycott, the same can be said of that famous West Indian opening pair of Gordon Greenidge and Desmond Haynes, England's John Edrich, who was another player you would not mind having with you in the trenches when the going got tough, and Graham Gooch, an England player with an outstanding Test record.

At three and four I have gone for Vivian Richards and Greg Chappell. Those two could hit the ball through mid-wicket like the bullet out of a gun, when it was pitched eighteen inches outside the off stump, something it is great to see a batsman do. They were both exceptionally strong on the on side, from where three-quarters of their runs came.

Viv Richards was the outstanding batsman of the 1976 tour to England, scoring 1,724 runs at an average of 71.83 in first-class matches and 829 runs at an average of 118.42 in the Tests, including his highest innings of 291 in the fifth Test at The Oval. On the 1980 tour he again topped both first-class and Test batting averages with 56.93 and 63.16 respectively. In all he scored 1,000 runs in a season in England ten times, topping the 2,000 mark once in 1977 when he scored 2,161 at an average of 65.48. A brilliant middle-order, right-handed batsman, he had a Test match average of 56.57.

Chappell was a stylish righthander who first toured England in 1972, when he hit 1,260 runs at an average of 70.00 in first-class matches and 437 runs at an average of 48.55 in the Tests. In 1975 he was not too successful, but two years later, when he captained the tourists, he was the leading batsman with 1,182 runs (average 59.10) in first-class matches, and 371 (average 41.22) in the Test series. He hit 1,000 runs during both his seasons with Somerset. One of the leading players to join Kerry Packer's World Series Cricket, he announced his retirement from Test cricket at that time, but resumed as Australia's captain in 1979. He played in a total of 82 Tests, scoring 6,746 runs at an average of 53.11 his highest Test score being 247 not out.

Then we come to Graeme Pollock at number five. Now, I believe he was the best left-handed batsman I have ever seen, and I've seen some great ones – Neil Harvey (Australia), Brian Lara (West Indies), Allan Border (Australia), and David Gower and Willie Watson (England)

Gower was a class act, and it is my firm belief that he should have played for England at least another three years after he retired from international cricket. I would never, ever, have left Gower out of any England side. In fact, he could still have been playing in my last season. He was such a fit lad and carried no surplus weight whatsoever.

However, although Gower was a marvellous touch player and had a first-class temperament, he was not a big net man, and there were people in charge of England at the time who thought that he would not knuckle down to serious practice, including the circuit training introduced as part of a new fitness regime. Therefore he was left out. It was a travesty, because Gower did not need all that fitness training. He was a fit athlete naturally: he always moved like a gazelle in the field, and was brilliant wherever you chose to put him.

There was also a criticism that he used to get out to balls that he could have left alone, but that is rubbish. Everybody gets out to bad shots, but what about the good shots that Gower played – those beautifully timed strokes off the back foot, played with such imposing elegance? He was a lovely player when in full flow and people would pay through the turnstiles to watch him.

Most people, I imagine, will also be surprised at Brian Lara's exclusion. After all, he holds the record for Test innings of 375. It may cause more surprise when I say that I rate India's Sachin Tendulkar as a better batsman than the West Indian star.

I first saw Tendulkar when he was just sixteen years old, playing in a one-day international tournament in Sharjah, where I was umpiring. He came up to me on the field and said, 'I've always wanted to meet you, Mr Dickie Bird. I've always been a big admirer of yours.'

'What's your name, son?' I asked him.

'Sachin Tendulkar,' he told me. 'My headmaster has given me permission to have time off school to come here to Sharjah to play for India.'

I could not believe it, yet he went out and made 86 against

such great West Indian fast bowlers as Malcolm Marshall, Joel Garner, Michael Holding and Courtney Walsh. It was a magnificent innings for a sixteen-year-old kid. I know it was only a one-day international, and there is a big difference between that and Test match cricket, but the sheer class shone through as soon as I saw him play.

I now feel that Tendulkar is the best player in the world today, and that when their respective careers have finished, Tendulkar will have scored more runs and have a better Test average than Lara.

The fact that I have had to leave players like these two out of my side gives you some idea of how highly I rate those batsmen I have nominated, all of whom had one thing in common: they all had so much time to play their shots. They waited for the ball to come to them, and did not lunge at it. That is the vital difference between a class player and an average player. The class player waits, and is therefore able to pick the line and the length far better.

If you think that I have possibly gone over the top in assessing Pollock as the greatest lefthander of them all, I remember Sir Donald Bradman being quoted in a newspaper many years ago as saying that Pollock was the best player he had seen, which coming from Sir Donald must mean something. Pollock really was something very special.

Other players I had to leave out of my top-of-the-order batting line-up were Australia's Ian Chappell, whom I rate as one of the best captains I have seen, and the Waugh brothers, Steven and Mark. They are three players I would love to have at my side if I was in the trenches facing enemy fire. Send for Waugh to win the war, I'd say.

Then there was Clive Lloyd, of the West Indies, a flamboyant attacking batsman and brilliant fielder; and Pakistan's Javed Miandad, who scored more than 8,000 runs in Test matches at an average of more than 50. They did not quite make it, either.

The all-rounder spot in my team goes to Sir Garfield Sobers. He was simply the best, to coin a phrase. He was three cricketers rolled into one: great left-handed batsman, arguably one of the best new-ball bowlers of his type – left arm over the wicket – and a brilliant close-to-the-wicket fielder.

As well as his ability to slant the ball across the batsman with his quicker stuff, and then nip one back with the next delivery, Sobers could also bowl slow left arm, and batsmen found it very difficult to spot his chinaman and googly. To be able to do all these things was a gift, a kind of special talent that is, I believe, born with you. If there has ever been a better all-rounder than Sobers in the history of the game I would have loved to have seen him play.

Sobers had all-round brilliance in every department. His record speaks for itself. He was the first Test cricketer to hit more than 8,000 runs in his career, that total including 365 not out for West Indies against Pakistan at Kingston in 1957–58, thus creating a new record at the time for the highest individual innings in Test cricket. He is one of the few bowlers to capture more than 200 Test wickets, and this, allied to his 109 catches, demonstrates his standing amongst the greatest players of all time. He captained the West Indies in 39 Tests, which was, at the time, yet another record. Of his five West Indian tours to England the most outstanding was in 1966, when his Test record was quite incredible – 722 runs at an average of 103.14, and 20 wickets at an average of 27.25. He played in a total of 93 Tests, scoring 8,032 runs at an average of 57.78 and taking 235 wickets at an average of 34.03.

His most famous feat in county cricket was to hit six sixes off a six-ball over delivered by M.A. Nash of Glamorgan at Swansea in 1968, and his best bowling was 9 for 49 against

Kent at Canterbury in 1996. He hit 1,000 runs in a season in England nine times and captained the Rest of the World in five matches against England. What a player!

Sobers was also a gentleman. When you think that he flew over from the other side of the world to appear on *This is Your Life*, it shows what kind of a man he is. That gesture was greatly appreciated. When I go to the West Indies he is always the first man to ring me and suggest a meal and a drink. For the world's greatest all-rounder to do that means so much. Money can't buy that kind of friendship and mutual respect.

Ian Botham (England), Imran Khan and Wasim Akram (Pakistan), Kapil Dev (India) and Michael Procter (South Africa) can all feel very unlucky not to have made it into my team.

I am a big admirer of Botham. He was a great competitor, a matchwinner who was capable of lifting the spirits of team-mates and the crowd with moments of sheer inspiration. It is unfortunate that he was unable to make the transition from successful England player to successful England captain, but perhaps Brian Close was right when he said that 'Both' had been given the captaincy too soon.

An England selector at the time, Close was the only one who saw the danger looming. He was violently opposed to the idea of making Botham captain. He was convinced that at the relatively young age of twenty-four the brilliant all-rounder was not yet ready for the additional responsibility. He was also far too naive and inexperienced, not to mention headstrong, to be able to cope with the man-management side of the job.

His approach to man-management amounted to little more than making sure nobody drank alone and everyone got their round in at the bar. But whatever his failings, he was absolutely convinced that he could do the job. In any case, as he said, 'If anyone offers you the captaincy of England you don't say "no," or, "not yet, come back in six months time." The only possible answer is "yes, anytime, anywhere."' I agree with him. There is no greater honour in sport than to lead your country and if you are asked to do it you cannot possibly turn it down.

One thing was for certain, Botham never needed any motivation to play for his country, and, even if he failed to make a go of it as captain by name, he still led from the front by his enthusiasm and will-to-win. I never had a moment's trouble with him. He accepted decisions and got on with the game. As he said himself, dodgy decisions even themselves out over a season.

Imran Khan and Kapil Dev were similarly invaluable to their teams, while Procter, like Richards, was another South African sadly lost to international cricket. I rated Procter not far behind Sobers. Towards the end of his career he played as the overseas professional with Gloucestershire, and even then, despite bad knees, he still roared in on pitches that had no pace in them at all, giving his usual 150 per cent. I admired him for that. He was a good batsman, good bowler and brilliant fielder, and he was a sad loss to international cricket.

Kapil Dev, incidentally, is the present-day record holder of Test wickets, with well over 400, while Allan Border, of Australia, who could almost be classed as an all-rounder himself, holds the record for Test runs, more than 10,000. I have therefore left both the leading wicket-taker and the leading run-getter in Test history out of my World team.

I now come to the wicket-keeping position in my side, and, although there were others who came to mind, such as Wasim Bari (Pakistan), Rodney Marsh (Australia), Bob Taylor (England), Jeffrey Dujon (West Indies), Farokh Engineer (India) and Ian Healey (Australia), it was not a difficult choice.

Without doubt, England's Alan Knott is the doyen of them all. I am a great believer in picking your best wicket-keeper, whatever else he may or may not be able to do. He can be a piano player, a butcher, a labourer, or a candlestick maker, but, as far as I am concerned, as long as he can keep wicket he should be in the team. People argue with me and say times have changed. They claim that in this day and age a wicketkeeper has to be able to bat as well. I disagree, but, in Knotty's case, that does not matter anyway. I have seen England reeling at 80-odd for 5 and Knotty has come fidgeting in to score a magnificent century which has saved a Test match. Not only was Knotty the best behind the stumps, he could bat as well. Consider the facts. In 95 Tests he scored 4,389 runs at an average of 32.75 and claimed 269 victims as wicketkeeper. For ten years he was regarded as England's number one, commanding an automatic place in the Test side until he joined Packer's World Series Cricket in 1977.

Of the current wicket-keepers only Jack Russell comes close to him. As well as being an outstanding competitor behind the stumps Jack, like Knott, is also a good batsman. One of the best innings he ever played was at Lord's in June 1996, when he hit a magnificent century against India. Then there was the Old Trafford Test against the West Indies in 1995. Had it not been for him we would have lost that match. He came in with England having lost a few wickets very quickly when chasing only 90-odd, and I was thinking, 'Heaven help us, they're not going to get these.' Then in comes Jack to steer his side home.

Of course, there was that memorable occasion in the winter tour of 1995–96 when he stuck with Michael Atherton against all the odds to save the Test match in South Africa, his skipper playing a marathon innings that must go down as one of the greatest backs-to-the-wall knocks of all time. Jack stood stubbornly at his captain's side to hold out for a draw. It was a magnificent effort by someone who critics claimed was not a good enough batsman to merit his place in the side.

Those are just three examples of his doggedness. There are many more, and I am amazed that he has not been a regular in the England side.

Jack lives on Jaffa Cakes, those chocolate covered biscuits with orange in the middle. He loves them. He does have a bowl of soup occasionally as well, but he is not very big and doesn't carry much weight, which is hardly surprising considering how little he eats.

It was Jack, incidentally, who provided me with my last victim in Test cricket, to an lbw decision at that. Saurav Ganguly was the bowler. Afterwards Jack came up to me and said, 'Don't say I never do anything for you, Dickie. That was a present for you after all these years. But I've got to admit I was plumb. Course, it had to be for you to give it, hadn't it?'

He is also an accomplished artist and I treasure the sketch he did of me.

To provide balance in the squad I had to have a couple of spin bowlers, and this gave me the biggest headache of all. There was no doubt about my off-spinner. That choice fell on Lance Gibbs, of the West Indies, with 309 wickets at Test match level (average 29.09). Probably the biggest spinner of the ball I have ever seen, he created a new Test record in his final Test against Australia in 1975–76 when he captured his 308th wicket. Raymond Illingworth (England) and Ashley Mallett (Australia) were good, but not in the Gibbs class.

But who to pair with him? There were three contenders: Shane Warne (Australia), Derek Underwood (England) and Abdul Qadir (Pakistan).

Take Warne. He is a magnificent bowler, one of the biggest

spinners of the ball around at the moment, with superb control of leg-spin, the flipper and the googly.

I have seen two prime examples of Warne's prodigious skill at first hand. At Sydney in November 1995, when Australia were playing Pakistan, Warne was bowling to Bishen Ali in the last over of the day. As Warne prepared to send down the final delivery, Ali, for reasons best known to himself, apparently tried to waste time. He took an eternity to settle into his crease, then he would stand up again, chunter at the fielders clustered round the bat, have another long look round, and resume his stance. He did this several times, and when he was finally ready, Warne said to me, 'Dickie, I'm going round the wicket.' He pitched the ball a yard outside the leg stump. Ali thrust his left pad at it. The ball turned, passed between his legs and hit middle stump. It was an unbelievable delivery and Warne could be excused for his unrestrained war-dance of delight.

There was, perhaps, an even better delivery during a Test in England in 1994 when Warne was bowling from my end to Mike Gatting. Again the Aussie ace pitched the ball a yard outside leg stump. Gatting played at it, but it turned almost square, beat him all ends up and clean bowled him middle and off. Gatting could not believe it. He just stared down the pitch, then back at his stumps, in amazement.

Some time afterwards I said to him, 'Gatt, if I'd been you I would have kicked that ball away.' I dared not say anything at the time because the poor chap was in a state of shock. It really was a truly remarkable delivery, and I don't think I have ever seen a ball turn so much. That is the quality of the man.

On a turning pitch, however, there was nobody to beat Underwood. He was unplayable in such circumstances. We were brought up in Yorkshire to believe that a slow left-arm bowler could do a better job than a right-arm leg-spinner who bowls googlies, because the left-armer always had the greater control. Underwood was a master of control. He also fired the ball in at speed, almost medium pace, which made him an absolute terror on a turning track. On the other hand, Underwood rarely troubled batsmen on a good pitch, despite the fact that he still varied his flight and bowled an immaculate length.

So we come to Qadir. Maybe he did not turn the ball as much as Warne, and maybe he was not as devastating on a turner as Underwood, but he finally got my vote because his variation was unmatchable. He could bowl leg-spin, googly, top-spin, flipper, all with an impeccable line and length. He, too, had masterly control, which was the essence of his success. In 1982–83 he became the first bowler ever to take 100 wickets in a season in Pakistan, and during the tour of England he was the leading wicket-taker in first-class matches with 57 at an average of 20.82. He got better and better, but sadly had problems with the Pakistan Cricket Board of Control, and was lost to Test cricket at least five years before he should have finished his international career.

As for the fast bowlers, to my mind Dennis Lillee was the best who ever lived. Freddie Trueman still argues with me about this. Fred thinks that he was a better bowler than Lillee, but then, he would. What is, perhaps, more interesting, is that Fred also rates Ray Lindwall as a better bowler than Lillee. I can only say that when I saw Lindwall it was towards the end of his career. It was obvious, even then, that he was one of the truly great fast bowlers of all time. At once graceful and menacing, Lindwall was able to send down an over of six very different balls with perfect disguise, an ability which derived from an exemplary action, with a run-up so smooth that someone once described it as 'being pulled on wheels by a wire'. Maintaining his rhythm as he gathered pace he would leap into his delivery stride, and, with a classic sideways action, send the ball on its lethal way.

Lindwall in full flow made for a thrilling spectacle, no doubt about that.

He took exactly half his Test wickets against England, and it was in this country that his skill blossomed. He relished the damper atmosphere of Britain which gave the ball more chance to swing. This was particularly evident in 1948 when, in partnership with Keith Miller, he produced some devastating performances. Alec Bedser described him as 'a fast bowler with a medium pacer's precise control'.

He was a modest man who once said, 'If you believe only half of what you read about me, I must have been a miraculous player, and I wasn't.' He could, however, be rather bluff, as on the occasion during 1948, so the story goes, when Len Hutton asked Keith Miller to introduce him to the great man. Hutton had batted against him often, but, surprisingly, they had never met off the pitch.

Miller assured Hutton that Lindwall thought the world of him and encouraged the Yorkshireman to go over and talk to Lindwall. Hutton did so, but returned moments later looking somewhat downcast. Asked what had happened Hutton reported, 'He said he was sick of the sight of me when I was batting against him and told me to bugger off.'

'There,' said Miller, 'I told you he admired you.'

For me there was just one slight flaw in Lindwall. I always thought he had a bit of a slinger's action. Lillee, for me, just had the edge over his fellow countryman.

Dennis played hard, of that there can be no doubt, but he is also a very friendly character, and whenever I go to Australia we always meet up, have a meal and a drink, and recall the good old days. When he was on the pitch it was no place for the fainthearted, but he always accepted decisions and got on with the game, very much like that other trouble-shooter, Ian Botham. I never had any problems with Lillee, although there was a time at The Oval in 1975 when I thought I might.

Lillee had asked me to change a rather battered ball which, in his opinion, was badly out of shape. I took a quick look at it, handed it back, and told him to complete the over. I could tell he wasn't happy, because his next ball was most unlike him, definitely not up to the standards expected from one of the greatest fast bowlers of all time in a Test match against the old enemy.

He tossed the ball over to his captain, Ian Chappell, and said, 'What can I do with that? I'm a fast bowler, not a miracle worker.' As you can imagine, I have deleted one or two expletives from that particular quote.

Chappell replied, 'Look, Dennis, I realise the ball is out of shape, but just get on with the over, and then I'll have a chat to Dickie about it.'

That did not suit Dennis, either, and he showed his disgust by sending down two good-length, well-flighted off-spinners, indicating in no uncertain terms that this ball could be used only by the slower bowlers.

I just stood there, with a deadpan expression, and said nothing, but when Chappell came up at the end of the over to ask for a better ball, I chuckled, 'I wouldn't change either the ball or the bowler, Ian. He's the best off-spinner I've seen all season.'

Lillee saw the funny side of it, especially when, being the fair and reasonable chap that I am, I immediately changed the ball for the next over.

For me, Lillee was very special. If there has ever been a better fast bowler I would have given all the tea in China to have seen him. He had a beautiful approach to the wicket; stood up in his delivery stride, left knee stiff as a poker; his follow-through was perfection; and his whole action poetry in motion. He had so much control and variation. It was wonderful for me to stand there and watch him.

When he first came over with the Aussies he was just a lad, hair down to his shoulders, and it was all raw aggression. If you talk to him now he will admit that in those days he had no idea where the ball was going. He sprayed it all over the place.

I remember when the Aussies were playing Lancashire at Old Trafford. He was bowling from my end and I spent nearly the entire day calling 'wide, wide, wide'.

Yet that was the start of a wonderful friendship. After that match, as we walked off, he put his arm round me and said, 'I'll tell you something, Dickie, when I come back to England you'll see a completely different bowler.' When he returned in 1975 I could not believe the improvement he had made. The transformation was complete. He had just about everything and went on getting better and better.

He came back after a serious spinal injury, and you have to admire him for that. He sweated blood and worked his guts out to get himself fit again. He admitted to me just how bad his back had been in 1972, but he followed the advice of Dr Frank Pyke, a lecturer in Physical Education at the University of Western Australia, and made a marvellous recovery.

Dennis was also one for having a laugh and a joke, often at my expense. For example, I was preparing to go out to umpire Lancashire's match against the Australian tourists at Old Trafford in 1975 when some of the Aussies pushed their way into my room.

'Hey, I'm not having this,' I barked. 'We're about to start a game of cricket. Get yourselves out of here.' And they did as they were told.

I did my usual last-minute check to see if everything was in place, but when I put my hand in my pocket to see if all my counters were there I felt a strange rubbery object. I pulled it out – it was a snake. Panic-stricken, I hurled it across the room and called for the attendant.

'For goodness sake,' I cried. 'There's a snake in here. Get rid of it.'

I was still feeling all shook-up when lunch arrived. I was ready for the break, if only to steady my nerves. Snakes and I don't see eye to eye. There was a tureen of soup on my plate in the dining room and I was looking forward to it. But when I lifted the cover off, snakes alive, there it was again. I jumped many a mile in the air and ran off shouting, 'There's a snake in my soup.' Somebody yelled, 'Don't tell everybody, Dickie, they'll all want one.'

But I was having none of it. I ran out terrified. When I eventually plucked up courage to return the snake had disappeared and so had my soup. All the players were doubled up with laughter.

'Don't worry, Dickie,' said Lillee, for it was he who had been responsible for the prank on both occasions, 'it was only a rubber one.'

Two years later, when the Aussies were over here again, Lillee had lots of problems at The Oval with the sightscreen at the Pavilion End. It was always difficult there because you had to move it on wheels and everybody seemed to be jumping up in front of it.

I kept shouting to the crowd, 'For goodness sake, please sit down. Then we can get on with the game. You're holding us all up.' And so it went on. Moving the sightscreen here, moving it back, going down to the attendants, appealing to the crowd, and I was getting more than a little fed up with it all.

Suddenly there was a tap on my shoulder. It was Lillee. He took off my white cap, put it on his own head, and started directing the stewards in moving the sightscreens, right there in the middle of a Test match.

That is what has sadly gone out of the game – the fun, the laughter, the spontaneity, the enjoyment. There is such a vast amount of money at stake now that if you smile these days you are in danger of being reported and fined. But having a laugh can help break the tension. It has worked so many times for me.

That great Australian Ian Chappell agrees with me. He once wrote, 'Dickie Bird has this knack. I have seen many times in Test matches when it looked as though all hell was going to be let loose and Dickie came along and calmed it down with a joke and a smile. Before we knew what was happening the Test was rolling along trouble free.'

Lillee went on to bowl in the Lancashire Leagues and learned so much more there, but he once said to me, 'Do you know, Dickie, I would never play county cricket, because seven days a week would take so much out of my body and it would shorten my Test career.' There's a lot in that. He did eventually play county cricket for Northamptonshire, but only after he had finished as a Test player.

New Zealand's Richard Hadlee is second only to Kapil Dev in the list of all-time wicket-takers at Test match level. He had a deceptively easy, graceful approach to the wicket, but bowled both away-swinger and inswinger with devastating accuracy and pace. He bowled right-handed, but batted left, and might well have also come into the reckoning as an all-rounder. His ability with both bat and ball was emphasised in 1983 when he took 21 wickets in the Test series in England at an average of 26.61 and also topped the Test batting averages with 50.16, scoring 301 runs. He was the first New Zealander to capture 200 Test wickets.

'Whispering Death' was the nickname given to Michael Holding. When he ran up on his approach there was scarcely a sound. With other fast bowlers I was always aware of them pounding up behind me, getting closer and closer, until they exploded into action by my side. With Holding it was different. It was so quiet. Just like the calm before a storm. He would glide over the ground, smoothly and noiselessly, until 'whoosh', he rocketed past me at the point of delivery, and the ball arrowed its way through the air at a frightening pace. He first made an impression in England when he toured here in 1976, heading the first-class and Test bowling averages with 55 wickets at 14.38, and 28 wickets at 12.71 respectively.

His West Indian colleague, Andy Roberts, was quite fearsome. He was very quick and had so much control. Batsmen never quite knew what to expect next, and he had them hopping about constantly. Former Australian captain Richie Benaud, now a television summariser, has been quoted as saying that, of his generation, he thought Roberts was the best of all the great West Indian quickies he had seen. Roberts's best season in England was 1974, when he took 119 first-class wickets at an average of 13.62. During the 1976 tour to England he took 28 wickets at an average of 19.17 in five Test matches.

The players I had to discard in the fast-bowling department included Malcolm Marshall, Joel Garner, Courtney Walsh and Curtley Ambrose – all West Indians – Waqar Younis (Pakistan), and John Snow and Bob Willis of England. Not to mention a certain Frederick Sewards Trueman.

Everyone agrees that Fred was one of the game's greatest characters. But he was also a tremendous competitor and a truly great fast bowler. In many ways it was a pleasure for me, and an honour, to have been in the same Yorkshire side. I can't put into words how I feel about that.

It is difficult to compare players of old and players of today, but I would rate Fred up there with the best of them all. I always have a good debate with him about who exactly was the best. When I state my case for Lillee he exclaims, 'Tha what? I thought tha were a friend o' mine.

I can bowl better now, off five paces, than 'e ivver could.'
And he believes it!

Trueman and Lillee had one thing in common. They both
had the benefit of a perfect natural action. I once asked Fred
if he ever had any coaching as a youngster and he told me that
he had not. His natural flair developed without outside help –
or hindrance – in the back streets of a little village just outside
Maltby. That explains why they both had such long careers.
They were born to it. In some ways it was no real effort for
them. They were also true professionals, competing very hard
and giving no quarter. In a sense that is the bond that joins
every Yorkshireman and every Australian. We are alike in so
many ways.

If I was a young fast bowler today I would seek Fred out and
pick his brains over a pint. He knows what he's talking about,
don't let anybody kid you about that.

I have spoken at many dinners with him and there has been
plenty of time to talk over so many things. What people do
not realise is that one of his greatest ambitions was to captain
Yorkshire. I think he would have made a good captain. Indeed,
he did captain Yorkshire to a great victory over the Australians
at Bramall Lane, Sheffield, when Brian Close was unavailable.
There is no doubt he would have liked the job permanently.

Fred always used to go into the visitors' dressing room before
a match started. He did not knock on the door, just threw
it open, stood there, pipe going full blast, and warned the
occupants, 'Now then, lads, I'm 'ere; I'm ready for you lot
today. Could be eight wickets in it for me wi' a bit o' luck.
Oh, aye, there's an owd friend from last season. I remember
'im. Standin' by t' square leg umpire when I bowled 'im if I
remember rightly. That's one of my eight for starters. Anyway
lads, best o' luck. Just remember, I'm waitin' for yer out there
in t' middle.'

The Yorkshire team would walk out on to the field with the two umpires and someone would say, 'Where's Fred?' And there he was, waiting for the opposition's two opening batsmen to come out. He would stand there at the bottom of the pavilion steps and say to them as they came past, 'Don't close t' gate, you won't be long out 'ere.'

If Fred had not missed so many Test matches for England because he upset certain people, he would have broken all wicket-taking records.

He loves to tell the story of a trip to the West Indies when that great side included the likes of Jeffrey Stollmeyer, Alan Rae, Frank Worrell, Everton Weekes, Clyde Walcott and Gary Sobers.

'I'll tell thee summat, lad,' he says, 'I 'ed all on 'em out, caught be'ind, an' given not out, before they 'ed made many runs at all.'

Playing the straight man to perfection I reply, 'Well, that was bad luck, Fred.'

'Aye,' he says, puffing his pipe.

'Did they get many runs in the end?' I persist.

'Oh, aye, 750 for four declared. But they didn't get runs off me tha knows. Couldn't get me away, lad.'

I love him. But I still think Lillee was the better bowler.

When selecting my team I also took fielding into consideration, although one of the best of all in the cover point area has had to be excluded. Derek Randall was in the class of Clive Lloyd, Viv Richards, Colin Bland and David Gower – and he really enjoyed his cricket.

He lived on his nerve ends out there in the middle, though. He was just like a jack-in-a-box. When I was out there umpiring and he was batting it was a sight to behold, what with me with my arms going, tugging at my jacket and white cap, and him jumping about all over the place like a cat on a hot tin roof. They should have set it to music.

But I feel the fielding in my world side is exceptional.

Barry Richards, Greg Chappell, Garfield Sobers, Sunil Gavaskar and Graeme Pollock were all magnificent close-to-the-wicket fielders; Viv Richards was absolutely brilliant in the cover and mid-wicket areas; Michael Holding and Richard Hadlee were supreme in the outfield; and neither Dennis Lillee nor Andy Roberts were slouches when on boundary patrol between bowling stints.

That, then, is my world squad. I would have loved to have been able to stand out there in the middle as umpire while that team was playing. They were all truly great cricketers who gave me and millions more throughout the world so much pleasure.

18

TOP TEST CAPTAINS

URING my career as a player and umpire I have seen a half
century of Test match captains come and go. Some have
been very successful, others have fallen quickly by the wayside,
and one or two were still hanging on when I decided to take my
retirement from the international scene.

The full list of the fifty Test captains during my time as an
umpire is as follows:

Australia: Ian Chappell, Greg Chappell, Graham Yallop,
Allan Border, Kim Hughes, Mark Taylor.

England: Raymond Illingworth, Mike Denness, Tony Greig,
Michael Brearley, Mike Gatting, David Gower, Graham Gooch,
Ian Botham, Michael Atherton.

India: Ajit Wadekar, Bishen Bedi, Sunil Gavaskar, Kapil Dev,
Mohammed Azarhuddin, Dulip Vengsakar, Srinavasaraghavan
Venkataraghavan.

New Zealand: Mike Burgess, Bev Congdon, Jeremy Coney,
Glenn Turner, Martin Crowe, John Morrison.

Pakistan: Intikhab Alam, Javed Miandad, Imran Khan, Salim
Malik, Waqar Younis, Wasim Akram, Majid Khan, Zaheer Abbas,
Wasim Bari, Wasim Raja, Mushtaq Mohammed.

South Africa: Kepler Wessels, Hansie Cronje.

Sri Lanka: Dulip Mendes, Vini Ranatunga, Avarinda De Silva.

West Indies: Rohan Kanhai, Clive Lloyd, Vivian Richards,
Richie Richardson, Courtney Walsh.

Zimbabwe: David Houghton, Andy Flower.

Of those fifty, if I had to pick out four as the best I have seen, they would be Raymond Illingworth and Michael Brearley of England, and Ian Chappell and Richie Benaud of Australia.

There are good arguments and strong cases to be made for quite a few of the others. Clive Lloyd, of the West Indies is an example, although he was fortunate in having such a great side under him from 1975 onwards, when they were, without doubt, the best in the world. Their success owed as much to supreme individual talent as to Lloyd's powers of leadership. The same applied to Vivian Richards, who took over from Lloyd. His team hardly needed a captain. The most difficult part of the job was that of tossing up and deciding whether to bat or field.

However, one gift that Lloyd had was to keep all the players from the different islands together as a unit in the dressing room – the Barbadians, Antiguans, Trinidadians, Jamaicans. There had always been intense inter-island rivalry and jealousies, which Lloyd, who was from Guyana, cleverly kept the lid on and thus allowed the natural talent to flourish.

Imran Khan, of Pakistan, was very much in the same mould, and did a superb job in welding all the different sects into a united team. He kept the team from bickering amongst themselves, which had always been a problem, and they developed into a very fine side indeed. Before Imran took over, whenever I had stood at matches involving Pakistan, as I looked around me I always had the feeling that there must be ten captains on the field, because each player would be putting in his ten penn'oth. Imran put a stop to all that, which is why he was so successful. There was only one captain, one leader, one man in charge – and that was Imran Khan.

I also rate Australia's Mark Taylor very highly as a captain. I saw him start, and he was still holding the job down at the beginning of 1997, although coming under increasing pressure as the performances of the team dipped below the levels expected, and he himself hit a very lean spell with the bat, finding runs very hard to come by.

I admire Taylor all the more for the way he has come through so much criticism. He was absolutely slated in the Australian papers. There were not only knives in his back, but in his stomach as well. For him to fight back and score a century in the first Test at Edgbaston showed tremendous character. Anyone else would have cracked. But not Mark. And that's the measure of the man.

However, Taylor retained the respect of the players, who would jump over the pavilion for him, and there is no doubt that he has done a tremendous job for Australian cricket, and also the game at international level. He will not tolerate dissent by his players. He tells them always to accept the umpires' decisions: when they have been given out they must go straight back into the pavilion. As an umpire I appreciate such a wonderful attitude, and I remain a big admirer of his.

Another man for whom I have a great deal of respect at the highest level in the game is Richie Richardson, of the West Indies. I always found him the perfect gentleman, and, like Taylor, he also did a lot of good in international cricket by insisting that it was always played in the right spirit. Sadly, he failed to earn the respect of his players, which I found very, very sad. In many ways they let him down.

Ajit Wadekar was another fine captain. When he led India in the early 1970s they recorded a series victory against every other cricketing nation in the world – a marvellous achievement. Wadekar became such a hero that they built a statue to him in Bombay. His record was exceptional, but even he was eventually stripped of the captaincy. All good things come to an end, and no one can go on for ever. The best merely survive that much longer.

It was difficult to leave Wadekar out of my top four, and the same goes for Australia's Allan Border, who was a great competitor with a wonderful never-say-die spirit,

Another Pakistan captain I rated was Mushtaq Mohammed, a fine cricketer in his own right. An all-rounder, he was a first-class batsman and bowled leg-spin and googlies. He played county cricket for Northamptonshire for a time, and, bowling from my end to Peter Graves of Sussex in one game, he sent down one of the most remarkable deliveries I have seen. Everyone talks of Australian leg-spinner Shane Warne as exceptional, and I have seen at first hand what that young man is capable of, but this ball from Mohammed more than matched anything that Warne has produced. He pitched the ball so far outside the off stump that I was going to call a wide. Then it turned. It was his leg-spinner, but an off-spinner to the lefthander, and it came so far back that it knocked the middle stump out of the ground.

I was so amazed that I could not help but jump up in the air and shout, 'Mushy, that was a ball of magic. A magic ball, Mushy.' He still talks about it to this day, and when I saw Shane Warne bowl Mike Gatting with a similar delivery in more recent times, memories of that Mushy magic came flooding back to me.

Sunil Gavaskar earned himself a place in the record books when he was responsible for the first – and possibly the last – known instance of a haircut stopping play in a Test match. This particular one took place at Lord's. Gavaskar kept complaining that his hair was falling into his eyes and hampering his run-making, and finally he turned to me in desperation and asked, 'Have you got a pair of scissors, Mr Dickie?'

Like all umpires, I invariably take a pair out to the middle with me, so I got them out of my pocket and cut off the offending locks with a gusto that left Gavaskar looking a trifle stunned. Seeing all the hair round our feet and gingerly feeling the top of his head to see if I had left any on at all, he reflected, 'Seems I won't have to go to the barber's again this summer.' I had given him a good, old-fashioned short back and sides, but at least he could see more clearly.

Bishen Bedi, who captained India, was another overseas player who turned out for Northamptonshire in the county championship. As well as being a good leader, he was one of the great slow left-arm bowlers, whose variation and flight were out of this world. There was no one who could match him for that.

He was also a very nice man, although I did manage to upset him during a game between Hampshire and Northants at Bournemouth. In those days umpires had to go into the visitors' dressing room to shower. I waited until I thought all the players had changed, and went in. There on the changing-room bench was Bedi's turban. Noticing that my shoes were rather dusty I decided to give them a bit of a polish, using the turban to do so.

I was rubbing away merrily when the shower curtain opened and out strode a very irate Indian – Bishen Bedi. I am not quite sure what he said, because he jabbered away nineteen to the dozen in his native tongue, but I gathered from his manner and expression that he did not entirely approve of my actions.

Greg Chappell also caught me in the shower in the Australian dressing room at The Oval after I had given him out caught. It had not been an easy decision. Chappell had played at an outswinger from Chris Old, jamming his bat hard into the ground as he did so. The noise of bat on ground drowned out all other sounds, but I was certain contact had been made with the ball, and up went the finger as players appealed for the catch.

So when Chappell approached me in the shower I feared the worst. He's going to have a go at me about that catch, I thought. He obviously didn't think he got a touch.

However, Chappell shook his head, grinned, and said, 'Damn you, Dickie, I thought I'd get away with that one.'

That was one decision I was thankful to get right, but Mike Denness made a wrong one when he captained England against Australia at Edgbaston in 1975, and it cost him his job.

In those days, once the game had started, the pitch was left to the elements during the day, being covered only overnight, so there was always the possibility that you could get caught on a sticky wicket. When Denness won the toss it was therefore surprising to find him putting the Australians in to bat. Why, I simply do not know. One theory is that there was cloud cover that morning and he thought the ball was going to swing. That he may have been advised by his selectors to insert the Aussies was another possible explanation.

Whatever the reasoning behind the decision, it backfired on Denness with a vengeance. The Aussies scored well over 300, and, with their last pair at the wicket just before lunch on the second day, England's opening batsman, John Edrich, who was fielding at the side of me at square leg, remarked, 'We're going to get caught on a helluva sticky wicket here, Dickie. Just look at those clouds ready to roll over. They're as black as the ace of spades. There's going to be an almighty storm, you mark my words.'

Sure enough, just as the last man got out, the heavens opened and pretty soon Edgbaston was awash. When the rain eventually abated the groundstaff did a magnificent job in making the pitch playable again. Tommy Spencer and I helped them to lash sawdust all over and play finally restarted at a quarter to four.

I said to Ian Chappell, the Australian captain, as we walked out, 'I've seen Birmingham when it's rain affected. England could be all out by the close of play.'

He just laughed at me. 'Come on, Dickie, don't be daft. It's not as bad as all that.'

At close of play England were 69 for 9. Lillee had taken 6 for 12 from my end in an unbelievable spell, helped, of course, by the pitch. Edrich played one of the finest knocks I have seen in a Test match, despite scoring only 37. In the circumstances, with the ball flying about all over the place from Lillee and Thomson, it was a superb piece of batting.

I was one of the first to congratulate him.

'Great knock, lad,' I told him. 'But, you know, Lillee wouldn't have got all those wickets if I hadn't told him how to bowl in those conditions. He were bowling far too short, so I told him to pitch 'em up.' Funny thing is, Edrich didn't seem too impressed!

On the other hand, Graham Gooch, playing in his first Test, got two noughts. England never recovered from that first innings disaster and the Aussies went on to win easily.

I had seen it coming, knowing that when it was rain affected, Edgbaston could be virtually unplayable. Yet I had never seen the ball swing there under overcast skies, as England apparently thought it would when the decision was made to give the Australians first use of the pitch. If I knew these things, why did Denness and his advisers not know them as well?

At the end of the match the England selectors sat down to appoint the captain for the remainder of the series. Denness got the chop – and that's how Tony Greig took over.

A lot of people blamed Denness for putting the Australians in, although he should not have to take all the flak. I firmly believe that he was under a lot of pressure to make that decision because it was thought that the ball would swing. He was not to know that storm clouds would gather the following day to wash away not only his chances of winning the game, but also his career as England captain.

Greig was therefore the captain when Clive Lloyd brought the West Indies to England the following year, which was when Greig, too, was guilty of an enormous blunder. Before the series started he said in a *Sportsnight* interview on television that he would make the West Indians 'grovel'.

It was a most unfortunate choice of words, and, in any case, I thought he was very foolish to make any kind of criticism of the tourists which might upset them, because they had four cannons ready to fire at the England team – Holding, Roberts, Garner and Croft – while Greig could call on only peashooters in his attack, apart from Bob Willis, who although a very good fast bowler, was certainly not as feared as the Caribbean quartet.

What Greig said in full context was, 'If the West Indians are on top they are magnificent. If they are down they grovel. And, with the help of Brian Close and a few others, I intend to make them grovel.' Greig admitted that he knew it was a controversial thing to say, and that he could easily be proved wrong, but that is what he felt.

I checked on the definition of the world 'grovel' in the *Oxford English Dictionary*, which says, 'To lie prone, humble oneself, often in the dirt or dust; abject; low; base.'

Such a statement was therefore bound to create fury in the West Indian ranks, and it must have added thousands to the attendance at all five Tests, as nearly all the West Indian supporters who could possibly afford it turned out to see Greig's words rammed back down his throat.

I do not for one moment think that Greig meant the remark in as insulting a way as my dictionary definition suggests. Most people were of the opinion that England had no chance against Clive Lloyd's side, and I believe Greig was merely trying to inject some confidence into his own players and fire them up. I am certain he was not being racist, either, because he has never been like that. It was, however, unfortunate that the words should have come from the lips of a man speaking in a South African accent, captain of England or not.

Next day Alec Bedser, Chairman of the England Selectors, defended Greig, saying that it was totally unfair to take the word 'grovel' out of context. What Greig meant, claimed Bedser, was that he was going to do his best to beat the West Indies, and he had merely been instilling the right attitude into his players.

Clyde Walcott, the West Indies tour manager, would not be

drawn, and was quite philosophical when questioned about the England captain's remarks. 'If Greig cares to make comments about us, it is up to him. I am not concerned. It seems to me that this is just another of those psychological moves – I will not call it warfare – that are made before a big match.'

As it turned out, the West Indies did anything but grovel. The series went very much as expected with a 3–0 win for the tourists, culminating in a massive 231 run triumph at The Oval, where I saw one of the best spells of sustained fast bowling I have ever witnessed at Test level.

On a flat pitch, which was beautiful to bat on, Michael Holding repeatedly beat the English batsmen by sheer pace through the air. He took 14 wickets for 149 runs in that Test – a remarkable feat. Had he produced that kind of performance at Lord's – a Test he had missed through injury – it would have been understandable, because conditions were favourable for pace. The Oval, however, was a batsman's paradise.

One of Holding's victims in the second innings just happened to be the beleaguered Tony Greig. As the England captain walked out through the members' enclosure and on to the grass, Holding turned to me and said, 'Dickie, I can do this man Greig for a pastime.'

I replied, 'Michael, I have noticed that throughout the series.'

Greig reached the middle, took leg stump guard off me, looked round, and set himself to face the first ball. In came Holding to bowl a medium-pace half-volley which pitched on the line of off stump. Greig leaned into the ball, head and shoulder nicely over the line, leg to the pitch of it, and dismissed the delivery imperiously for four. It was a truly handsome-looking shot and all the English supporters leaped to their feet chanting, 'Greig, Greig, Greig.'

As the ball was returned from the crowd to Holding, he

walked past me polishing it vigorously, chuckling ominously, 'Dickie . . .'

I said, 'Yes, man?'

'Get ready. Get ready for this ball.' The expression on his face filled me with apprehension.

Holding walked back many a mile, turned, then set off on that flowing run of his, faster and faster, until he exploded into action right beside me and released a delivery as quick as anything I have seen. I was frightened to death just standing there watching as it rocketed towards the England captain.

Greig had developed a habit of standing with his bat poised in the air as the ball was being bowled. The bat was still on its way down as the leg and middle stumps went cartwheeling past the startled wicket-keeper on their way towards the boundary. It was an absolutely magnificent yorker, and Greig never saw it.

Now it was the turn of the West Indian supporters to celebrate. They threw their Bacardi bottles and Coca-Cola cans all over The Oval, and they were so jubilant that they streamed on to the pitch. One big chap, magnificently attired and obviously with more than two 'a'pennies to rub together, came up to me and put his arms around me.

I stood there nervously, wondering, what my next move should be.

The big man said, 'Mr Dickie Bird, professor of cricket.'

'That's me, my friend,' I replied.

He put his hand in his pocket and pulled out a wad of fivers and tenners, peeling off fifty quid's worth. He said, 'I want you to give this fifty pounds to Michael Holding for bowling Greig.'

I said, 'Thank you very much, man,' and stuffed the notes into my back pocket.

That fifty pounds was safely invested into the Halifax Building Society. I have seen Holding many times since that day, and I have said nothing to him about that money. I am not going to, either, because it has made me a bob or two through the years. I only hope Michael doesn't read this book!

Not only was Holding one of the best fast bowlers of his generation, but what many people do not realise is that, as a youngster, he was the 400 metres track champion of Jamaica, and could have gone on to compete in the Olympic Games. However, cricket came first, and he had a glittering career in his chosen sport. Athletics' loss was certainly cricket's gain.

As for Greig, despite his indiscretion during that television interview, which had all sorts of repercussions, and despite his team's heavy defeat in that series, I still rated him as a good captain. He was a keen competitor who always played to win. There was nothing negative about him, his thoughts were always positive, and I admired him for that. He led from the front and never asked others to do what he was not prepared to do himself, which is why his players supported him to the hilt.

Greig certainly had a tough time of it in that 1976 series. Every time he walked out on to the field the West Indian supporters shouted abuse at him from start to finish. He did not have a moment's peace. Yet he was resilient enough to survive to captain England again in the series against India the following year.

All the captains I have mentioned are admirable candidates for my top-four award, but none of them could quite match the qualities of Illingworth, Brearley, Ian Chappell and Benaud. As far as I am concerned they had everything, being tremendous matchwinning competitors. They believed in their own judgement, and were great readers and thinkers of the game, astute in spotting weaknesses in the opposition while playing to their own team's strengths. Each had the full backing and respect of their players, whom they moulded into a unit, and they knew how to get the best out of them.

I believe captaincy is a gift, just as much as natural playing talent is a gift. It is born in you. Some men are born to lead, and those four were of that breed.

Benaud was the only one of the four who captained Test teams before I was appointed to the international panel, but I was privileged to see him in action while I was a player myself, and there is no way that I could leave him out of the top quartet.

He captained Australia in twenty-eight out of the sixty-three Tests in which he played, and never lost a series. What a record that is! He was also the first cricketer, on 6 December 1963, to reach the double of 2,000 runs and 200 wickets in Tests, having since been joined by Gary Sobers, Ian Botham, Kapil Dev, Imran Khan and Richard Hadlee. These days he is a respected television commentator, and I rate him as the best in that sphere, too.

During my playing days another captain I held in high esteem was England's Peter May, who led his country on forty-one occasions, a record which Michael Atherton broke during the 1997 series against the touring Australians. As far as the success rate is concerned, however, there is simply no comparison between the two.

Ian Chappell was captain of the Australian team which toured England in 1972 and 1975, and he had also been a member of the 1968 team. On all three visits he reached 1,000 runs, a feat he achieved six times in Australia. Of his three double centuries the highest was 209 for the Aussies against Barbados at Bridgetown in 1972–73. As well as England, he toured South Africa, the West Indies, India and Sri Lanka, and played in seventy-five Tests from 1964 to 1980. He came out of retirement to play for Packer's World Series Cricket.

Ian once told me that he so admired Ray Illingworth that he used to invite him out for a drink just so that he could pick his brains and learn from him. He was a good pupil, and it's no surprise in the circumstances that both should feature in my top four.

Illingworth was one of the game's outstanding thinkers and theorists. He was incredibly thorough in his knowledge of the strengths and weaknesses of every single opponent, and was a master of field placings and bowling changes. He did not throw bouquets around and was a hard taskmaster, but his methods brought success and earned him the respect of people in the game, who recognised his excellent leadership qualities.

He was a Yorkshire and England all-rounder from 1951 to 1968, completing the 'double' six times. During that period he also appeared with success in twenty-nine Tests, touring Australia in 1962–63. A difference between himself and Yorkshire at the end of 1968 led to his appointment as captain of Leicestershire for the 1969 season, and then an injury to Colin Cowdrey resulted in him captaining England for the six Tests of that year. In 1970 he continued to lead England in the series against the Rest of the World, and the following year he was captain of the MCC team during their tour of Australia and New Zealand. In all, he captained his country in thirty-one out of the sixty-one Tests in which he played up to 1973.

Brearley took a lot of stick, particularly from the Press, who claimed that he was not a good enough batsman, and while it may be fair to say that he commanded a place in the Test team more for his flair as a leader than for his batting, he was a far better batsman than a lot of people gave him credit for. He managed 1,000 runs in a season on eleven occasions, going on to top 2,000 one year, and he hit a marvellous 312 not out for the MCC against North Zone in Peshawar in 1966–67. Both his double centuries were also for the MCC abroad.

It is not always the most prolific runmakers who make the best captains, and Brearley was an exceptional captain in thirty-one of the total of thirty-nine Tests in which he played, including the overseas tours of 1966–67, 1977–78, 1978–79 and 1979–80. If there was any deficiency in the run-gathering department – and

287

I question that – he more than made up for it by the way he led the side.

If there is one criticism I can make of Brearley it is that I was not always sure what he was talking about. He complained that I was neurotic; said I was the kind of man who had to keep going back to the front door to make certain he had locked it. Anyone who knows me will tell you that I am not a bit like that . . .

I also remember Mike saying to me one evening something along the lines of, 'Dickie, there is no such thing as an absolute certainty, only the certainty that befits the subject. What is certain or accurate for a carpenter is not certain or accurate for a geometer.'

All I can say to that is that when it comes to giving lbw decisions, I have to be absolutely certain, whatever Mike Brearley might think, and there have been times when he has had me to thank for that!

It is a crying shame that we have not been able to get Brearley interested in coming back to help shake English cricket out of its lethargy and recapture some of the former glories, because he knows the game inside out. He has a brilliant brain, achieving honours degrees in everything he has undertaken, and he now has his own practice as a highly successful psychoanalyst. Such intelligence and deep knowledge of cricket makes him an ideal candidate for a leading role and it is sad that he has been lost to the game.

If Brearley were available I would make him my supremo of English cricket. I would appoint him as chairman of selectors, very much involved in the coaching side as well, with two good men to assist. He is quite definitely the man for the job. No doubt about it. With Brearley at the helm I am certain that English cricket would soon be lifted out of the Test match doldrums.

19

THIRD UMPIRES, BIG SCREENS AND LIGHT METERS

THE introduction of electronic aids had me seeing red in Hobart, Tasmania. Or not seeing red, to be more accurate.

It was the first morning of the Test match between Australia and Pakistan. I had been travelling for thirty hours and I was still somewhat jet-lagged. Thankfully the first hour passed quite uneventfully, but then Australia lost a wicket and David Boon came in to bat.

He was going along nicely when there was a call for a quick single. Boon, not the fastest between the wickets, struggled to make his ground. An appeal went up and immediately I thought, 'That's out.' But I felt obliged to go to the third umpire which I did. I waited for the decision – a green light for not out, a red light for out. Nothing happened.

I thought to myself, 'What's going on?' There were about 38,000 in the ground, a full house, and I could hear them all shouting, 'Come on, Dickie, get on with it.'

Just then a light flashed up on the scoreboard, but it wasn't red, or green. It was white. I shouted up to the little room where the third umpire was sitting.

'What on earth does that mean?'

'It means the system has broken down and the decision is left to you,' came the reply.

'You must be joking,' I said. Anyway, I went back to the middle.

'That's out, David,' I said. And off David Boon went, no problem. But I thought, 'I hope I've got that right.' When I went in at lunchtime I was told that the television people had played it back several times and he was out – by six inches. It was a good job I did get it right, because if I had got it wrong with the pictures being shown all over the world . . . oh, dear me! And there was I, in my innocence, thinking that electronic aids were supposed to help.

Then there was the time when South Africa were playing in a one-day international series in Pakistan. South Africa were getting into a position to win the game and there was a run-out appeal which was referred to the third umpire. Again red and green buttons were in operation. This time the third umpire pressed the wrong one. The batsman, David Richardson, was well in but the out button was pressed by mistake.

After the match the third umpire went up to Richardson and said: 'I am so sorry, Mr Richardson, I do apologise. I pressed the wrong button. I pressed the out button instead of the in button. You should have been in. And I pressed out. I do apologise, a thousand times.'

And Richardson replied, 'It's a bit late to tell me this now, after the match.'

It was another very crucial decision.

However, I do think that generally the system has been a tremendous help for close run-outs, close stumpings and hit wickets. If you ask any umpire in the world he will tell you that the close run-out is the most difficult decision to make when it is purely down to the human eye.

The third umpire can also probably help with line decisions on the boundary. If ever there is any doubt in my mind, I run from the centre of the field ninety yards or so – no way can you tell from there – and I look the player straight in the eye and I say, 'Young man, I want you to tell the truth. Did you catch that ball fairly inside the boundary, or did you touch the rope? I am a Christian and a churchgoer, and I want you to be honest with me. The good Lord is looking down on us and I don't want you to tell any lies.'

That seems to work, although if I am honest with myself I think that possibly one or two of them might have told a little fib from time to time. The good Lord only knows.

However, I would not like to see the electronic aids intrude any further. I certainly would not like them to be used for lbw, caught behind and bat-pad decisions. So many things have to be taken into consideration for those three types of dismissal.

Take the lbw decisions, for example. Every lbw involves angles and opinion. You have to take into account the point from which the bowler delivers the ball – the return crease or the back line; how much did it do off the seam; how much did it swing in the air. A batsman may be in front of his stumps and look plumb on the television pictures, but when everything is taken into consideration the ball could well be missing the leg stump by eighteen inches by the time it has finished its line.

The cameras have to be in the right places. This is what Richie Benaud and all the commentators have said. I think they are too high. The only man in the right position to judge is the umpire. Some people think that the wicket-keeper is perfectly placed, but he is not. There is a moment when the wicket-keeper is blinded and in the worst position to make judgement, not the best. It has to be down to the umpire.

Even then, he must be a hundred per cent certain that the batsman is out. That is how I have always worked and it is the only fair way. Any benefit of doubt has to be given to the batsman. I like to see a bowler get close to the stumps, bowl wicket to wicket and make the ball hold a straight line. Then the bowler has a chance of an lbw. When the bowler is bowling wide of the return crease, the ball is nipping back off the seam and the batsman is playing forward, he has no chance as far as I am concerned.

People have claimed that I am a 'not-outer' when it comes to lbw decisions, but I counter by telling them that I was once involved in a world record of lbw dismissals. There were seventeen of them in a Test match I umpired between the West Indies and Pakistan in Port of Spain in April 1993. Mind you, I only gave six. My colleague, Steve Bucknor, was responsible for the rest.

One player who always complained that I never gave him any lbws was Jim Cumbes, the former Lancashire, Surrey, Worcestershire and Warwickshire bowler, who also played in goal for West Brom and Aston Villa at football. We always got on well together – still do for that matter – but there was one game in particular when he was feeling more than a little peeved because I had turned down three very strong lbw appeals against Graham Roope.

After the third appeal, from the sixth and last ball of the over, Jim wandered back dejectedly towards me to take his sweater, a resigned expression on his face.

'When are you going to give me an lbw, Dickie? I don't think I've had one off you in the whole of my career.'

So I tried to explain to him where he was going wrong.

'Jimmy, listen to me lad. They were all nip-backers, and tha' can't get lbws wi' nip-backers. Tha' should know that. Now, if yo' were to hold one up, then you've got a chance.'

'Huh,' he muttered, nodding in the direction of the huge gasometer next to The Oval ground. 'I reckon if he was in front of that bloody gasometer you wouldn't give him out, Dickie.'

'Not if it were a nip-backer, Jimmy lad, not if it were a nip-backer,' I agreed.

Unless the batsman and the ball are wired up to some complicated electronic eye system, catches at the wicket from slight edges cannot be settled with complete certainty. Anyone thinking back to a particular incident in the West Indies v England Test at Edgbaston in 1973 will, I am sure, agree on that. The tourists were convinced that Geoff Boycott should have been given out when they appealed for a catch behind by Deryck Murray off the bowling of Keith Boyce. I was at square leg and in no position to pass an opinion. All I do know is that Arthur Fagg, one of the greatest umpires there has ever been, ruled in Boycott's favour and never wavered.

The television people showed the incident time and again. I watched it with the recording slowed down so much that the ball was barely moving, but it was still impossible to be positive. Arthur relied on his experience both as an umpire and top-class batsman.

However, as far as the changes related to electronic aids are concerned I think they have generally been for the better, but there is a danger. I have always been a big believer in accepting the umpire's decision. Accept it and get on with the game; in the end it evens itself out. People may argue about whether the umpire was right or has dropped a king-sized clanger. That's fair enough. It's part of the game. But there is a point beyond which it is dangerous to proceed and I believe we have reached that point. If we go further we will be taking something away from the umpire and his authority will be undermined to an unacceptable degree. The umpire has always been part and parcel of the game and it would be very sad if he was relegated to a secondary role by pieces of electronic gadgetry, no matter how sophisticated.

It could happen; already umpires are beginning to lose confidence in making decisions. Take the case of Tony Clarkson. He is a Yorkshireman who played county cricket for Yorkshire and then went to Somerset. He is now on the first-class umpires' list, but had a nightmare baptism to his career in the middle.

His first match was a televised Benson & Hedges Cup tie at Edgbaston. Warwickshire were playing Leicestershire and there was an appeal for a run-out involving Leicestershire's Ben Smith. As Clarkson saw it, Smith was out. That would have been his decision had there been no recourse to an electronic aid. But he decided to go to the third umpire, Mervyn Kitchen, for confirmation. Kitchen came back to him and said, 'I am very sorry, Tony, but I do not have a clear enough picture. I cannot help you. The decision is down to you.' So Clarkson said, 'Well, what decision can I give now?' And Kitchen replied, 'There is only one thing you can do. Give him not out.'

When they eventually played the incident back on television from another angle it showed that Smith was well out, as Clarkson had initially thought.

In the next match Clarkson came to join me for another Benson & Hedges tie, this time between Worcestershire and Yorkshire. The television cameras were there again. There was another run-out appeal, a close decision that was down to Tony. He gave not out. When we came off he asked the third umpire if he could have helped had he gone to him for a decision. He was told no because, once again, the picture was not clear enough; that was twice in successive matches for Tony. Thankfully, this time later television action replays proved that his decision had been right.

There was also the famous incident in Cape Town, when South Africa played England in the final Test. This time

Graham Thorpe was the batsman involved in a close run-out call. South African umpire David Orchard immediately gave Thorpe not out, apparently forgetting that the third umpire was available. It is easily done in the heat of the moment. It has happened to me in a Test match, England v Australia at Headingley, when I gave Mark Waugh out on a run-out appeal. There would have been all hell let loose had I got it wrong.

That time in Cape Town the South Africans would not accept the decision. They kept on appealing until Orchard repeated, 'Not out.' Hansie Cronje, the South African captain, began pressurising the umpire further, which I think was wrong. Consequently Orchard decided to go to his colleague, Steve Randell, and consult with him.

'Look,' he said, 'I think I ought to go to the third umpire.' He then went to Graham Thorpe and said, 'Do you mind if I ask the third umpire for a decision?'

'Mind? Of course I mind,' Thorpe replied. 'You have said not out twice, quite clearly. You have made your decision. You should not allow yourself to be pressurised.'

But Orchard did go to the third umpire and was told that Thorpe had failed to make his ground, so he gave the batsman out. It was the right decision in the end, after all the palaver. Thorpe was clearly out. But I do feel that, looking back – and he has admitted this – David should have stuck by his original decision. He had said not out and that should have been it. He would have been admired for sticking to his guns. But he changed his mind as a result of pressurisation and that cannot be tolerated.

People may wonder how we communicate from the middle with the third umpire in his little room. These days we are equipped with a walkie-talkie which is clipped to a pocket. So, in addition to making the signal for a playback decision and being shown the red or green light for out or not out, as the case may be, we can also talk to the third umpire if necessary. His decision, by the way, is based on either BBC or Sky television pictures which are replayed to him by the producer.

Those walkie-talkies are usually no hindrance to us, but I certainly regretted having one during a match between England and the West Indies in 1995 at Headingley. I raced to my position to make judgement on a run-out at the same time as Jimmy Adams was racing in from mid-on to field the ball. We collided and I came off worse; after all, he is a strapping six-footer. I fell to the ground, landing on my walkie-talkie. I can still feel the bruise to this day.

When I was a young hopeful playing with Barnsley in the Yorkshire League against Sheffield United at Shaw Lane, I was involved in a run-out with a certain Geoff Boycott. But then, who hasn't been?

There were 3,000 people in the ground. We had bigger gates in those days than Barnsley Football Club, who were struggling in the fourth division; and we had a very good side. On this occasion I was taking strike. I was on 49 not out and set for the biggest collection ever taken at Shaw Lane when I reached my 50. I drove the ball to long-on for a comfortable two.

'Come one,' I shouted to Boycott, and set off. I was nearly at his end when I realised that he had not budged. He was standing there, leaning on his bat, a wicked glint in his eye, and as I reached him he said, 'Keep on running lad, right into the pavilion.' And there I was, run out for 49 by twenty-two yards! No need for any electronic aid there.

Then, of course, there is the big screen. I am totally against that. Every decision an umpire makes during a Test match – that's five days for six and a half hours every day – is scrutinised on the big screen. Now, you are going to get wrong decisions, umpires are far from infallible. It can easily cause problems in the crowd if they see clearly on the big screen that a decision has gone against their team. It puts even more pressure on the men in the middle.

Say there's an lbw shout. They all go up, even the chap at long leg. You say not out. The incident is immediately replayed on the big screen, with forty-odd thousand people in the ground looking at it, as well as the players on the field. If the umpire seems to have got it wrong you can see the players shaking their heads and thinking, 'We've got a right Charlie here.' They can so easily lose faith in that umpire and begin to question every decision. If they start to appeal for everything, shouting and bawling, and it's shown umpteen times on the action replay, it merely holds up the play unnecessarily. People these days pay far too much money to watch cricket anyway without having to suffer additional stoppages. Yet the authorities tell me that the crowds enjoy watching all the action on the big screen. I don't see how they can, although I have to admit that as they watch that recording up there you can hear them all start oohing and aahing.

I never look at it. I've made my decision and that's it. I've been umpiring for twenty-eight years and I have never seen an action replay of one of my decisions. I never watch myself umpiring whether on the edited highlights at night or on the Nine O'clock News. If I did, I would probably have gone crackers by now.

The problem is that, in this day and age, because of the vast amounts of money which have come into sport, everyone wants perfect decisions and that is an impossibility.

Sky Television have tried, many times, to have umpires wired up for sound. Thank goodness the Test and County Cricket Board have refused. It is bad enough as it is, because there is usually a microphone fitted into the foot of the middle stump and we have to be very careful what we say, especially in the heat of the moment.

One of the first times I came across this was in the World Cup in Lahore. I kept kicking dust over it so that it couldn't pick up any sound. The technicians kept cleaning it during lunch and tea and in the intervals between innings. They just couldn't understand how so much dust could keep getting in there. I didn't tell them.

There is also a camera fitted into the middle stump to provide a further insight for the televiewers. I've nothing against that. It does no harm and provides an interesting shot. Those cameras, incidentally, are worth thousands and thousands of pounds. Umpires are told to be sure to guard the middle stump so that nobody pinches it. Our own safety doesn't appear to be taken into account, but then I suppose we're not worth that much money.

Perhaps the best innovation as far as electronic aids are concerned is the light meter. This has been a tremendous help, particularly to yours truly. I have been known to have the occasional problem with bad light. Indeed, I get down on my knees every morning and every night, put my hands together and say, 'Please, dear Lord, no bad light.'

Light meters were first introduced in 1978 largely as a result of an unfortunate incident at Trent Bridge in the second Test, when New Zealand were beaten by an innings and 119 runs. The umpires, David Constant and Tom Spencer, had a dilemma on the Saturday morning, with light drizzle falling from grey skies. They knew they might have to come off because of the light, but they were also aware that the public were demanding action.

They elected to play, but after only two balls had been bowled they realised that conditions were unsatisfactory, so they brought the players off. Under the regulations the pitch could not be covered until play had been abandoned for the day and the consequence was that New Zealand eventually had to bat on a wet surface some four hours later. They were dismissed for 120 and understandably felt badly done by as they followed on.

A big debate followed, during which a photographer just happened to mention that, according to his light meter, the conditions when play was proceeding in the afternoon had been exactly the same as when they started in the morning. That comment planted the seeds in some official minds. Why not issue light meters to umpires?

Barrie Meyer and I were given a brief lecture on how the meters worked by Patrick Eagar, the famous photographer who specialises so brilliantly in cricket, and were told to use them in the third Test at Lord's. Not surprisingly, we had five days of beautiful sunshine, so the light meters never came out of our pockets.

But crowds still have a go at me when I do get the light meter out.

'Put it away, Dickie,' they yell. There is no arguing with it, though, or with those big lights on the scoreboards which send the message shining clearly to the spectators. When the light starts to fade one bulb comes on. As it gets worse, two bulbs light up, then three, then four. When you get five, it is just about pitch black.

Nevertheless people do take some convincing. If it chucks it down with rain they are disappointed, but they understand. If it's a case of bad light, that upsets them, because they have paid good money and they want to see some action. If they bring their families it can cost a fortune, so their reaction is understandable.

I have, however, seen some wonderful games in conditions which a computer would have ruled as unfit. The best example was the famous Gillette Cup semi-final between Lancashire and Gloucestershire at Old Trafford. We finished at nine o'clock when it was really dark. The moon shone bright and clear in the night sky, as did the lights on Warwick Road station, but nobody seemed to care. It was one of the greatest games I have ever umpired and it seems like only yesterday.

The outcome of that semi-final emphasised an interesting point which not many people really appreciate. It is often more difficult for the fielding side in very bad light, for once the ball is hit, no one is really sure where it has gone. It might be in the air, but the chances of a catch are remote. The bowler has to hit the stumps to be sure of a wicket in such circumstances.

All these questions are in the mind of an umpire as he seeks to make a decision with regard to bad light, even when he has the help of the light meter. Can the players pick up the ball clearly? Who is bowling? We have to decide when we think it is too dangerous to continue. If we have spinners operating we don't come off. Obviously with the quicker bowlers, the danger is much more acute. Apart from the batsmen there is the possible danger to fielders to consider, if they are unable to see the ball and it comes quickly and directly at them.

We do try to keep the game going as long as we possibly can. I sometimes take a reading from my light meter, look around me at the gathering gloom, and wonder if my electronic aid has been doctored to keep us out there.

But the danger of someone being hurt always affects our thinking. It was brought home to me by an incident when the West Indies were playing Gloucestershire at Bristol. Syd Lawrence was bowling and the West Indians were offered the light by the umpires. Phil Simmons was batting at the time and he decided to carry on. Unfortunately he got hit a tremendous blow on the side of the head. If he had not been a mere five minutes away from one of the best hospitals in the world for that type of injury he would have been dead.

There was, in contrast, a famous occasion when I had to bring the players off because the light was too bright. It happened in the summer of 1995 when England were playing the West Indies at Old Trafford. The sun was shining on some adjacent greenhouses and it was reflecting on to the stands. All around the ground there was this blinding light. I thought for a minute we were on the road to Damascus. We had to come off because the slip fielders and batsmen could not see the ball. Officials had to cover up the greenhouses with the black sheeting they use for the sightscreens at Sunday League matches.

But that wasn't the end of it. The light began to reflect off the Press box windows at one side of the ground and on to some hospitality boxes at the other end. Again, it was shining into the eyes of the players on the field. It took some time for us to work out where it was coming from. I was featured on the main news that night yelling at the people in the hospitality boxes, who must have wondered what on earth was going on. But they took it in good part.

'Don't worry about it, Dickie,' they shouted back to me. 'Come up and have a beer.' And I could have murdered one!

I always took some stick at Old Trafford, being a Yorkie in the middle of all those Lancastrians I suppose. On another occasion when England were playing the West Indies, as we came off the field a Lancashire supporter was waiting for me, standing grim-faced at the top of the steps by the members' enclosure.

'You're here again, Bird,' he snarled. 'Every time you come to Old Trafford you bring them off. And here you are, bringing them off again. What is it this time, for goodness sake? Bad light?'

'No sir,' I replied, 'it's lunch.'

301

20

NEUTRAL UMPIRES

THERE has been a lot of talk in recent years about neutral umpires, and that has puzzled me. As far as I am concerned every umpire in the world is neutral, by which I mean he does not take the part of one side or the other.

In my experience, when it comes to giving a decision, whether it be a difficult lbw, a catch close to the ground, or a run-out, an umpire never takes into consideration who the batsman is, or what team he is playing for. He gives the decision as he sees it.

So, when the captains of the Test-playing nations called for neutral umpires, what they really sought were independent umpires, those who were free from any perceived allegiance to either of the competing teams.

The general opinion now is that the switch to one independent umpire and a home umpire, as opposed to two home umpires, has been a good thing for Test cricket, because players accept decisions more readily, and it has eliminated any suspicion of bias.

Now there is a move towards two independent umpires, and this will surely be the next step. There is one big drawback, however. My greatest thrill in Test match cricket has been to umpire at Lord's, which I regard as my second home. There is nothing to beat a Lord's Test for atmosphere and a sense of occasion. I do not think it can be beaten in any sporting arena, whether it be football's World Cup, the Olympic Games, or boxing's World Heavyweight Championship.

It is every English umpire's ambition to stand at a Lord's Test. Likewise, it is every West Indian umpire's ambition to officiate at a Test in Bridgetown or Port of Spain; every Pakistani umpire's ambition to stand at Lahore or Karachi; every Australian's to be there in Sydney or Melbourne; every New Zealander in Auckland or Christchurch; every Sri Lankan in Colombo; every Zimbabwean in Harare; every Indian in Calcutta or Bombay.

That ambition, that honour, that delight, of umpiring at the top venue in his own country will be denied every official if the double independent plan comes into play, and it will be a sad, sad day.

Personally, I would like the system to stay as it is, if it was a matter of choice between one independent umpire or two, but most umpires would tell you that they feel the system in which each nation has its own panel of Test officials is the best.

It was former Pakistan captain Imran Khan who led the call for independent umpires, and, with the backing of other captains, he got his way. He believed that there was bias with home umpires. I did not go along with that at the time, and I still think he was wrong.

It is hardly surprising that former England captain Mike Gatting should agree with Imran, after the notorious dust-up he had with Shakoor Rana in Pakistan in the winter of 1987–88. As far as I am concerned, Gatting was wrong to argue with the umpire. I can understand and sympathise with a captain feeling frustrated when he reckons he is getting the rough end of the stick with regard to decisions, but that is no excuse for the kind of finger-jabbing lecture that Gatting gave to Shakoor Rana. He should have accepted the decisions and got on with the game. In the long run these kind of things invariably even themselves out, despite what anyone says to the contrary.

It was certainly a powder-keg confrontation. Reagan meeting Gorbachev was nothing compared to this, so much so that Ian Botham was quoted as saying that if he had been out there he would probably have ended up doing thirty years' hard labour.

What Gatting should have done, if he felt so aggrieved, was mention it in his match report on the umpire at the end of the Test. I think if he could have his time over again, that is what he would do. He did, as a matter of fact, write an apology to Shakoor Rana afterwards, but under duress. He claimed, 'Our self-respect has been taken away by our Board. The only reason they got my apology was because I was ordered to. And the only reason we took the field afterwards was for cricket and the youngsters who are starting the game.'

Gatting scribbled a note which read, 'Dear Shakoor Rana, I apologise for the bad language used during the second day of the Test at Fisalabad [sic]. Mike Gatting.'

Shakoor Rana accepted it, saying, 'That's enough, that's good, that's what I wanted from the start. It could have been done straightaway.' Many observers, however, thought that the apology did not go far enough, and the Press over there remained very critical of Gatting.

Writing in the *Gulf News*, Bikram Vohra summed up the feeling of many of his countrymen as follows:

Pakistan and England went back in the field after a two-day affair that has ensured cricket will never be the same again. I read Mike Gatting's apology, the apology that ostensibly broke the stalemate. Never have I seen a more abysmal display of contriteness. If that litany of block letters scrawled on lined paper of the sort generally used by school children to do their lines for punishment after class constitutes an apology, then there is nothing else one can say.

But really, such a churlish, insincere scribble and Umpire Rana says this is what he wanted in the first instance. It is incredible. To underscore his triumph Shakoor Rana poses with this silly note and allows himself to be photographed, as if he'd attained salvation in sport. I cannot believe that Mr Rana would have taken a stiff stand only to surrender his ground over such a blatantly transparent 'concession' from Gatting.

Surely a principle should be made of sterner stuff. Evidently, there was pressure to capitulate, which situation one can understand, but then it would have been far more salutary not to display that note and just say the apology had been tendered, period. And get on with it. By the exhibition of the sloppy scrawl Mr Rana has, in my mind, lost a major point. Gatting's sulkiness, and the fact that he was allowed to get away with the most unhandsome apology in the world makes a total mockery of the act anyway.

As you can see, feelings were running very high and it was an incident that left a nasty taste. It certainly tarnished the good name of cricket. But it should not have happened. I have always maintained that no player, not even the captain, should dispute an umpire's decision, or decisions, on the field of play. In this instance Shakoor Rana felt he was doing the right thing at the time. Gatting should have accepted it. I have stood with Shakoor Rana in Test matches and he is a good umpire, make no mistake about that.

I once stood with Shakoor Rana in a county match between Essex and Sussex at Ilford early in 1981 at a time when overseas officials were being invited over here to gain experience. Sussex scored 436 for 4 before they declared to take full advantage of the conditions, which were beginning to help the slower bowlers. The Sussex spinners made a good start, including their captain, John Barclay, who, as I watched from square leg, was exchanging words with Shakoor Rana.

It was not really any of my business, so I did not take much notice until Shakoor Rana came marching over to me. 'I am giving this bowler a final warning,' he said. 'He is running on the pitch, and I am not standing for it any longer.'

With that he returned to the bowler's end, where Barclay was busily inspecting the pitch with a puzzled expression on his face.

Seconds later Shakoor Rana was back again. 'I want you to come with me. The bowler does not agree with my ruling, and I cannot report him to the captain, because he is the captain.'

In such circumstances the opinion of the bowler or the square leg umpire is irrelevant, but not one to miss an opportunity to try to pour some oil on troubled waters, I went over to have a look for myself.

'He says I'm running on to the pitch,' complained an indignant Barclay, 'but I'm doing no such thing. Have a look for yourself. Can you see any marks?'

By this time all the players had gathered round, studying the disputed area with eagle eyes. I sensed there could be a bit of bother ahead if I did not handle the situation diplomatically, so I just said to Barclay, 'You've had an official warning. Just accept it and get on with the game. There is no point arguing about it.'

Thankfully Barclay did as I asked, and, to my even greater relief, Shakoor Rana, having made his point, was satisfied with Barclay's bowling – and that of his colleagues – for the rest of the innings.

On that occasion we were, to all intents and purposes, both independent umpires, yet there was still a dispute. The problem is that everyone wants perfect decision-making, and that is impossible. You will never achieve perfection. You can have

A cold and breezy Bristol on the day I showed
Princess Diana my coloured long johns.

Displaying my three World Cup final awards.

Receiving the Yorkshireman of the Year award
from the Earl of Harewood in 1996.

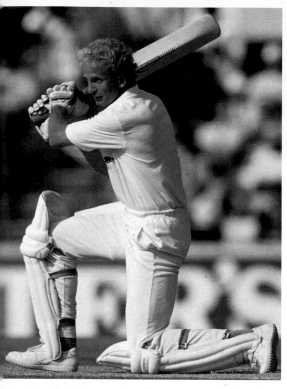

David Gower, summed up in one word – class. He should have gone on playing for England longer than he did.

Dr Ali Bacher, who has done so much for cricket, not only in South Africa, but throughout the world.

Waiting with the West Indians for confirmation of a run-out decision against Michael Atherton. I thought it was out and so I told them – thankfully it was.

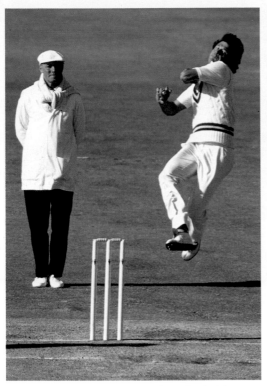

Imran Khan, a great all-rounder who held Pakistan together as captain.

Allan Donald, the fastest bowler in the world today, fires one down at England captain Michael Atherton on South Africa's return to Test cricket at Lord's.

One of the greatest deliveries ever bowled in Test cricket as Shane Warne dismisses Mike Gatting in the 1993 Old Trafford Test between England and Australia. I was umpiring and still couldn't believe the amount it turned.

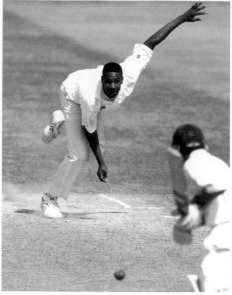

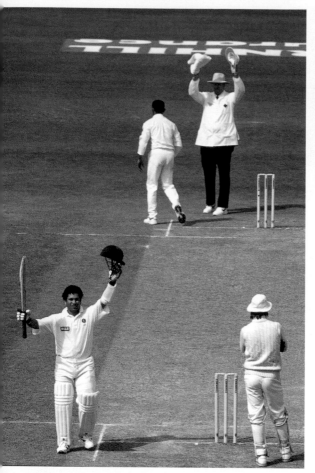

Above: One for the future, nineteen-year-old fast bowler Alex Tudor of Surrey, an England player in the making. Ashley Cowans of Essex is another to watch out for.

Left: Sachin Tendulkar of India is destined, I believe, to score more runs than Brian Lara in Test cricket.

Below: The first over of my final Test and I have to give England captain Michael Atherton out lbw to Indian bowler Srinath.

Above: Anthony McGrath, one of Yorkshire's up-and-coming young prospects.

Right: Another teenager of great potential, Ben Hollioake of Surrey, who has already played for England.

Below: Darren Gough, England's number one strike bowler, has Brian Lara, one of the best batsmen in the world, caught by Alec Stewart.

After my one hundredth international I was invited to dinner at the House of Lords by Lord and Lady Mason, along with friends John and Pat Perry of the Livermead Cliff Hotel in Torquay.

After the 'People of the Year' presentation at the London Hilton in 1996, with recipients Lisa Potts, Captain Mike Lobb and Steven Redgrave.

I was delighted to be awarded an honorary doctorate at Sheffield Hallam University in recognition of outstanding services to cricket.

In the Long Room at Lord's with Godfrey Evans, Lord Cowdrey, Brian Johnston and Colonel John Stephenson, signing copies of Jack Russell paintings.

Over and out. Walking out for my final Test at Lord's as England and Indian players form a guard of honour.

all the electronic aids in the world, but you are still going to get mistakes, and we must all accept that.

The introduction of independent umpires has given me an opportunity to officiate all over the world, which is something I have thoroughly enjoyed. To stand at Tests in different countries, to visit strange cities and towns, has been a marvellous experience.

What I did find a little difficult to come to terms with were the different conditions in other countries. Not just the pitches, but the weather. Any umpire will tell you the same. We had all become so used to umpiring in our own country that it came as a jolt to the system to have to stand in a dust-bowl in temperatures of well over 100 degrees in places like India, Pakistan, the West Indies, Sri Lanka and Australia.

I celebrated my sixtieth birthday when umpiring the series between the West Indies and Pakistan in the Caribbean in April 1993, but by the third Test I felt more like ninety. In that heat. I had done three back-to-back Tests in twenty-one days. To make matters worse, a metal band had camped right outside the umpires' room. The Grimethorpe Colliery Band it was not, and I was brassed off.

I also had to contend with a pitch invasion from a chap with a long, flowing beard wearing a ballgown. He was being chased across the field by another fellow in a frock coat, a very large hat and frogman's flippers. It turned out that they were Gravy and Mayfield, two clowns who operated in front of the disco in the double-decker stand at St John's in Antigua. I thought it was all part of a bad dream. The heat must have got to me. I was hallucinating, that must be it.

To make matters worse I was also hit on the backside by a throw from Keith Arthurton and I had to have treatment from Dennis Waight, the West Indies physio. He had to use some pain-killing spray, which meant that I had to drop my trousers, lift up my umpiring jacket and tuck my shirt out of the way, all at the same time. Well, I got into such a tangle that I let my trousers fall round my ankles and everyone got a glimpse of the Bird underpants. Not a pretty sight. I was certainly caught with my trousers down that day.

Local umpire Clancy Mack took over when I was unable to continue after tea. He turned down an lbw appeal by Waqar Younis against Desmond Haynes, but gave Brian Lara and Keith Arthurton out lbw at the same score. Richie Richardson became another lbw victim. It was then that the local band struck up a refrain of 'Bring back, bring back, oh bring back my Dickie to me . . .'

That series, incidentally, was almost called off. I was sitting at home, bags packed, waiting to fly out when it was flashed up on all the news bulletins that there was a doubt about the series because Wasim Akram the Pakistan captain, Waqar Younis, Aqib Javed and Mushtaq Ahmed had been accused of smoking pot on the beach.

I did not know what to do, so I got in touch with chief executive David Richards at the ICC headquarters at Lord's, and he advised to me go, so I did. When I got there I found the place humming with television crews, radio and newspaper reporters, all clustered round the hotel in Port of Spain waiting for the Pakistan team to arrive.

It was decided to delay the Test for one day while police tried to sort things out with the Pakistan Cricket Board of Control, management and players. On the day the match should have started I was relaxing around the swimming pool with my West Indian colleague Steve Bucknor, the West Indian team and several of the English Press lads, just waiting to see what was going to happen. I honestly thought I would be on the next plane home.

However, late that afternoon word came through that things

had been sorted out, the Pakistan players involved had been cleared by the police, and we were able to start the Test a day late. The West Indies eventually won in a match that contained a world record seventeen lbws.

Two years later I felt as though I was Daniel about to enter the lion's den when I flew out to umpire the series in Australia against the visiting Pakistan team. During the previous series between the teams in Pakistan, two Australian players, Shane Warne and Tim May, their spin bowlers, reported to their Cricket Board of Control that Salim Malik of Pakistan had offered them a bribe.

Because of that there was a lot of ill-feeling between the rival camps and everyone said there would be a lot of trouble and much more controversy in the return matches in Australia. I was in the middle of it all again.

It is very sad when we read and hear about allegations of this kind in what is still the greatest game in the world, and I hoped that the teams would see sense and play the game in the proper spirit. Thankfully they did, and I had no trouble with them at all, much to my relief. I did the first match in Hobart and then the one in Sydney, and the only indication of an undercurrent of bad blood was the fact that none of the Australian players spoke to Salim Malik.

When he was batting in the Sydney Test he turned to me and said, 'I'm glad you're here, Dickie.'

'Why's that, then?' I said.

'Because, apart from my batting partner over there, you're the only person in this stadium who will talk to me,' he replied.

Incidentally, the Test in Karachi during that previous series was one of the best I have umpired. The pitch was turning and of great help to Shane Warne and Mushtaq Mohammed, two of the best spin bowlers of their type in the world. But, ironically, the star was Salim Malik, who was at the centre of the bribery allegations. He was magnificent and played a big part in winning the Test for his country with some superb batting in very difficult conditions.

When Mushtaq went out as last man to join Inzumman Haq, Pakistan still needed 89 to win despite Salim Malik's heroics, and the Aussies were saying to me, 'It's all over, Dickie. We've won it now.' But those two batsmen knocked off the runs, all 89 of them, for the last wicket. It was a remarkable effort.

As you can see, in all these series the heat was on, in more ways than one. In such conditions it is so important to take in stacks and stacks of fluids and salt tablets because you lose so much in sweat. You can dehydrate very quickly, and that is dangerous. The other side of the coin is that when umpires from hot countries come over to England, they have to buy long johns and thermal underwear to keep themselves warm. One or two have even umpired in gloves.

You would think, though, that rain would be less of a problem once you had left the shores of England, but not a bit of it – at least as far as I am concerned.

For example, when I went to Sharjah in the United Arab Emirates to umpire a one-day series involving the West Indies, India, Australia and Sri Lanka, they had seen no rain for years. However, one evening there was a torrential downpour. It rained all night and when I woke up next morning there was three or four inches of water all over the bedroom floor. A porter had to carry me out of bed and down into the foyer.

Magnificent though the Sharjah Continental Hotel was, it had never been tested by rain, and the roof had sprung a leak. I suppose it should not have surprised me: rain and bad light have followed me around throughout my umpiring career.

I once umpired a Test between Zimbabwe and New Zealand in Bulawayo, and before I flew there from Harare I was warned that there was a drought in that area which had lasted for months and months. Yet just as I walked down the steps from the plane at the airport in Bulawayo it started to teem down with rain. No one had ever seen rain like it, and everyone went down on their knees thanking me for bringing an end to the drought.

There was, of course, a price to pay, as the Test match was delayed because the ground was under water.

I have made a lot of good umpiring friends on my travels. One of the biggest, in more senses than one, was the popular Indian Swarup Krishan Reu, sadly no longer with us, who officiated in the final Test between India and England in Bombay in 1984. There was some criticism of him, and, significantly, he did not appear again after that series. However, I rated him as a very fine umpire.

He was quite a character, too. He chewed betel nuts and spat frequently, rather like one of those cowboys in an old Wild West film. All he needed was a spitoon. He offered me a chew one day, but, despite assurances that it tasted similar to tobacco and would put hairs on my chest, I managed to resist the temptation.

As we walked out together for the first time in the game between Pakistan and Sri Lanka, he said to me, 'I have often prayed that one day I would be umpiring with you.' Me, Dickie Bird, an answer to another umpire's prayer! I was extremely flattered.

I could not help but tease him about his girth. 'I bet you have a few problems in England with those left-arm spinners as they try to go round the wicket,' I said to him.

He looked at me and grinned. 'Too right, Dickie. Your Derek Underwood would never bowl from my end. He said he could not go round the wicket and me as well. And as for poor Phil Edmonds, he was always complaining that I upset his rhythm.'

How far should we go with independent umpires, though? Where will it all end? And is there really any need for them at all? I am a Yorkshireman. I played for Yorkshire. Yet I umpire their matches in the county championship. My colleagues who played for other counties umpire their matches. So why should it be any different at international level?

I am very proud of having played for Yorkshire – and Leicestershire – but when it comes to making decisions for and against those two counties, I never give my previous association a thought; or the fact that I am now an honorary life member of both clubs.

Some years ago I was umpiring a match between Northampton-shire and Yorkshire at Northampton. I stayed in a pub in Abingdon, just down the road from the ground, and some of the Northants lads were there as well. Inevitably talk turned to the rivalry between the counties and I stuck up for the White Rose in the face of some good-natured ribbing.

One of the customers, obviously a keen Northants fan, tugged at my arm. 'Here,' he said, 'I don't think you should be talking like that when you're standing in a match between the two teams. What will people think?'

I looked him straight in the eye. 'Don't you worry about it,' I told him. 'In here I'm a Yorkshireman. Out there in the middle I'm an umpire. That's the difference.'

Having said all this, independent umpires are here to stay, and I can claim the distinction of being the first one under the auspices of the International Cricket Council, standing in Zimbabwe at their inaugural Test against India in Harare in October 1992.

It was there that I had one of the worst experiences travelling abroad. I was mugged in the centre of Harare at twelve thirty on a Saturday afternoon, with hundreds of people milling around. Taking no chances, I had my hand firmly on my wallet, which was in my trouser pocket, when I felt someone brush up against me. I took my hand out of my pocket momentarily, and someone shouted, 'Your wallet's on the floor.' I reached down to pick it up, and all my money had gone, about two hundred pounds. Thank goodness I was fully insured, but I couldn't believe the way it was done so quickly.

The National Grid have played a prominent role in launching the independent umpire project, and have done a tremendous job in sponsoring the World International Panel of Test Umpires, ploughing lots of money into it. From the moment an independent umpire walks out of his door at home to the moment he returns from the other side of the world, the National Grid pay for everything – salary, hotel, travel and any other sundry expenses. If two independent officials are introduced for Test matches, it will cost them double. Should the National Grid pull out at the end of their existing contract and no other sponsors can be found, however, then we could be in big trouble.

The National Grid also made 12,000 umpires' coats available to local cricket clubs affiliated to the National Cricket Association in England and Wales to mark my record half century of Test appearances, and they sponsored the umpires for that summer's one-day internationals and Test matches between England and Australia.

The coats had special features which I had helped to design – thigh-length straps on both sides and at the back for sweaters, stud fasteners down the front, two standard pockets at the front with access slits to the trouser pockets, plus a two-section breast pocket with the unique National Grid/Dickie Bird 50 Tests logo.

National Grid chairman David Jeffries said, 'We are delighted to be associated with the NCA in giving new encouragement to the national game at grass-roots level.'

On a personal note, I have to thank the National Grid for the most wonderful surprise when they presented me with a life-sized bronze bust on my retirement from the international scene, for my 'outstanding services' as an umpire. David Jeffries handed it over to me at a special ceremony, and it was later delivered to my home by their Press Officer, Trevor Seeley. I don't know how on earth Trevor got the thing into his car. It is so heavy that it took two men to lift it out at my end.

One umpire who was not at all keen on the introduction of the so-called third umpire was Steve Bucknor, of Jamaica. He said quite openly prior to the second Test between South Africa and India in Johannesburg that he would not call for the help of the television camera, and would make all the decisions himself, right or wrong. He believed that decisions should be left solely to the umpire, and that the electronic aids were undermining his authority. The Indian captain, Azharuddin, argued that there was no point in introducing electronic aids if the umpire refused to use them, and was highly critical of Bucknor's attitude.

Almost inevitably, an incident occurred which highlighted the difference of opinion. There was a strong appeal for a run-out against the South African batsman, Jonty Rhodes, when he was on 28. All the Indian players went up. Bucknor, true to his word, did not go to the third umpire. He gave the decision as he saw it. Not out.

The television replay showed that Rhodes had been well out of his ground when Srinath's throw hit the stumps direct, and it also showed that Bucknor was some yards out of alignment with the crease at the crucial moment. Rhodes went on to get 91 which helped save the match for his side.

Before then Bucknor had been so disapproving of television replays as an aid to making decisions. Today, not surprisingly, he thinks they are the best thing since sliced bread.

Another thing which can make umpiring a lot easier is the state of the pitch. If it is a very good one you find there are far fewer difficult decisions than on a bad one, when something happens every other ball.

In the early sixties I always remember our captain at Leicestershire, Maurice Hallam, going to great lengths to try to turn a tide of results which had anchored us at the bottom of the county championship table. He came up with this great idea of roughing up the pitch to help his spinners – we had some good slow bowlers in those days, such as John Savage and Chopper Smith. Hallam roughed up both ends on a length and filled the holes with sand. Hallam did this against Essex at the time when that great off-spin bowler Jim Laker was playing for them. Laker was one of the best slow bowlers in the world, so I didn't think it was a particularly good idea to mess about with the pitch, and I was proved right, because Laker took 9 for 12, and Essex gave us a hiding.

Essex's captain, Trevor Bailey, went out on to the middle before that match, sat there in a deckchair and declared, 'All I need now is the sea. I'm on the beach!' He knew . . .

Nowadays umpires can also call on match referees to help in Test series, and I am all for it. It is good for the game to have another adjudicator on hand, and that is what a referee is. He is there to see that the game is played in the right spirit and within the laws. If there is any dissent he has the power to step in and punish the offender with a fine, or even, as a last resort, suspension. Referees, incidentally, are also sponsored by the National Grid.

If we are to have referees, however, they must be strong. All those I have worked with meet that criterion: people like John Reid, the former New Zealand captain, Ramon Subba Row of England, West Indian Clive Lloyd and Peter Burge of Australia. Referees nowadays go out with the two captains for the toss of the coin before the start of the game. This stems from an incident between Pakistani captain Salim Malik and Ken Rutherford, the captain of New Zealand. When Malik was asked to call he jabbered away in Pakistani and Rutherford had no idea whether he had won the toss or lost it, or whether he was batting or fielding.

In order to maintain high standards of umpiring, I feel it is so important for any would-be officials to have played the game on the first-class county circuit. It certainly helped me enormously, and all county championship umpires, with two notable exceptions, have done the same.

The only two umpires to have worked their way right through to umpiring at Test level without having first played county cricket are Don Oslear and Nigel Plews, which is a tremendous achievement.

There is nothing to say that you must have played first-class cricket in order to become a county umpire, nor does it necessarily mean that all umpires who have played at that level are better than those who have not. However, if you have played to that standard yourself you know what the players are thinking, what they are doing, what they are trying on. You know all the tricks, all the wrinkles. And you command their respect, which is so essential.

Football league referees very seldom have the advantage of experience gained from playing at that level, nor are they employed in a fulltime capacity. To pay the bills they need to have another career as well as taking charge of matches once or twice a week.

Umpires are fulltime professionals, employed now by the England and Wales Cricket Board which, I am convinced, is an advantage.

It is important for budding officials to have someone to look up to, to learn from. When I first went on to the Test panel

I stood with people like Syd Buller, Charlie Elliott, Tommy Spencer, Dusty Rhodes and Arthur Fagg – great umpires all of them. They set the standards for me to follow, and I respected them. I hope I have not let them down.

21

MUSCLING IN ON TRAINING AND FITNESS

C IRCUIT training seems to be 'in thing' these days when it comes to keeping fit, and I believe it does more harm than good.

The exercises that players are asked to do put a strain on the spine, the hamstrings, ankles and knees, particularly if they are done on hard indoor floors. It is especially bad for younger players whose bones have not fully developed, which is why we are getting so many stress fractures amongst youngsters.

I am a big believer in getting fit for cricket by using the muscles you need for cricket. Build up in pre-season with sprints, jogging – but only on grass, where there is a cushion, and not on hard surfaces – and general loosening exercises, but as soon as possible get out into the nets and into the middle to bat and bowl. There are other exercises you can do relating to cricket, such as throwing the ball on the turn, running, bending, picking the ball up and throwing it back to the stumps, catching practice and running between the wickets.

This system gets you fit by playing cricket, and once the

hard work has been done pre-season, players should then be kept as fit as they need to be by turning out in matches seven days a week, without all this circuit training. Players can be on the field seven hours a day, yet they still have at least an hour's circuit-training session beforehand. They must be exhausted before they even go out into the middle. They are at it all over the world, and at county level, too. Out they go with their physios before each day's play, and I look on and wonder . . .

In my days at Yorkshire, we got fit by playing cricket. I'll use Freddie Trueman as an example. When we reported back after the winter break on 1 April, he would bowl off one pace. On the second day he would extend that run by a few more yards, and so it went on throughout the month. By the end of it he was off a full run and ready for the start of the new season.

I've talked to a lot of the great Test players of the past, including Freddie Trueman and Alec Bedser, and they all agree with me that circuit training does little, if any, good.

David Gower was one great player who believed in using the muscles that you need for cricket, and he was hardly ever injured. You would never find David Gower doing circuit training, or anything like that, yet he was magnificent in the cover point area: so quick, so lithe in his movements. Geoffrey Boycott was another. He would practise in the middle for hours and hours, and work things out in the nets. Mind you, he could possibly have practised his running between the wickets a bit more.

Freddie Trueman tells the story of one trip by boat to Australia for a Test series. The athlete Gordon Pirie was included in the party so that he could lead the players in running sessions round the deck in order to keep fit. Fred said to him, 'I'll run round the deck if you can put all your medals on the table so that we can see what you've won.' Of course, Pirie hadn't brought them with him so he couldn't, so Fred didn't run.

Most modern players say that Trueman, Bedser, Gower, Boycott and Birdy live in cloud cuckoo-land, that times have changed. They say that the game is not like it was in our day, and that we have moved on. Maybe so. But are things better? Cricketers these days spend a lot of time playing football, if a match is rained off, for example, which is something that I would not allow if I was in charge of a county cricket club. Bad injuries can be incurred through football, and it has been known for a player to be sidelined for a full season as a result.

I would also ban running on hard surfaces, indoors or out. When you see all these joggers running up and down the roads and lanes throughout the country, you know that there will always be jobs for physios and orthopaedic surgeons. Many joggers find, in later years, that they have serious problems with the spine, ankles, knees and ribs, and the same will happen to cricketers if they continue to put too much pressure on those areas, either by the wrong exercises or by exercising in the wrong environment.

We never used to have so many stress-related injuries. People were injured, but there were not nearly as many bone injuries and hamstring, calf and muscle pulls as there are today, and I believe it is down to circuit training and other associated exercises. Far be it from me to suggest that these training methods are anything to do with England's lack of success in recent years, but they could well be a contributory factor.

Nor do I feel that it is a good thing for players, and especially youngsters, to practise indoors too much. Not only are bad habits developed by playing indoors, but players become more susceptible to injuries, particularly bowlers, who put so much stress on the spine when pounding along on hard floors.

Players tend to bowl short indoors, where a full toss or half-volley would be equivalent to a good-length ball outside on grass. A batsman can also commit himself to the front foot indoors, knowing he can get away with it because the bounce will be true. You can't do that on grass, where the ball holds up and the pace is slower. These are just some of the reasons why I feel that practising indoors does more harm than good.

I could be upsetting a lot of genuine people who run indoor schools, but it is what I feel. If you have to play indoors, then simply enjoy it. Do not try to be too technical, and do not think you can play the same way when you get outside on grass in a match. The only place to iron out faults is in the nets, or in the middle itself.

Looking back over my own career I think I practised too much indoors. If I could turn the clock back and have my time over again I would not spend so much time inside. It *does* – and I must stress this – get you into some bad habits.

When I played county cricket I used to go down to Oakwell, the home of Barnsley Football Club, and do a bit of training with the players there. The manager in those days was a chap called Tim Ward, who was a cricket fanatic and played for Stainborough, one of the local teams in the Barnsley area. After training we would sit in the big bath in the dressing room talking about cricket. Never football. All the lads used to join in, and we had so many of those sessions that one of them said to me one day, 'If tha keeps comin' down 'ere like this, Dickie, gaffer will be signin' thee on.' Tim loved his cricket, and in later years, when he retired, he used to go and watch Derbyshire.

I've had some useful treatment for injuries down at Oakwell, too, in the days of Fred Semley and then Norman Rimmington, a former goalkeeper for the club, who is another cricket lover. Norman is now the Barnsley kit man, and a great character.

As an umpire I have developed my own way of keeping fit, doing a lot of walking, for example, which is tremendous exercise. I also do twenty to twenty-five minutes of general light exercises every morning without fail. I have had a lot of trouble with my spine, as well as my knee, and therefore one exercise I concentrate on more than any other is trunk curls, to strengthen the bottom of the spine. I also do arm and leg movement exercises, and cycle on my back. I sometimes even practise raising my index finger, just to keep it in trim! I believe that those morning exercises do me much more good than the miles and miles run by joggers on the roads, or by modern cricketers pounding up and down the hard indoor surfaces.

Many of my umpiring colleagues keep fit by playing golf, and that is certainly good exercise. I have never played golf myself, although I would have liked to have done. However, I would have wanted to make myself into a very good player, and to do that you need to practise constantly, which I have never had the time to do. If it was snooker or bowls, whatever sport, I would feel the same. I never have been one for doing things by halves. Whatever I have tackled, I have wanted to be one of the best, and that takes practice.

David Shepherd, a colleague of mine, whom you may have noticed is of rather more ample proportions than yours truly, never does any exercises as far as I can make out, apart from his little jig when the Nelson – the score of 111 – goes up on the scoreboard. Yet he never seems to be injured, and I can't even remember him having a cold. Perhaps that tells us something . . .

Once when he was playing for Gloucestershire, however, he was forced to go on a cross-country run with the rest of the players one morning. He was quite a size even in those days, so it was hardly surprising that he should soon be lagging miles behind the rest. He jumped on to a milk float, sat on the ledge, holding on for dear life, with the bottles tinkling merrily around him and his legs wobbling in the air. He was first back to the county ground at Bristol, and the other lads could not believe it when they huffed and puffed their way into the ground to see Shep there with a smirk of superiority on his face. He certainly had plenty of bottle on that occasion.

Another former Gloucestershire county player hardly renowned for his fleetness of foot was Andy Stovold, who is now the coach at that county, where he is doing a lot for the youngsters.

I always remember umpiring a match between Gloucestershire and Lancashire at Old Trafford in the days of Michael Procter. Proccy was captain of Gloucestershire at the time, and during a period of inactivity due to bad weather – well, this was Old Trafford! – he said to me, 'How quick do you reckon you are, Dickie?'

I rather prided myself on how quickly I could race into position from behind the stumps in order to judge a run-out, and replied, 'Well, I'm not that bad on the old sprints.'

Proccy said, 'Do you think you could beat Stov?'

Having seen Andy Stovold in the field, I had, in all modesty, to answer in the affirmative.

Proccy simply said, 'Mmm, that's interesting,' and left it at that.

I thought no more about it until the end of the season, when I had Gloucestershire again, this time down at Bristol. Before the match Proccy took me on one side and asked, 'Have you got a minute, Dickie?'

'Why?' I said.

'Well, I've been thinking over what you said earlier in the season and I've arranged for a hundred-yard sprint between you and Andy Stovold. At the end of the match we're going to mark out the distance and we're going to put it over the PA system that if any spectators want to stay they will be able to see a rare athletics challenge between an umpire and a player – Dickie Bird against Andy Stovold. And there is no way,' he added, 'that you are going to get out of this one, Dickie.'

So, after the game, I lined up with Stov on the starting line of a hundred-yard 'track' marked out in front of the pavilion. All the crowd had stayed on to see the fun.

I beat Stov easily. He was still playing, remember, in his prime, I would have been about fifty at the time. To be honest, he did not take much beating. He was hardly the fastest player on the county circuit. They still talk about that sprint challenge to this day down in Bristol. Stov doesn't, though. Never mentions it. Funny, that . . .

I wouldn't have fancied taking on someone like Derek Randall. Now he was quick, but was it a question of fitness, or just natural athleticism? Geoffrey Boycott wasn't quick, but he was fit. He kept himself fit, and worked at it. He made himself into a great batsman by constant practice. He was a very, very poor fielder early in his career, but he made himself into a good one by practice, practice, practice. It wasn't extra training that brought the improvements, but working hard at particular aspects of his game.

Graham Gooch is different in more ways than one. He has his own views and ideas, and he is a big believer in this new fitness fad. I don't know whether it ever made him a better player, but I do know, to my cost, that he was one of the hardest strikers of the ball I have ever come across.

Gooch once drove a full toss from Aussie leg-spinner Bob Holland straight back down the pitch like a tracer bullet during a Test match at Old Trafford. I have never seen anything like it. Or, perhaps, more accurately, if I had seen it I would have said that I had never seen anything like it. The first thing I knew was when the ball hit me smack on the ankle. Down I went in agony. When I pulled myself together and realised what day it was, I was already being treated by the Aussie physio. I finally tottered to my feet, thinking that Goochie would come over and apologise, but all he said was, 'What do you think you're playing at, Dickie? You robbed me of four runs, there.'

Then there are all the diets. I don't believe in any of them. They are bound to weaken the body, and you need strength to perform to your limits, whether it be batting, bowling, fielding – or even umpiring. Eat everything in moderation, that is my philosophy, and I have followed it all the way through my career, both as a player and then umpire. Certain foods are obviously important, such as fruit and vegetables. Garlic is good, too, and red wine helps the circulation of the blood, but again in moderation. There have been times when I have strayed off the straight and narrow, I have to admit. When I start on chocolate, for example, I'm terrible. I can eat a full box of chocolates at one sitting, so that is something I have to watch. Not smoking also helps to keep you fit, and it is vital not to drink too heavily.

One thing that has always helped me keep fit through my career is the health food, Bio-Strath, which is taken in tablet form. This was first recommended to me by Sir Stanley Matthews many years ago. He is one of the fittest men I know, so I was only too eager to take his advice. The tablets are regularly sent to me by Keith Pollitt from his firm, Cedar Health Ltd, in Cheshire. Every time I see Sir Stanley he says, 'Still taking the tablets, Dickie?'

When players go abroad, they usually like to eat the local food, whether it be India, Pakistan, Sri Lanka, or wherever, and most of them have no problems at all, but I have always been wary. I always insist on drinking bottled water, and eat fruit you can peel, such as bananas and oranges. I always eat fried stuff, chips and such like, with some Heinz baked beans, and, of course, chocolate. One thing I do like abroad, however, is the Nan bread in India. If I stick to foods like these I never have any problems. I've had the occasional dodgy tummy – the dreaded Delhi belly – like everyone else, but nothing serious, and I have always been able to enjoy my visits to foreign countries throughout the world.

Sometimes I take food with me, such as Mars bars and gingerbread men from the local village bakery. You know what they say about a Mars a day, and as for the gingerbread men, biting the heads off is the best bit!

As you can see, I like plain food, and Derek Randall, the former England and Nottinghamshire player, is obviously made in the same no-nonsense mould. He was never quite sure what to make of foreign dishes and on a tour of India in 1976, as he tucked into some caviar, he observed, 'This champagne's a bit of all right, but the blackcurrant jam tastes of fish.'

22

OVER AND OUT

E NGLAND v India, Lord's, 20 June 1996, an emotional
occasion I will remember as long as I live: the start of
my final Test match. Even the weather, which had played
havoc with my nerves over the years, had to pay its particular
tribute, a shower of rain putting the scheduled start time back
from eleven o'clock to half past. As I stood surveying the grey
skies I did wonder whether it was once again going to rain on my
parade, but thankfully the rain blew over, and that was the last
we saw of it during the five days.

When the time came to get things underway I wondered
why the security guards were keeping me back, along with
my Australian colleague, Darrell Hair, but I was soon to find
out. I will never forget the feeling I had when I walked from
the umpires' room and down the steps through the Long Room,
where all the members rose, to a man, from their tall seats and
stood to clap us through. It was the same in the members'
enclosure, and when we stepped on to the green I saw that
England captain Michael Atherton had arranged for both teams
to line up in a guard of honour. Meanwhile a full-house Lord's
stood to applaud me all the way out to the middle.

Oldtimers told me that the reception I received was even
bigger than the one afforded Sir Donald Bradman when he

walked out at The Oval for his last Test. If that is so, then it was a truly remarkable compliment. As I made that walk, a lump in my throat, tears in my eyes, and handkerchief in my hand, I heard MCC Secretary Roger Knight announce over the public address system that the MCC had made me an honorary life member – the first umpire in history to receive that honour.

Seeing how overcome I was, Darrell Hair offered to take the first over while I recovered my composure, and strolled over to the Nursery End, thinking that Srinath would bowl the first over from there. Instead, however, the Indian came to my end, and it was a good job my eyes cleared quickly, because I had to give Atherton out lbw in that first over.

After all Michael had done for me in lining up the teams in my honour only a minute or two before, I suppose it was not very nice of me, and as he walked past on his way back to the pavilion he had a rueful smile on his face. I knew what he was thinking: 'Given out lbw by Dickie Bird, of all people, and in his last Test, too.' He could hardly credit it.

However, during the lunch interval 'Athers' came up to me, put his arm round me and said, 'I was out, Dickie. You were right. I was plumb. Don't worry about it.' A nice touch, and typical of the man, and it gave me a lot of satisfaction. It goes back to having the respect of the players, something that has always meant a lot to me, and there it was, right to the last.

What is sport if you cannot have a laugh? It seems to me that hardly anybody laughs any more. A lot of the enjoyment has gone out of the game in that respect. It is all too serious. As far as I am concerned, once you stop enjoying yourself it ceases to be a sport. I never stopped enjoying cricket right to the end, but I was probably the only silly bugger who did.

When they heard that I was retiring from international cricket, Test players throughout the world said I was daft, and that I should carry on. I had always said that I wanted to go out at the top, and to bow out at Lord's, because that had been my second home throughout my career. Here I was being given that opportunity, with my appointment to the India Test, and I thought it was for the best. If I had gone on for another year and started to slip, with people criticising me for bad decisions, that would have hurt me more than anything. I wanted to leave the international arena with pride and dignity, at the top of my profession.

People have told me that I did well in that final Test, and I did feel as though I had done a good job. I had to deal with some very tough decisions over those five days, and three of them, I believe, were as good as anything in my career. All three involved appeals for catches behind the stumps, two being Indian batsmen, and the third Englishman Ronnie Irani on the last day. I gave not out for all three, judging that on each occasion the ball had glanced off the player's shirt. Those decisions were later vindicated by television replays. I therefore completed that last Test thinking that there was no way my standards were slipping. I could have gone on for another twelve months and bowed out with the big one, England v Australia in the Ashes series of 1997.

I began to doubt that I had got my final decision right. I should not have quit. I should have gone on to the full retirement age. Life is all ifs and buts, though, and you always look back and wonder if you did the right thing.

With hindsight, the England v India Test was one of the best matches I have had, so I console myself with the knowledge that I did what I wanted to do: I quit at the top.

The day before that farewell appearance I had been invited into the boardroom at Lord's for drinks, where I was presented with a framed montage of photographs illustrating my career, including one of the most famous ones, showing me sitting on the covers in the middle of the pitch during that bomb-scare Test, with thousands of spectators gathered around me. The inscription read: 'From the Test and County Cricket Board, presented to Harold Dickie Bird MBE from all his friends on the board on the occasion of his 66th and final Test at Lord's, June 20–24, 1996, in recognition of his wonderful services to the game as a first-class umpire since 1970. Well done, Dickie lad.'

Cornhill also presented me with a framed cricket scene in silver, acknowledging the fact that I had stood at their first, fiftieth and hundredth internationals.

The previous night I had been invited to the England v Holland European Championship football match at Wembley, and England played so well in beating the Dutch 4–1 that the FA's Chief Executive, Graham Kelly, said that I had to go again. The visit had been arranged by FA member Doug Insole, who is also a very powerful man at Lord's. Doug rightly thought it might relax me in the build-up to my final Test, and it did. I really enjoyed the evening, especially when the lads on the England subs' bench saw me and gave me a wave as I sat in the Royal Box. I'm glad I brought the team some luck. Perhaps I should have gone back when they played Germany.

I also took the opportunity to have a chat with the Neville brothers, of Manchester United, who were in the England squad. I had not seen them since I nursed them both when they were toddlers out on holiday in Barbados, Gary on one knee and Phil on the other.

The BBC documentary of my life, *A Rare Species*, which was to win the Documentary of the Year award, with *Football's Coming Home, Euro '96* in second place, was shown on television immediately after the match, and everyone in the banqueting suite wanted to watch it. This was not possible, however, because the FA wanted to show the highlights of England's magnificent victory, and Middlesbrough manager Bryan Robson, the former England captain, who was involved in the national team's coaching set-up, told me, 'Don't worry,

Dickie, I wouldn't miss it for the world. My wife's taping it for me.'

My previous visit to Wembley was when I umpired a World XI v Rest of the World match there, and it chucked it down for most of the day. There was certainly more water on the field than in the referee's room – I went for a shower and all that came out was an apologetic trickle. I complained to Lord Denis Howell about it afterwards. As a sports minister in the previous Labour government and a former football league referee, as well as vice-president of Warwickshire County Cricket Club, I thought he might be able to get something done. I never did find out if he had managed to get it fixed.

A week after that Euro '96 highlight I was walking off the field at Lord's and only then did it really hit me. So many thoughts, so many memories, whirled around crazily in my head, and I said to myself, 'Well, that's it, Dickie lad. You'll never umpire a Test match ever again. That's it. Finished. Over and out.'

Meanwhile tributes were pouring in from all over the world, including ones from His Royal Highness the Prince of Wales, Prince Philip, and the then Prime Minister the Right Honourable John Major, which were read out at a dinner, arranged by the Lord's Taverners, in the banqueting suite at Leeds United Football Club.

Tributes have continued to pour in, and I have been overwhelmed by them. Within a year of announcing my retirement I had received more than eight thousand letters and cards, which were strewn knee deep all over my study floor as I desperately tried to answer them. It was an impossible task, and I had to get some help to sort them out. There are still boxes full waiting for a reply. All I can say to people who sent their best wishes is that I appreciated them all and am very sorry if I have not replied personally.

Kind words from all the cricket boards of control throughout the world and from all walks of life, have meant more to me than all the riches in the world.

However, there was one publication, supposedly written as a tribute, which I was annoyed about. *Free As a Bird*, a biography which the publishers Robson Books invited David Hopps, of the *Guardian* newspaper, to write, was done without any consultation with me.

The beauty of the saga was that I received David Hopps' contract in triplicate through my letter box. It was addressed to him but mistakenly sent to my house.

Free as a Bird came out to coincide with my last Test, and it had me in a bit of a flap, on top of everything else.

I had considered retiring twelve months earlier, and had even mentioned it, in passing, to Lord's, who asked me to give it another year and then see how I felt. In January 1996, I went down to stay with my friends John and Pat Perry at the Livermead Cliff Hotel in Torquay, determined to come to a decision. There was hardly a soul around as I walked for miles and miles along the shoreline in that lovely Torbay area, and I was able to give the matter a lot of deep thought.

I had already had long chats with John and Pat, Lord and Lady Mason, Lord Howell of Aston, and *Barnsley Chronicle* Sports Editor Keith Lodge – all very good friends of mine. They all offered me the same advice: quit while you are still at the top. Deep down, I knew they were right. Now was the time to go. So, after long and hard deliberation I rang Lord's from Torquay and told them of my decision to retire from international cricket.

This time, I said, it was final. There was no turning back. I wanted to make way for younger officials, to give them a chance. After all, I was already five years older than the previous oldest Test umpire, Syd Buller.

When Lord's issued a press release a few days later, it seemed that every single representative of the media had descended on

Torquay. The Livermead Cliff Hotel had never known anything like it. It was a good job it was out of season, otherwise they would not have been able to cope with all the newspaper, radio, television and magazine people, as well as the guests. It was sheer bedlam. John Perry was a tower of strength through it all. He organised the interviews for me, bringing some order out of all the chaos, and it was amazing that I managed to say a few words to everybody, although that was not the end of it. The clamour for interviews went on for days afterwards, and it has not really stopped since.

A rumour had circulated some years earlier, while I was standing at my one hundredth international, that I was thinking about retiring then, but there was not a lot of truth in that. My colleague Barrie Leadbeater had sparked that one off, claiming that I told him during that England v West Indies one-dayer at Lord's in 1988 that I was about to announce my retirement. Barrie tells the tale that he warned me, 'Whatever you do, Dickie, don't announce it too quickly. The weather is not too clever. If you announce your retirement too soon and the match is washed out, you'll be stuck on ninety-nine internationals for the rest of your life.' It's a good story, but should be taken with a pinch of salt.

It is quite unbelievable the number of radio and television programmes I have been asked to do since announcing my retirement for real: *Desert Island Discs* with Sue Lawley; *Songs of Praise* with Sir Harry Secombe; *A Question of Sport* – it was great to beat Ian Botham's team – *Through The Keyhole*, when they guessed me straightaway because of all the white shoes lined up in the bedroom; *Noel's House Party* and *The Generation Game* on the same evening; *Breakfast with Frost*; *Newsnight*, and the award-winning documentary *A Rare Species*.

I also appeared on *The Big Breakfast*, and they wanted to interview me in bed with a fella called Lily Savage.

'No way,' I said.

They argued, 'But we've interviewed Gary Lineker, Frank Bruno and your mate Ian Botham on that bed, and they had no objection.'

I said, 'Well, you're not getting Dickie Bird in there, I can tell you that now. I'm not going to leap into bed with a bloke dressed up in a wig and a nightie and wearing lashings of make-up. If you want to interview me, then you'll have to do it while I'm sitting on a chair. Otherwise I'm taking t' next train back to Barnsley.' So that's what they did. I wasn't going to stand for any of that in-the-bed nonsense.

I found lots of awards coming my way. I was honoured at a national People of the Year ceremony, and I was both proud and humble when I saw some of those who had also been chosen. I felt they all deserved to be there much more than me.

I was also voted Yorkshireman of the Year, an award I received from Lord Harewood in a special ceremony at Harewood House in December 1996, having been unable to attend the big dinner in the Leeds United Football Club's banqueting suite because I had previously agreed to speak at a builders' dinner. If I promise people I am going to do something for them, I won't let them down if I can possibly help it. As it happened, Lord Harewood, who had also won an award, could not make it either, so we had a cosy presentation of our own, in which he received his award and then handed me mine.

Leeds University made me an honorary Doctor of Law, a way of honouring individuals who are distinguished by their contribution to public life. I was also granted an honorary doctorate from Sheffield and Hallam University, for 'outstanding services to international cricket and cricket in general.' I was due to receive the doctorate at Sheffield City Hall in November 1996, but, this being Dickie Bird, there was the usual hitch.

The day of the award dawned clear, but cold. I was due to

have lunch at the university prior to the ceremony, which was scheduled for three o'clock in the afternoon. So there I was at home, getting ready for the big occasion, when I glanced out of the window and noticed that it had started to snow quite heavily. If it's not bad light or rain, it's snow. Very soon the lane leading to my cottage was almost knee deep in the stuff, and I couldn't get my car out of the garage.

In desperation I rang for a taxi. If anyone could get through it would be a taxi driver, but even he could not make it along Paddock Road to the top of the lane, so I had to arrange to meet him on the main A61 road that links Wakefield, Barnsley and Sheffield. We then had to pick up Lady Mason in Barnsley – Lord Mason was on official duty in the House of Lords so could not attend – and my sister Marjorie from Worsbrough village. With difficulty we managed to negotiate our way to Lady Mason's, but it was impossible to get up the side road to where my sister lived. Hopping out of the taxi, I rang Marjorie from the pub at Worsbrough Bridge and asked if she could walk down to meet me there. She looked just like a snowman when she arrived.

The traffic was chaos, bumper to bumper, with lorries skidding across the road and blocking our pogress. It was a terrible mess. It took us three hours to do seven miles and then we had to give up. There wasn't a snowball in a hot oven's chance of reaching Sheffield, so we turned round and went home. It took an absolute age. When I arrived home at my cottage, I made myself a cup of tea, flopped into my favourite chair, and wept.

However, the story did have a happy ending. The university rang to say that they could present me with my degree two days later, and I had a magnificent time. I still had a bit of a problem, though, as I was due to speak at a dinner just outside London that same evening, and it was late afternoon by the time the ceremony was over. I had planned to take the train, but one of the university officials, Alex Pettifer, would hear none of it. He arranged for a car to take me all the way to London, and thanks to him I made my evening appointment in comfortable time.

I arranged a special retirement dinner, to which I invited all my closest friends, in the Brooklands Restaurant in Barnsley. I have travelled all over the world, wining and dining in all the best hotels, but Brooklands takes some beating. The owner, Jim Gratton, has been very good to me, and I am indebted to him and his wife for all they have done. Going to Brooklands for a meal every Sunday lunchtime that I am at home is one of my relaxations and the Grattons certainly did me proud on this occasion.

These days I like to look back and think of all the great players of the modern era whom I have seen start and finish their Test careers – Sunil Gavaskar, Dennis Lillee, Michael Holding, Imran Khan, Kapil Dev, David Gower, Graham Gooch, Ian Botham, Clive Lloyd, Martin Crowe, Joel Garner and Viv Richards, to name but a few – and the teams they played for.

When I first started umpiring Test matches in 1973 the Australians beat the West Indies 5–1 in Australia. Clive Lloyd said that he would go back there next time with a battery of fast bowlers who would win the series for them and make them the strongest Test side in the world, and he did just that. He brought in four quickies, one at one end, a second at the other, with two more resting at third man and fine leg waiting to take over. There was no respite, no getting away from them. This was something completely different. They had no spin bowlers. On a turning pitch Lloyd always said that he would still win with the fast bowlers because of their exceptional pace through the air.

Way back into history fast bowlers had always hunted in pairs – Hall and Griffith, Statham and Trueman, Snow and Willis, Lillee and Thomson, Lindwall and Miller – but never four at a time. The West Indies doubled up the traditional pairing, with a quartet of world-class bowlers to strike fear into any opposition: Michael Holding, Andy Roberts, Joel Garner and Colin Croft – not to mention Malcolm Marshall, who was to come along a little later, and then Curtley Ambrose and Courtney Walsh.

Look at some of the batsmen the West Indies also had at their disposal: Gordon Greenidge, Desmond Haynes, Vivian Richards, Larry Gomes, Rohan Kanhai, to name but a few.

The West Indies became the most powerful Test side from 1976 and held that position for almost twenty years, but, looking back, I can think of a side that could have challenged them for their crown: the South Africans of the 1960s, before they were banned from international cricket. What a contest that would have been, and I would love to have seen it.

That South African side included Barry Richards, Michael Procter, Graeme Pollock, Peter Pollock, Tiger Lance, Trevor Goddard, Eddie Barlow and Denis Lindsay. Five world-class all-rounders in the line-up – Proctor, Goddard, Barlow, Lance and Pollock – and England are currently struggling to find *one*.

South Africa had beaten Australia in two Test series in the early 1960s, and that showed what a good side was beginning to develop. Their captain was Ali Bacher, now Dr Ali Bacher, who is one of the top administrators in South African cricket and doing a very good job for them.

In the last few years the West Indians have gradually declined. Players have grown old together and, for the first time in twenty years, there are no suitable replacements coming through. Consequently Australia have resumed their position as the best Test side.

I stood at Tests featuring the Australians in the early seventies, when Ian Chappell was captain. They had a great side in those days, including those two magnificent fast bowlers, Dennis Lillee and Jeff Thomson, with Max Walker a very fine support bowler. Variety was provided by Ashley Mallett, one of the best off-spinners at the time. With those two top-notch cricketing brothers, the Chappells, in the middle order, and a truly great wicket-keeper in Rodney Marsh behind the stumps, there was a solid backbone to a superb team.

I have always admired the Australian approach to the game. They are always so sharply honed and totally dedicated. You can never write them off, they are so competitive. They are fully committed to the cause, with an aggressive streak, and are superb fielders, both in the outfield and close to the wicket, and always feature strong batting from orthodox batsmen and attacking bowlers. They put an emphasis on the physical aspect of the game: they are fit, tough, ruthless even.

Australian players believe totally in themselves, honestly thinking that they are the best, but, from my experience, they have always played within the laws of the game. People have complained to me about the Aussies' sledging, but I can say that I have had no problems whatsoever with that from any Australian Test player. I treated them as professional men and found that, in return, they were straight and honest with me. The same qualities run right the way through any Australian side, even when the players change. It seems to be ingrained in our friends from the other side of the world.

Pakistan are also a very strong side right now. Peter Burge, who is a referee with the National Grid, told me that he had seen all the best bowling duos, from Lindwall and Miller to the present time, and he rated Waqar Younis and Wasim Akram as the best pair of them all. These two continue to spearhead the Pakistani challenge.

I can also see Sri Lanka coming through. They did superbly well in the last World Cup and I believe they could develop into a Test side capable of beating the best.

Zimbabwe are another emerging nation, but, like New

Zealand, they could suffer through lack of numbers. They simply don't have enough players to choose from.

So what about England? Well, I think they are well equipped from a batting point of view. The first six on the winter tour of New Zealand provide the nucleus of a good side. What worries me, however, is the bowling. It was nice to see Robert Croft, of Glamorgan, coming through, because I like to see spinners in the Test arena, and I have always rated Phil Tufnell, but we do seem to have problems on the bowling side.

However, I think I saw a glimmer of light there last winter. I have never been one for putting my head on the block with regard to young players, because you can so easily end up with it being chopped off. I have seen magnificent kids up to the age of eighteen, fine players, who then just fall by the wayside for one reason or another, usually because they lack the toughness and application of the Australians, but if I had to stick my neck out it would be for Chris Silverwood, of Yorkshire. If he remains fit, keeps his feet on the ground, and maintains his current development, he could spearhead the England attack for a few years to come. I like him because he has a natural aggression, is quick and swings the ball late. I feel he could go a long way, and we certainly do need a top-class strike bowler.

Silverwood's county colleague, Darren Gough, from my home town of Barnsley, is the best we have at the minute, and if we can get him firing on all cyclinders, along with Andy Caddick of Somerset, then we could have the makings of a decent team.

I am of the old school, and believe in operating with two spinners in a side if at all possible. That produces a balanced attack. The problem, of course, is that we have not managed to find an all-rounder to replace Ian Botham. Players of his calibre do not come on the scene every day, rather once in a lifetime. I also believe that a Test side should play its best wicket-keeper, irrespective of his ability with the bat, but that debate has already been aired elsewhere.

On the whole I am fairly optimistic for the future of English cricket at international level, but the series victory over New Zealand last winter proved nothing. New Zealand were a very ordinary side, poor even by Test standards, so no one should read too much into that minor triumph.

I have mentioned Silverwood and Gough, of Yorkshire, and the White Rose county continues to boast the best youngsters in the country. What worries me is what happens to so many of them. I went on record as saying that a lad called Anthony McGrath was close to the England team, but he has not quite developed to the level expected of him. Why? One of the reasons, I feel, is that he has not been allowed to open the innings with Michael Vaughan, another good player. His position is as an opener, not at five or six, which puts pressure on him to go for quick runs and abandon his preferred style of play. Such tactics have held back his development.

The answer is for Martyn Moxon, true professional that he is, to bat further down the order, leaving McGrath to open with Vaughan. Moxon would do a good job in the middle order. People may argue that he is still a fine opening batsman, and I go along with that, but at his age I believe he has to make the sacrifice in order to allow a very promising young player to come through.

Moxon, another Barnsley product, is a player I rate very highly. England must have had some excellent players in the last fifteen years for Martyn not to have played more at Test level. He has been very unlucky not to have been called upon by his country much more, and all my fellow umpires, who have seen him regularly at close quarters, will back me up on that.

I suppose it is possible that one day a Test umpire will break my record of 159 internationals. For most of the twenty-four years that I umpired in Test matches, every cricketing nation had its own panel of officials, so the most I ever got in a twelve-month period was three Tests, usually only two. Since the National Grid International Panel came into operation, with umpires officiating all over the world, it is possible for an official to stand at up to ten Tests in a twelve-month period, so my record could go one day. It would still take a long time for anyone to break it though, and they would be damned tired when they did. However, nobody will get to their sixty-fourth year and still be doing Tests, like me. That will never happen.

My final count was sixty-six Test matches, although I still feel that the record should show sixty-seven. The International Cricket Council declined to number the Bicentennial Test in that total, which I think they should. On top of those, I stood at ninety-two one-day internationals, including four World Cup tournaments and three World Cup finals.

I do hope that I can still be used in some capacity in cricket. I would very much like to pass on my vast experience and help umpires throughout the world, not necessarily on the laws of the game, but with how to handle players, and try to make them mentally strong and able to stand up against the massive appealing which has crept into the game. You can have all the ability in the world, but if you are not mentally strong you will have big problems.

A good umpire must have five qualities: honesty, concentration, application, dedication, and the calm confidence to inspire and retain the respect of the players. That is what I would try to instil into up-and-coming umpires. If I could help in that way I would feel that I was putting something back into a game that has given me so much. I want to be involved. I need to be involved; even after I've drawn my old-age pension.

There is only one decision I would change if I could have my career over again: I would not leave Yorkshire for Leicestershire.

That was my one big mistake. I should have stayed and fought for my Yorkshire cap, as it would have meant so much to me.

On the other hand, one of the best decisions of my life was to become an umpire. Everything has stemmed from that. I can go anywhere in the world and I am recognised. Everyone knows me, from Smith to Lord Roseberry, as the old song has it. Letters from all over the world, addressed simply, 'Dickie Bird, Test Umpire, England,' are delivered to my home without the slightest problem.

I look at it this way. The good Lord gave me a gift, and I hope I haven't let him down. I have always said that if I cannot give an hour of my time to go to my local Methodist church at Staincross in order to thank Him for everything that He has done for me, then it's a bad job.

I have always tried to be pleasant to people – that costs nothing. I chat to kids and old ladies alike, and I've always been willing to sign autographs. At close of play I used to line up the youngsters – and some not so young – and sign every one of their books, photographs and scraps of paper, even cigarette packets. I appreciate such requests all the more because before I came on to the scene it was unheard of for people to want the autograph of an umpire.

Being friendly, courteous and nice pays. Badmouthing people is unwise, and it rebounds on you. Do as you would be done by, that is my motto. I have always done my best to help and encourage others, and to bring a smile to the proceedings. I have always been loyal to the Establishment, remembering what my father always told me: 'Stay loyal to those who employ you and they, in turn, should stay loyal to you.'

All these things, I feel, have helped build my reputation, and, of course, my name helps – it is not one that people can easily forget. I would like to think that somewhere along the line, though, I must have made one or two good decisions as well . . .

Appendix I

WHAT CRICKET LOVERS SAY ABOUT DICKIE BIRD

A T A dinner arranged in Dickie Bird's honour by the Lord's Taverners, the following messages were read out. HRH the Prince of Wales wrote:

> I can only assume, as you are actually reading this message, that bad light has not stopped play this afternoon. Dickie Bird is not only an enthusiastic ambassador for the game of cricket, he is also a splendid man and a great character. We must be thankful that there are such marvellous people about. I suspect that Test matches in this country will never be quite the same again now that he has retired from international umpiring. He has become such a national monument I was going to suggest that Dickie should eventually be mounted, stuffed and displayed in the Lord's pavilion, but as I suspect he might object to this I do think that at least he should perhaps hand over the famous light meter which could have a display cabinet of its own somewhere.

The message from Prince Philip read:

> I am very disappointed that I cannot join what I am sure
> will be a full house of Taverners and their guests to pay
> tribute to one of cricket's great characters. There have been
> many outstanding umpires before and there will be many in
> the future, but none will have done more for the game of
> cricket than Dickie Bird in his long career. We all know
> the star players, but it is just as well to be reminded of
> the vital role of the umpires, not just their ability to make
> the right decisions, but also their influence on the whole
> tone of the game. Few, if any, have brought that special
> balance of humour and firmness that is so characteristic of
> Dickie Bird.

And John Major said:

> If Dickie has anything to do with it, it promises to be a
> memorable evening. This country has produced some of the
> finest umpires in the world, and none more so than Dickie.
> He was a true original, respected by players and fans alike for
> his unerringly accurate judgement, loved for his eccentricities
> and sense of humour. The game was certainly never dull
> when Dickie was umpiring. His harangue of the hospitality
> boxes at Old Trafford when sun stopped play against the
> West Indies was just one moment which will live long in
> the memory. Cricket lovers the world over will miss him
> greatly. I know I certainly will.

Big names in the cricket world also paid public tribute and
here are just a few examples.

> What you see is what you get with Dickie. There has never
> been any hatred in him, and in this day and age you cannot
> say that about too many people. He will go down in history
> as the greatest Test umpire ever. (Raymond Illingworth)

> Dickie has been so much more than a Test umpire. He has

contributed hugely to the humour of the game. (Matthew Engel, Editor of *Wisden*)

Dickie Bird is an umpire who is prepared to acknowledge players while standing out as an excellent operator, certainly the best I have ever seen. Umpires throughout the world could learn so much from him. (Sir Richard Hadlee)

Dickie was fair, honest and consistent. What more could a player ask for? Simply the best. (Michael Holding)

A lovable man and always a joy to meet. But remember, behind all the fun and laughter is one of the world's best cricket umpires, who is never browbeaten by loud, threatening appeals, and only gives a player out if he is absolutely sure. He can be very strict if a player runs down the pitch or bowls too many bouncers. He stands no nonsense from anyone. (Brian Johnston)

The best Test umpire I have ever seen. There will never be another to touch him. (Viv Richards)

The ideal umpire, one who has played the game at county level and has a genuine understanding of the people he is controlling during a game. He is a friend and a great official. (Dennis Lillee)

Dickie Bird was one of the most respected and best-loved personalities of his day. He has so many attributes. Lucky to have been a good player himself, he has something of Frank Chester's efficiency, Alec Skelding's sense of fun, Frank Lee's sensitivity, Syd Buller's courage and calm, the clever touch of Dusty Rhodes, the dignity and bonhomie of John Langridge, Arthur Fagg's perception of the game and Charlie Elliott's interest in the welfare of the players. (Sir Colin Cowdrey)

Nobody transmits a love for the game as surely as Harold

Dennis Bird, and I, for one, will miss his presence in the Test match arena, a stage which has brought him a reputation unsurpassed in his field. (David Gower)

Dickie is respected throughout the world for invariably being both fair and firm. (Geoffrey Boycott)

There will only be one Dickie Bird. He is unique. Lovable, excitable, passionately in love with the game. He was a great umpire, no doubt about that. (Brian Close)

Dickie Bird enforced Law 42, section 8, better than any other umpire in my experience. That is the law regarding intimidatory bowling. He never shirked from the battle. (David Graveney)

The West Indians love him because of his sense of humour and the way he talks to them. He is a real lovable man. He was never shy of making the tough decisions and making them decisively. (Sir Garfield Sobers)

I shall miss Dickie. His record of appearing in four World Cups, easily the best of the world's leading umpires, may never be beaten. (Umpire David Shepherd)

When I think of umpires the name of Frank Chester springs to mind, lifting the status of his profession by dint of his personality, coupled with the excellence of his judgement. To write of Dickie Bird in the same breath is a high compliment which I believe is not undeserved. When both were in their prime a mistake was a rarity, and they therefore enjoyed the confidence of the players. (E.W. (Jim) Swanton)

His greatest quality, I feel, is that he has been able to cope with the difficult players and not upset them. He has humoured them, but still controlled them and got them playing the game in the right way. (Henry Blofeld)

Dickie has managed to be in the centre of the picture to

everyone's greater pleasure, yet never at the expense of doing his job. With a magical balance he has contrived on one hand to be a character, a comic and an entertainer, and on the other an absolutely impartial and dedicated arbiter, as near flawless in his decision-making as it is humanly possible to be. (Christopher Martyn-Jenkins)

A man of humble tastes and honest opinions, tempering justice with mercy, presiding at great cricket events, a born worrier, yet happy in his work. That is Dickie Bird. (John Woodcock)

He has been an outstanding ambassador on behalf of our country, and has gained the respect of the whole cricketing world. (Lord Mason of Barnsley)

For the last twenty-four years Dickie Bird has graced the international cricket circuit with his mannerisms, eccentricities and unparalleled ability to make the right decisions at the right time and in the right place. He is a character. No doubt about that. And he does play to the gallery. There will never be another quite like him. And there will never be a better umpire. (Keith Lodge, Sports Editor of the *Barnsley Chronicle*)

There has been no one to touch him as an umpire. He is the best and fairest of them all. He is a great bloke and completely bonkers. (Ian Botham)

Michael Parkinson wrote in the *Daily Telegraph*:

To say Dickie Bird loves cricket doesn't get anywhere near describing what exactly he feels for the game. It is a bit like saying that Romeo had a slight crush on Juliet, or Abelard had a fancy for Heloise. The game consumes his life and defines its horizons. It shapes the very posture of the man. Like a tree bent and moulded by the prevailing wind, so the curve of Bird's spine, the hunch of his shoulders, the crinkled eyes as he inspects the world, have been sculpted through a lifetime's dedication to cricket. He is, nowadays, one of the landmarks of the game – an umpire as famous as any superstar, as much respected by cricket as he is loved by the public.

A letter to the *Daily Express* from a member of the public, Denise Robertson, sums it up:

For years I have tried to understand cricket. You can't watch the faces of those you love come alive at the mention of Lamb or Boycott and not understand their animation. One of them, driving me through Yorkshire recently, pointed out Botham's house in tones so reverent he might have been describing the last resting place of the Holy Grail. But the rules of cricket are incomprehensible. One ball follows another and sometimes they jump up and down and shout 'Howzat' whereupon one player walks off and another replaces him.

The language is strange, too: leg before, silly mid-off and the repeated mention of Dickie Bird. 'Silly name, silly game,' I have always thought. Until last week's *Desert Island Discs*. The castaway was the legendary umpire Bird, and in forty magical minutes he brought cricket alive for me. Now I understand the siren music of leather on willow. It was there in his voice as he spoke emotionally of the game he loves and the men who play it. His romantic choice of records included Nat King Cole's 'When I Fall in Love'. Shirley Bassey's 'Till' reminds him, he said, of a time before he gave his heart to cricket and relinquished the prospect of wife and family.

He made me understand keen committee men in clubs up and down the country, patient wives rubbing at grass stains, the charmer who sells raffle tickets, and the man behind the roller. These individuals keep cricket alive, and Dickie Bird is one of them, a cricket lover rather than a member of the cricketing establishment. When he spoke of the fast-approaching day when he stands in the Long

Room at Lord's for the last time as a professional umpire, his voice almost broke. I hope he knows he will reign for ever in the hearts of cricket lovers. Since he let me share his desert island, he has a very special place in mine.

Appendix II

DICKIE BIRD'S CAREER

DICKIE Bird's cricketing career started as a player with Yorkshire and Leicestershire but it is as an umpire that he has become well known. He has been umpiring first-class cricket for twenty-seven years, standing at 159 international matches, and has achieved every honour it is possible to achieve in the umpiring world. In England, he has officiated at all the major Cup quarter-finals and semi-finals and umpired the finals of the Gillette Cup, NatWest Cup and the Benson & Hedges Cup, all at Lord's. Worldwide, he has stood in thirty-six major Cup finals. In 1987, Dickie was appointed a member of the World Cup panel of umpires. He turned down a fortune twice by refusing to join Kerry Packer and the rebel tour of South Africa, remaining loyal to the TCCB and the established game.

In 1977 he was voted Yorkshire Personality of the Year and in 1996 Yorkshireman of the Year. Also in 1996 he was awarded an honorary doctorate by Sheffield and Hallam University and a year later an honorary Doctor of Laws degree by Leeds University, both for outstanding services to cricket.

A qualified MCC advanced cricket coach, Dickie is an honorary life member of the MCC, Yorkshire CCC and Leicestershire CCC. He was awarded the MBE in 1986.

MAJOR INTERNATIONAL MATCHES UMPIRED BY DICKIE BIRD

Three World Cup finals: West Indies v Australia at Lord's, 1975

West Indies v England at Lord's, 1979

West Indies v India at Lord's, 1983

Four World Cup tournaments

Sixty-six Test matches (a world record)

Ninety-two one-day internationals (a world record)

The Queen's Silver Jubilee Test match: England v Australia at Lord's, 1977

The Centenary Test match: England v Australia at Lord's, 1980

The Women's World Cup in New Zealand, 1982

The Women's World Cup final: England v Australia at Christchurch, 1982

The Rothmans Cup in Sharjah, UAE, 1983, between Australia, Pakistan, India and England

The Rothmans Cup final: Pakistan v India at Sharjah, 1983

The Asia Cup in Sharjah, UAE, 1984, between Pakistan, India and Sri Lanka

The Rothmans Cup in Sharjah, UAE, 1985, between Pakistan, India and the West Indies

The Asia Cup in Sri Lanka, 1985, between Pakistan, Sri Lanka and Bangladesh

The Asia Cup final: Pakistan v Sri Lanka at Colombo, 1985

The Champion's Cup in Sharjah, 1986, between Pakistan, India, Sri Lanka and the West Indies

The MCC's Bicentenary Test match: England v Rest of the World at Lord's, 1987

The Sharjah tournament, 1993, between the West Indies, India, Sri Lanka and Pakistan

Test matches

No	Season	Match*	Venue	Colleague
1	1973	New Zealand	Headingley	C.S. Elliott
2	1973	West Indies	Edgbaston	A.E. Fagg
3	1973	West Indies	Lord's	C.S. Elliott
4	1974	India	Old Trafford	D.J. Constant
5	1974	Pakistan	The Oval	W.E. Alley
6	1975	Australia	Edgbaston	A.E. Fagg
7	1975	Australia	The Oval	T.W. Spencer
8	1976	West Indies	Trent Bridge	T.W. Spencer
9	1976	West Indies	Lord's	D.J. Constant
10	1976	West Indies	The Oval	W.E. Alley
11	1977	Australia	Lord's	W.L. Budd
12	1977	Australia	Trent Bridge	D.J. Constant
13	1978	Pakistan	Edgbaston	K.E. Palmer
14	1978	Pakistan	Headingley	K.E. Palmer
15	1978	New Zealand	Lord's	B.J. Meyer
16	1979	India	Lord's	K.E. Palmer
17	1979	India	Headingley	B.J. Meyer
18	1980	West Indies	Old Trafford	K.E. Palmer
19	1980	Australia	Lord's	D.J. Constant
20	1981	Australia	Edgbaston	D.O. Oslear
21	1981	Australia	The Oval	B.J. Meyer
22	1982	India	Old Trafford	B.J. Meyer
23	1982	India	The Oval	A.G.T. Whitehead
24	1982	Pakistan	Lord's	D.J. Constant
25	1983	New Zealand	The Oval	D.G.L. Evans
26	1983	New Zealand	Trent Bridge	B.J. Meyer
27	1984	West Indies	Edgbaston	B.J. Meyer
28	1984	West Indies	Old Trafford	D.O. Oslear
29	1984	Sri Lanka	Lord's	D.G.L. Evans

* All matches are v England unless otherwise stated.

No	Season	Match*	Venue	Colleague
30	1985	Australia	Lord's	D.G.L. Evans
31	1985	Australia	Old Trafford	D.R. Shepherd
32	1985	Australia	The Oval	K.E. Palmer
33	1986	India	Edgbaston	B.J. Meyer
34	1986	New Zealand	Lord's	A.G.T. Whitehead
35	1986	New Zealand	The Oval	D.R. Shepherd
36	1987	Pakistan	Old Trafford	B.J. Meyer
37	1988	West Indies	Trent Bridge	J. Birkenshaw
38	1988	West Indies	Headingley	D.R. Shepherd
39	1988	West Indies	The Oval	K.E. Palmer
40	1989	Australia	Lord's	N.T. Plews
41	1989	Australia	Edgbaston	J.W. Holder
42	1989	Australia	The Oval	K.E. Palmer
43	1990	New Zealand	Trent Bridge	J.H. Hampshire
44	1990	India	Lord's	N.T. Plews
45	1991	West Indies	Headingley	D.R. Shepherd
46	1991	Sri Lanka	Lord's	J.H. Hampshire
47	1992	Pakistan	The Oval	D.R. Shepherd
48	1992–93	Zimbabwe v India	Harare	D. Robinson
49	1992–93	Zimbabwe v NZ	Bulawayo	D. Robinson
50	1992–93	Zimbabwe v NZ	Harare	K. Kanjee
51	1993	WI v Pakistan	Port of Spain	S.A. Bucknor
52	1993	WI v Pakistan	Bridgetown	L. Barker
53	1993	WI v Pakistan	St John's	S.A. Bucknor
54	1993	Australia	Old Trafford	K.E. Palmer
55	1993	Australia	Headingley	N.T. Plews
56	1994	NZ v Pakistan	Auckland	R.S. Dunne
57	1994	NZ v Pakistan	Wellington	B.L. Aldridge
58	1994	New Zealand	Trent Bridge	S.A. Bucknor
59	1994	South Africa	Lord's	S.G. Randell

* All matches are v England unless otherwise stated.

No	Season	Match*	Venue	Colleague
60	1994	Pakistan v Australia	Karachi	T. Hayat
61	1994	India v WI	Bombay	S.K. Bansal
62	1995	West Indies	Headingley	S. Venkataraghavan
63	1995	West Indies	Old Trafford	C. Mitchley
64	1995	Australia v Pakistan	Tasmania	D. Hare
65	1995	Australia v Pakistan	Sydney	S.G. Randell
66	1996	India	Lord's	D. Hare

* All matches are v England unless otherwise stated.

INDEX

B